The
Trouble with
Resurrection

The Trouble with Resurrection

From Paul to the Fourth Gospel

Bernard Brandon Scott

POLEBRIDGE PRESS
Salem, Oregon

Cover and interior design by Robaire Ream
Cover illustration by Robaire Ream

Library of Congress Cataloging-in-Publication Data
Scott, Bernard Brandon, 1941-
 The trouble with resurrection : from Paul to the Fourth Gospel / Bernard Brandon Scott.
    p. cm.
 Includes bibliographical references and index.
 ISBN 978-1-59815-020-9 (alk. paper)
 1. Jesus Christ--Resurrection. 2. Bible. N.T.--Criticism, interpretation, etc. I. Title.
 BT482.S36 2010
 236'.8--dc22
                         2010037451

2   3   4   5   6   7   8   9   10

Table of Contents

Cameos and Charts

Preface

Resurrection is the central belief in Christianity, and what and why early Christians believed has always fascinated me. I have spent the majority of my career investigating the historical Jesus, but I have remained intrigued about how early followers got from Jesus on earth to Jesus in heaven.

Doubt and uncertainty are part of our discussion. Often we are in gray areas where we know less than we think we know. The trick is to know when we are on *terra firma* and when it is shifting beneath our feet. I will try to be as honest as I can and ask of the reader an equal openness and criticalness. We often will be dealing with hypotheses, and there is a temptation to say, "Well, it's just a hypothesis." The word "just" is often used to dismiss. But a hypothesis is the way we assemble data in order to make sense of them. We have no option but to engage in hypothetical thinking, otherwise we just quit thinking.

We also are often tempted to argue, "Well, it *could* have happened." "Could" is another knotty word. Almost anything could have happened. The real question is, "What is the probability of its having happened?" With history we are always dealing in probabilities, in what is likely.

Housekeeping

Translations are a major problem. All translations are both good and bad, all are mistranslations. All are interpretations. There is no such thing as a neutral translation. That is why they are titled "Versions." For the New Testament, I will use the Scholars

Version (SV, *Complete Gospels,* 4th edition, Salem: Polebridge, 2010) where available, otherwise NRSV. For the Hebrew Bible the NRSV will be the standard, and for Maccabees I will use the NAB. Translations of the Septuagint (LXX), the Greek translation of the Hebrew Bible, are my own, while those of the Non-Canonical gospels are from *The Complete Gospels.* When I use my own translation or modify other translations it will be noted (BBS Trans). We are not trying to understand an English translation, but an ancient Greek composition, so we cannot avoid the issue of Greek. I realize that some eyes will glaze over at the mention of a Greek word, but ignoring the fact that translations are versions is what leads to fundamentalism. Paying attention to the differences between Greek and English where necessary is critical to understanding what the ancient writings meant.

Frequently I display the English translation in the breath (lines) cola of the Greek. This perhaps will enable the reader to understand how the expression is taking place in the Greek and remind us that we are not discussing an English paragraph. The Greek has no real punctuation, all letters are capitals, and it lacks paragraphs. The writings we are discussing will be displayed in full so that you will not have to go in search of the evidence.

This is a scholarly book written for the non-scholar. Since it explores new and different topics, it is, I hope, cutting edge. And since I think scholarship is important and should not be hidden away in an ivory tower, this book is written in a style and format that I trust will engage us all. It does not employ the scholarly apparatus of footnoting and referencing. Some topics, issues, or evidentiary materials that a reader needs but would interrupt the flow of the discussion will be exhibited in boxes. A list of further reading is appended at the end of each chapter. This is meant to help a reader go deeper, but is by no means all that I have consulted in writing the chapter.

By convention we refer to the authors of the gospels by their traditional names: Mark, Matthew, Luke, John, Thomas, etc. All our gospels are anonymous and we do not know who wrote them, but we need some way to refer to them and the convention is handy, yet misleading—the names name only the anonymous. The situation is different for Paul. We have a group of genuine letters written by the apostle Paul, and another group of letters ascribed to Paul, but almost certainly not written by him. When quoting from the latter I will indicate that Paul is not the author. (See *The Authentic Letters of Paul, A New Reading of Paul's Rhetoric and Meaning*, trans. Arthur J. Dewey, Roy W. Hoover, Lane C. McGaughy, and Daryl D. Schmidt. Salem: Polebridge, 2010).

Thanks

While giving thanks in a preface is traditional and conventional, I hope the reader will not skip this part. My debts are real.

I have many folks to thank. First of all my many students who keep asking, "Well, what really happened?" This is my attempt to answer their questions. The real secret of teaching is that I learn more than the students. They are my teachers and their questions often drive me on.

Various parts of this book have been worked out with lay groups. Their responses and questions have often guided me, forced me to rethink, indicated what was difficult, and what mattered. Special thanks to the folks at Snowstar in Canada, especially Dell, Chris and David. An extended speaking tour in Australia under the sponsorship of Common Dreams provided yet another occasion. Rex, Dick, Marie, Jeremy, Cecile, Grey, Wes, Sean all provided Aussie hospitality. Thanks to Andrew Bell for an amazing trip to Kakadu. Ernie and Frank at SPAFER in Birmingham, AL, and Jim Smith and the New Perspectives group in Goshen, IN, provided yet more conversation and stimulation.

Larry Alexander of Polebridge Press has kept this project on schedule. Tom Hall has done his usual expert job of copy editing. Roy Hoover gave the manuscript a careful and critical reading. Arthur Dewey over the years has endured my questions and doubts about the gospel of Peter and other questions on Christian origins. A special thanks goes to my long time conversation partner Joseph Bessler. Joe has encouraged, challenged, probed, doubted, and laughed when appropriate. Margaret Lee is not only an intellectual partner, but a life one.

Abbreviations

1,2 Chr	1,2 Chronicles
Col	Colossians
1,2 Cor	1,2 Corinthians
Dan	Daniel
Deut	Deuteronomy
Eccl	Ecclesiastes
Eph	Ephesians
Exod	Exodus
Ezek	Ezekiel
Gal	Galatians
Gen	Genesis
Heb	Hebrews
Hos	Hosea
Isa	Isaiah
Jer	Jeremiah
Josh	Joshua
Judg	Judges
1,2 Kgs	1,2 Kings
4 Kgs	4 Kingdoms LXX
Lam	Lamentations
Lev	Leviticus
LXX	The Septuagint
1,2,3,4 Macc	1,2,3,4, Maccabees
Mal	Malachi
Matt	Gospel of Matthew
Num	Numbers
Q	The Q-Gospel
Qoh	Qoheleth
Pet	Gospel of Peter
Phil	Philippians
Prov	Proverbs
Ps(s)	Psalm(s)
Rom	Romans
1,2 Sam	1,2 Samuel
Sir	Sirach
1,2 Thess	1,2 Thessalonians
Thom	Gospel of Thomas
1,2 Tim	1,2 Timothy
Tob	Tobit
Wis	Wisdom of Solomon
Zech	Zechariah

Introduction

The Problem
with Resurrection

res•ur•rec•tion n. 1. The act of rising from the dead or returning to life. 2. The state of one who has returned to life. 3. The act of bringing back to practice, notice, or use; revival. 4. Resurrection Christianity a. The rising again of Jesus on the third day after the Crucifixion. b. The rising again of the dead at the Last Judgment. (American Heritage Dictionary)

The dictionary defines our problem. "Resurrection" in English refers to "rising from the dead" or specifically in Christianity to Jesus' rising from the dead. The dictionary indicates that a non-religious meaning, #3, is derived from the religious meaning.

This is not the situation in the first century. In Greek the noun *anastasis* means "standing up" and the verb *egeiro* means "to get up." These are common, everyday Greek words. When Simeon address Mary in the temple, he prophecies, "This child is linked to the fall and rise (*anastasin*) of many in Israel" (Luke 2:34). The Greek word for "rising," *anastasin*, is used in this quote in its normal Greek sense. Only later because of Christian usage does it take on the meaning of "resurrection" in the sense we find it in a modern dictionary. In the Fourth gospel when Jesus gets up from table to wash his disciples feet, in Greek the verb is *egeiretai*—"So he got up from the meal" (John 13:4). The Greek word *egeiro* too is a common, everyday Greek word that takes on a special religious sense only later.

When Paul writes, "Now if our message is that the Anointed has been raised from among the dead, how can some of you possibly be saying that there is no such thing as the resurrection of the dead?" (1 Cor 15:12) we read and understand "raised from the dead" and "resurrection of the dead" as religious and theological terms, whereas in the Greek they are not technical theological terms. One might translate Paul's question, "Now if our message is, 'He is gotten up from among the dead,' how can some of you say, 'There is no standing up from among the dead?'" We employ a religious and theological code; they are using everyday Greek words metaphorically in a religious sense. Thus our translations make it difficult for us to get back to what Paul wrote.

Other things mislead us in our understanding of resurrection.

- The liturgy of Easter Sunday. This feast focuses our attention on a visual image connected to a narrative, frequently one in the gospel of John.
- Resurrection art. Most of the classical images, primarily those from the Renaissance forward, focus on stories from the gospel of John. One can see this in the number of images based upon Mary Magdalene being told, "Do Not Touch" (*Noli Me Tangere*) or the doubting Thomas. Caravaggio's graphic image of Thomas inserting his hand into the side of Jesus is only one of many famous examples, the problem is that the gospel of John and its stories of the resurrection are not only among the latest texts of the New Testament, but they are actually atypical.

Visual images form a cultural memory and our use of the theological term "resurrection" determines what we are looking for. Resurrection becomes a thing, an object, so we go looking for it and of course find it.

Frank McCourt tells a story about Humpy Dumpty that il-lustrates our situation.

> And for a whole class period there's a heated discussion of "Humpty Dumpty".
>
> > Humpty Dumpty sat on the wall,
> > Humpty Dumpty had a great fall;
> > All the king's horses
> > And all the king's men
> > Couldn't put Humpty together again.
>
> So, I ask, what's going on in this nursery rhyme? The hands are up. Well, like, this egg falls off the wall and if you

study biology or physics you know you can never put an egg back together again. I mean, like, it's common sense.

Who says it's an egg? I ask.

Of course it's an egg. Everyone knows that.

Where does it say it's an egg?

They're thinking. They're searching the text for egg, any mention, any hint of egg. They won't give in.

There are more hands and indignant assertions of egg. All their lives they knew this rhyme and there was never a doubt that Humpty Dumpty was an egg. They're comfortable with the idea of egg and why do teachers have to come along and destroy everything with all this analysis.

I'm not destroying. I just want to know where you got the idea that Humpty Dumpty is an egg.

Because, Mr. McCourt, it's in all the pictures and whoever drew the first picture musta known the guy who wrote the poem or he'd never have made it an egg.

All right. If you're content with the idea of egg we'll let it be but I know the future lawyers in this class will never accept egg where there is no evidence of egg.

(Frank McCourt, *'Tis*. New York: Scribner, 1999. pp. 353–54)

Humpty Dumpty and the missing egg describe our situation. Once traditions become fixed, they provide the lens thorough which everything is viewed. It becomes common sense. A recent survey of Americans found that a large majority believed in the physical resurrection of Jesus, despite Paul's calling this into question. The liturgical practice of reading John 20 on Easter morning reinforces this notion, and our use of the technical theological term "resurrection" buttresses this. Once we think there is an egg in the narrative of Jesus' getting up from the dead, we do not see that it is not there and we do not see what other things might be there. We need to develop a strategy to keep the egg out of what we are reading so as to see what is actually there.

Starting

Starting often determines the ending, and this is never more true than with the issue of resurrection. Where to start an inquiry about the emergence of resurrection in early Christianity is not only a central problem, but it will likely determine where we come out. Even more, what do we call it? Resurrection, a theological term, or standing up or getting up, an ordinary term? Beginning to see our problem? I have read more than one argument that was totally logical and convincing except for the foundation on which it was premised. Care about our starting point is critical. The egg is resurrection, and we know that egg is there even though it may not be. We have to look by not looking, as Emily Dickinson says, "Tell all the Truth but tell it slant—" (1129).

Let us begin by agreeing to set aside the question of what happened. For many this is the critical question, either to prove that Jesus did rise from the grave on the third day or to show that such an event is totally impossible. Let us agree not to ask this question because all we will find is an egg or no egg. If we start from faith, that often means what our church believes or what I was taught. I often find students rejecting what they discover a New Testament writing means because it does not agree with what they believe or what they were taught. Their logic is that it can't say that because that is not what I believe. On the other hand, those who start with the position that what it says is incredible have the same problem, only in reverse. I propose a sympathetic reading of an author. Let's first find out what the writing means: What do the authors really say, what are they trying to say? We will let the writings themselves be our guide, not our need to prove or disprove them.

Astronomy offers a useful analogy at this point. When astronomers look into the night sky, they are not viewing the stars directly, but the light that flows from the stars and galaxies. Even though the light they see is hundreds and thousands of light years old, it is much younger than the star from which it came. Astronomers are aware that with more powerful telescopes they can see further back into the history of the cosmos. But they can see only so far, they cannot see all the way back to the beginning.

Historical methodology is somewhat analogous to astronomy. Historical methodology will let us see back as far as our writings go, but it will hardly let us see before that. We must practice the discipline of asking the right questions and not assuming that we can see further back than we actually can.

How far back can we see? The writings of the apostle Paul. These are the oldest surviving writings of the movement that became Christianity. Over and over again I am going to insist on the importance of chronological order. Without it, whatever we are trying to discover falls apart. This is opposite to the direction found in the liturgical materials and paintings, which draw their inspiration from the end of the New Testament canon, not from its beginning. To return again to the analogy of astronomy, the brightest stars are the youngest and the closest. To see deeper or earlier, one needs a more powerful telescope. The evidence will be darker and more faint. The bright images of the fourth gospel are not the earliest, but among the latest. It's to Paul, whom we hardly think of in connection with resurrection, that we must turn.

There is an important corollary to following chronological order. We will not fill in the gaps or supposed gaps with later writings. This strategy is frequently employed with the result that the later determines the earlier. The gaps should be left as gaps. This is part of a conservative methodology—to deal with what is in the writings, to take it at face value, to understand how it came to be.

Chronological order means not beginning with what happened on the third day or at the empty tomb. No, the starting point is the apostle Paul, and for the simple reason that his writings are chronologically first in the New Testament. Common sense would appear to dictate that we begin with the gospel portrayals of the resurrection, but these all come much later than Paul. He is writing in the late forties and fifties, whereas the first gospel, that attributed to Mark, is post 70, the gospels of Matthew and John are late in the first century, and Luke and Acts perhaps in the second century.

Next after Paul in chronological order is the Q-gospel. This is a reconstructed writing that probably dates from Galilee sometime in the 50s and early 60s. Most discussions of resurrection skip the Q-gospel because it has no mention of resurrection. But after our study of Paul, I hope it will be evident that Q has not skipped resurrection: it simply does not have the egg!

Only after we have dealt with the apostle Paul and the Q-gospel will we turn our attention to the post-70 gospels, again in chronological order.

I predict that by the time we get to the last gospel account of the resurrection, John 21, we will find the question "what happened" to be a very different question than if we had begun with it.

1 The First Reference

The earliest writing in the New Testament is Paul's first letter to the Thessalonians, composed around 50 CE. Most likely this was not the first letter Paul wrote to a community, just the first to survive. This reminds us how accidental is much of our evidence. In the opening Thanksgiving of that letter occurs the earliest extant reference to Jesus' getting up from the dead. Paul has heard a report concerning the Thessalonians,

> how you have turned away from lifeless images
>> in order to serve the living and real God
> and to wait for God's "son" from heaven,
>> whom God raised from among the dead,
>> Jesus, who will rescue us from the condemnation that is
>> sure to come.
>> (1 Thess 1:9–10)

This letter is addressed to a community with whom Paul has good relations. The letter is somewhat gossipy, the Apostle is missing the community. Unlike most of Paul's letters, this one is not dealing with a controversy or putting out a fire in a newly founded church. Near the letter's conclusion, Paul answers some questions that have arisen in the community about those who have "fallen asleep," to which we will turn our attention in chapter 4.

When this letter was written about 50 CE, the new movement of Anointed-believers was less than twenty years old. There are no gospels, no connected stories of Jesus' life and teachings. Our common sense rebels at this idea, but modern gospel scholarship has firmly concluded that Mark created the first connected narrative about Jesus. These early Jesus movements did not start with a catechism or handbook. In Paul's letters we see him figuring it out as he goes along, responding to new circumstances as they arise.

In the Thanksgiving of the letter to the Thessalonians Paul fondly recalls the reports he has had about them by narrating their journey from being worshippers of lifeless images (idols) to the service of the living and real God.

These few lines tell us a number of important things. Those to whom Paul is writing were pagans (gentiles), but have converted from worshipping lifeless images or idols to serve the Jewish God. The phrasing "turned to God from idols" and "to serve a living and real (or true) God" is very Jewish. It is also pleasingly balanced—"turned/to serve." This language comes to Paul from Hellenistic Judaism, but it has deep roots in Israel's sacred writings. Tobit 14:5–6 nicely points to a similar usage.

> After this they all will return from their exile and will rebuild Jerusalem in splendor; and in it the temple of God will be rebuilt, just as the prophets of Israel have said concerning it. Then the nations in the whole world will all be converted and worship God in truth. They will all abandon their idols, which deceitfully have led them into their error.
>
> (Tob 14:5–6)

Where the NRSV translates "converted" the Greek has *epistrephō*, "to turn," the same verb as Paul uses. Notice also the constellation of other similar terms: truth and idols all set in an eschatological context. In the Acts of the Apostles and later Christian writings, "turn" becomes a technical term for "conversion."

Idols is the standard Jewish term for false gods; it does not refer to the cult statue. For second temple Judaism idolatry is the sin that lies at the root of all sins. "For the idea of making idols was the beginning of fornication, and the invention of them was the corruption of life" (Wis 14:12). As a Jew, Paul shares this conviction and follows the formula that idolatry leads to immorality and also that if immorality is present, at its root is idolatry. This connection is clear in the argument in Rom 1:18–25. Paul's argument is predicated on the assumption that idolatry leads inevitably to immorality. In Galatians he worries that his converts will slip back into idolatry and immorality.

In the past, when you had no knowledge of God, you were
  dominated by powers that were not really divine.
Now that you know God, or rather, God knows you, how can
  you return to those impotent and impoverished cosmic
  powers,
let alone wish to be their menial servants again?
For example, you are still involved in observing days and
  months, seasons and years, as if that determined your fate!
I'm afraid my efforts on your behalf have been a waste of time.
  (Gal 4:8–11)

In the Thanksgiving "to serve the living and real God" is a
misleading translation. The Greek *doulein* is connected with slavery. The noun means "a slave." Translators tend to translate "serve"
when the meaning is positive or associated with God, as in our
quote from 1 Thessalonians; they use "slave" when the meaning
is negative or associated with false gods, as in the Galatians quote
immediately above. In this way we end up serving God and slav-
ing for idols. But this is clearly tendentious. Since slavery is such a
powerful social model in the ancient world and a very widespread
phenomenon, we should not hide it in our translations with the
weak word "serve." Thus a more correct translation of Paul's
phrase from the Thanksgiving of 1 Thessalonians would be:

how you turned away from lifeless images,
    to be a slave of the living and real God

"To be a slave" denotes the total devotion and dependency of the
convert on God. Paul often describes himself as a slave in the
Address of his letters. "Paul, a slave of Jesus Christ" (Rom 1:1).

"Living" and "real" modify God to distinguish God from the
false gods, the idols from whom the Thessalonians have converted. Proverbs makes the point well.

Every word of God proves true (real);
he is a shield to those who take refuge in him.
  (Prov 30:5)

In the romance Joseph and Aseneth (circa 100 BCE to 200 CE), the
pagan Aseneth, who is to be Joseph's wife, makes reference in her
first speech to these same notions.

But I have heard many saying that the God of the Hebrews
is a true God, and a living God, and a merciful God, and

> compassionate and long-suffering and pitiful and gentle, and
> does not count the sin of a humble person.
>
> (Joseph and Aseneth 11:10)

If real or true denotes this God from false gods, living denotes
God as creator. In the Genesis creation account, God creates the
living creatures (1:20, 21, 24, 28). Sirach draws this conclusion:
"He who lives forever created the whole universe" (Sir 18:1); and
in Jubilees (circa 100 BCE), Abraham in his final speech to Isaac
says:

> I hated idols, and those who serve them I have rejected. And
> I have offered my heart and spirit so that I might be careful
> to do the will of the one who created me because he is the
> living God.
>
> (Jubilees 21:4)

The phrasing, "turning from idols" "to serve the living and
real God" is almost a Jewish cliché to denote what the gentiles
must do. This way of describing the Thessalonians' narrative
does not indicate that they have become Jews but that they have
become righteous gentiles. This status is important to notice. For
Paul the world is not divided into Jews and Christians, but Jews
and gentiles. At this period, there are no Christians. That is why
I have preferred to refer to Paul and his converts as Anointed-
believers.

That Paul's language should come from such a thoroughly
Jewish matrix ought not to surprise us. Paul after all was a Jew.
This should alert us to expect that the rest of this language will
find its home in Judaism.

The present situation of the Thessalonians is described as "to
wait for his 'son' from heaven." If the first two lines describe for
Second Temple Judaism (515 BCE–70 CE) the hoped for story of
pagan conversion to the worship of the Jewish God, this third line

Idols

Do not turn to idols or make cast images for yourselves: I am
the Lord your God (Lev 19:4).

The Lord your God you shall fear; him you shall serve, and
by his name alone you shall swear (Deut 6:13).

Anointing of David

The Lord said to Samuel, "How long will you grieve over Saul? I have rejected him from being king over Israel. Fill your horn with oil and set out; I will send you to Jesse the Bethlehemite, for I have provided for myself a king among his sons." . . . When they came, he looked on Eliab and thought, "Surely the Lord's anointed is now before the Lord." But the Lord said to Samuel, "Do not look on his appearance or on the height of his stature, because I have rejected him; for the Lord does not see as mortals see; they look on the outward appearance, but the Lord looks on the heart." . . . Samuel said to Jesse, "Are all your sons here?" And he said, "There remains yet the youngest, but he is keeping the sheep." And Samuel said to Jesse, "Send and bring him; for we will not sit down until he comes here." He sent and brought him in. Now he was ruddy, and had beautiful eyes, and was handsome. The Lord said, "Rise and anoint him; for this is the one." Then Samuel took the horn of oil, and anointed him in the presence of his brothers; and the spirit of the Lord came mightily upon David from that day forward (1 Sam 16:1–13).

adds a very new ingredient. Who is this son of the Jewish God and what does it mean to call him "son of God"? Since this language is very Jewish, we should avoid reading into Paul Christian assumptions from a later period, but should first attempt to understand Paul's language on Jewish terms. Son of God in Judaism has several possibilities, but the most natural one is its association with King David and so its identification with the Anointed, a word that in Hebrew means "anointed with oil," since Israel anointed its kings. Anointed implies anointed by God and so "son" would be a synonym for Anointed. In Hebrew *messiah* is the word for anointed, while in Greek it is *christos* (Christ).

The son is awaited "from heaven." This locates the son in the space of the Jewish God, the heavens. The Greek word *ouranos* which is here translated by "heavens" primarily means sky. We distinguish in English between sky and heaven with two different words; but Greek and Hebrew use one word for both these ideas. Whether the ancient Greeks and Hebrews would have understood

David as Son of God

Moreover the Lord declares to you that the Lord will make you a house. When your days are fulfilled and you lie down with your ancestors, I will raise up your offspring after you, who shall come forth from your body, and I will establish his kingdom. He shall build a house for my name, and I will establish the throne of his kingdom forever. I will be a father to him, and he shall be a son to me. When he commits iniquity, I will punish him with a rod such as mortals use, with blows inflicted by human beings. But I will not take my steadfast love from him, as I took it from Saul, whom I put away from before you. Your house and your kingdom shall be made sure forever before me; your throne shall be established forever. In accordance with all these words and with all this vision, Nathan spoke to David (2 Sam 7:11–17).

> I will tell of the decree of the Lord:
> He said to me, "You are my son;
> today I have begotten you.
> Ask of me, and I will make the nations your heritage,
> and the ends of the earth your possession.
> You shall break them with a rod of iron,
> and dash them in pieces like a potter's vessel" (Ps 2:7–9).

this subtle distinction is unclear, since their conception of the cosmos was quite different from ours. The sky is a literal boundary, a firmament, separating earth the dwelling of mortals, from heaven the dwelling of immortals, the god(s). The boundary is only a couple of thousand feet up. Their notion of the heavens is physical; ours abstract or "spiritual," a word whose meaning I will leave for a later discussion.

While Paul normally uses "eagerly await," (for example, Rom 8:19), the word used here appears a number of times in the Septuagint (LXX).

> We all growl like bears;
> like doves we moan mournfully.
> We wait for justice, but there is none.
> (Isa 59:11)

Septuagint

The Septuagint is the Greek translation of the Hebrew Bible. According to legend 72 translators in Alexandria, Eygpt under the orders of Ptolemy II Philadelphus, produced translations in perfect agreement. The abbreviation LXX (70 in Roman numbers) derives from the legend. The translations vary in quality. The Hebrew Biblical texts found at Qumran at times agree with the LXX against the standard Masoretic Hebrew text. The Canon of books in the LXX is more extensive than in the Hebrew Canon and this has led to the difference between the Catholic and Protestant Canons. The Catholic church followed the LXX tradition, while the reformers adopted the Hebrew Canon.

Again in a somewhat similar passage:

> You who fear the Lord, wait for his mercy;
> do not stray, or else you may fall.
> (Sir 2:7)

"Await" begs the question of how the son got to heaven. It implies that Jesus has been exalted to heaven, again a model borrowed from the LXX. (See chapter 6 for an extended discussion of this model.) "Await" also implies "return" and so indicates that this language belongs to Jewish apocalyptic. The last line drives this home: "Jesus who will rescue us from the condemnation that is sure to come." This implies the Jewish apocalyptic scenario in which God will redeem or rescue Israel by destroying her enemies. We have also seen God's wrath in the Jer 10:10 quote above, and the Sibylline Oracles, book 3 (163–45 BCE) exhibits this same pattern.

> It is a thousand years and five hundred more
> since the overbearing kings of the Greeks reigned,
> who began the first evils for mortals,
> setting up many idols of dead gods.
> On account of them you have been taught vain thinking.
> But when the wrath of the great God comes upon you,
> then indeed you will recognize the face of the great God.
> (Sibylline Oracles 3:551–57)

Finally, we come to "whom he [God] raised from the dead." The Greek for "he raised from" is *ēgeiren*, which means to "to get up" or "to rise up" as in "to get up from bed or sleep." This phrase could literally be translated as "whom God got up from the dead." To rise or to get up from sleep functions as a metaphor for moving from one state to another, from the dead to the living. The image is of the dead asleep in the ground and raising them up from the ground/grave as one arises out of bed. The language is metaphorical, not literal.

Since both lines bracketing this line came from Jewish apocalyptic, we should not be surprised that "raised up from the dead" also comes from apocalyptic. We have seen that these lines from Paul imply a Jewish narrative in which Israel as the slave of the living and true God looks forward to the worshippers of idols turning to this true God. If they do not turn, they can expect God's wrath. Paul is thinking in cosmic terms, not individualistic terms. His language implies a scenario. Now we must investigate where Paul's language of rising from the dead came from and how it fits into that scenario. But before we can investigate 'raising up from the dead' we must take an overview of Israel's view of life after death. This will involve two stages: first, ancient Israel's view and then the crisis in 167–163 BCE created by Antiochus Epiphanes' attempted destruction of the Jewish religion.

Works Cited

Sibylline Oracles: Charlesworth, James H., ed. *The Old Testament Pseudepigrapha, Vol 2, Expansions of The "Old Testament" and Legends, Wisdom and Philosophical Literature, Prayers, Psalms, and Odes, Fragments of Lost Judeo-Hellenistic Works.* Translated by John Collins. Garden City, NY: Doubleday, 1985.

2 After Death in Ancient Israel

In the religious culture of the ancient Near East, Israel was the odd one out. Belief in life after death was well established among Israel's neighbors, but for the longest time Israel remained adamant in its denial of life after death. Alan Segal in his masterful study *Life after Death* summarizes the issue well:

> That the Bible lacks a concrete narrative of the afterlife, as we have seen so often manifested in the pagan cultures around it, must, we suspect, not be just accidental or deficient; it must be part of the Biblical polemic against its environment. In contrast to the plethora of different ideas about life after death, in the great river cultures surrounding Israel, early Bible traditions seem uninterested in the notion of an afterlife. Practically every scholar who systematically surveys the oldest sections of the Biblical text is impressed with the lack of a beatific notion of the hereafter for anyone. (p. 121)

The most likely reason for this denial of an afterlife in ancient Israel is the threat such a belief poses to monotheism. The dead were viewed as powerful, almost as gods. Any dealing with the dead and their powers would open the way to the dreaded sin of idolatry. The dead could and did influence this world, and descendents of the dead were engaged in keeping them under control. On the anniversary of their death, their descendents would eat with them in sacred meals. These Canaanite traditions posed a threat to monotheism and so Israel denied such beliefs.

Ancient Israel's Position

We who have grown up in the Christian west, heavily influenced by beliefs about life after death and the Greek notion of the immortality of the soul, are often surprised at this total rejection on Israel's part. A number of the Psalms make this point so clearly that little commentary is necessary.

> Hear my prayer, O Lord,
> and give ear to my cry;
> do not hold your peace at my tears.
> For I am your passing guest,
> an alien, like all my forebears.
> Turn your gaze away from me, that I may smile again,
> before I depart and am no more.
>   (Ps 39:12–13)

Earth is the place of humans, and when they die and depart, they are no more, as the Psalmist notes. Our days are numbered, life is fleeting, what we sow we may not gather.

> Lord, let me know my end,
> and what is the measure of my days;
> let me know how fleeting my life is.
> You have made my days a few handbreadths,
> and my lifetime is as nothing in your sight.
> Surely everyone stands as a mere breath.
> Surely everyone goes about like a shadow.
> Surely for nothing they are in turmoil;
> they heap up, and do not know who will gather.
>   (Ps 39:4–6)

This meditation on the shortness of our days and the finality of it all leads not to despair but to wisdom: "that we may gain a wise heart." Or as Samuel Johnson quipped, "Depend upon it, Sir, when a man knows he is to be hanged in a fortnight, it concentrates his mind wonderfully."

> For all our days pass away under your wrath;
> our years come to an end like a sigh.
> The days of our life are seventy years,
> or perhaps eighty, if we are strong;
> even then their span is only toil and trouble;
> they are soon gone, and we fly away.
> Who considers the power of your anger?

> Your wrath is as great as the fear that is due you.
> So teach us to count our days
> that we may gain a wise heart.
>   (Ps 90:9–12)

This finality of death is reinforced by the notion that only here on earth can God be praised. "The dead do not praise the Lord." Therefore, the Psalmist concludes, we should praise the Lord during the time we have.

> The heavens are the Lord's heavens,
> but the earth he has given to human beings.
> The dead do not praise the Lord,
> nor do any that go down into silence.
> But we will bless the Lord
> from this time on and forevermore.
> Praise the Lord!
>   (Ps 115:16–18)

Sheol

Unsurprisingly, a culture that does not affirm life after death does not speculate about it. Unlike the surrounding cultures, Israel does not produce anything like the Egyptian *Book of the Dead* or the Mesopotamian Epic of Gilgamesh. Israel does have Sheol, which is envisioned as the abode of the dead, but this is not life after death in the western, Christian sense. There is no elaboration or speculation about it. This is not a place of conscious or beatific life but a place of the dead, and reference to it occurs almost exclusively in wisdom literature.

As in death itself, in Sheol there is no praise of God, for only the living can praise God.

> Turn, O Lord, save my life;
> deliver me for the sake of your steadfast love.
> For in death there is no remembrance of you;
> in Sheol who can give you praise?
>   (Ps 6:4–5)

Sheol can be used interchangeably with death itself. When David celebrates his liberation from the hands of Saul, he sings,

> I call upon the Lord, who is worthy to be praised,
> and I am saved from my enemies.
> For the waves of death encompassed me,

> the torrents of perdition assailed me;
> the cords of Sheol entangled me,
> the snares of death confronted me.
>> (2 Sam 22:4–6)

The same themes as above reappear: the living praise the Lord, death is a place of despair. Death and Sheol are identified. Sheol is identified with the grave and so is pictured as down. In Proverbs the warning against adultery concludes,

> Her house [adultery] is the way to Sheol,
> going down to the chambers of death.
>> (Prov 7:27)

Often times Sheol is referred to as the Pit (in Hebrew a pit, cistern, well). When Isaiah describes the end of the king he remarks:

> But you are brought down to Sheol,
> to the depths of the Pit.
>> (Isa 14:15)

In Wisdom literature the path of wisdom leads up, by implication to heaven, and that of the wicked leads down to Sheol and death.

> For the wise the path of life leads upward,
> in order to avoid Sheol below.
>> (Prov 15:24)

No wisdom exists in Sheol—there all is death. In Ecclesiastes, Qoheleth warns that one must act now (*carpe diem*, so to speak) because,

> Whatever your hand finds to do, do with your might; for there is no work or thought or knowledge or wisdom in Sheol, to which you are going.
>> (Eccl 9:10)

In Ecclesiastes we see the typical attitude—in death there is nothing. Only in life can God be praised.

Sometimes English translations can be misleading, especially because we are reading with much later presuppositions. A particularly difficult word to translate in this case is the Hebrew *nefesh*, frequently translated as "soul." The Psalms frequently describe the *nefesh* as what exists after death in Sheol.

> What man is he that liveth, and shall not see death?
> Shall he deliver his soul from the hand of the grave?
>> (Ps 89:84 KJV)

In the King James Version the problem clearly appears. The NRSV makes an effort to avoid the problem.

> Who can live and never see death?
> Who can escape the power of Sheol?
> (Ps 89:48)

The NRSV recognizes the problem of translating *nefesh* and so avoids the deceptive word "soul." In the west, especially since Plato, soul has been understood as immortal and as the real, existing person. Israel has no such notion. *Nefesh* as applied to the living means "person" or "personhood," and as applied to the dead it means something like "shade." It is not life after death in a beatific sense nor, as the quotes make clear, is it something desirable.

Ancient Israel, unlike its neighbors, has no elaborate conception of life after death.

- Only the living can praise God.
- After death there is the grave, Sheol.
- There is no promised future life.

For Christian readers of the Hebrew Bible this conclusion, while shocking, is evident. In the prophet Hosea's condemnation of Israel, this finality is make clear.

> Shall I ransom them from the power of Sheol?
> Shall I redeem them from Death?
> O Death, where are your plagues?
> O Sheol, where is your destruction?
> Compassion is hidden from my eyes.
> (Hos 13:14)

Ironically, this passage the apostle Paul later will employ in a much different sense (see chapter 9).

Popular Belief

Whenever we read an ancient text we need to remember that we are reading the literature of the elites. By default elites read and write, not the common folk. Even more, the Hebrew Bible largely reflects the point of view of the exiles who had returned from Babylon (539 BCE). They idealized the past.

The tribes of Israel settled in the land of the Canaanites, who had extensive rites in association with the dead. The dead were spirits and divine ones. The dead continued to be members of the family and so participated in family rituals and meals. Since the dead were powerful, they had to be placated with offerings.

Both material and literary evidence supports ancient Israel's interaction with Canaanite practice. In archaeological excavations, burial sites of ancient Israel cannot be distinguished from those of their neighbors, the Canaanites. The Hebrew Bible also exhibits extensive evidence of these practices, or rather of efforts to suppress them.

One of the most famous of these stories is Saul's consulting the medium (KJ: Witch) of Endor. After Samuel has died, the narrative notes that "Saul had expelled the mediums and the wizards from the land" (1 Sam 28:3). The placement of this note immediately following Samuel's death is interesting. If the narrator has to note their expulsion, their presence must have been prominent. Saul now faces the Philistines, and Yahweh has gone silent. Because Saul cannot communicate by dreams or prophets, he seeks out a medium:

> Then Saul said to his servants, "Seek out for me a woman who is a medium, so that I may go to her and inquire of her." His servants said to him, "There is a medium at Endor." So Saul disguised himself and put on other clothes and went there, he and two men with him. They came to the woman by night. And he said, "Consult a spirit for me, and bring up for me the one whom I name to you." The woman said to him, "Surely you know what Saul has done, how he has cut off the mediums and the wizards from the land. Why then are you laying a snare for my life to bring about my death?" But Saul swore to her by the Lord, "As the Lord lives, no punishment shall come upon you for this thing." Then the woman said, "Whom shall I bring up for you?" He answered, "Bring up Samuel for me." When the woman saw Samuel, she cried out with a loud voice; and the woman said to Saul, "Why have you deceived me? You are Saul!" The king said to her, "Have no fear; what do you see?" The woman said to Saul, "I see a divine being (Hebrew: *elohim*) coming up out of the ground." He said to her, "What is his appearance?" She said, "An old man is coming up; he is wrapped in a robe." So Saul knew that it

was Samuel, and he bowed with his face to the ground, and did obeisance.

    (1 Sam 28:3–14)

This vivid story preserves a memory of a time in ancient Israel when consultation with the dead was extensive: Saul, deprived of Yahweh's voice, turns to a medium to consult the dead Samuel, whom she describes as a god (*elohim*, one of the names for God in Hebrew*)* and Saul worships him as a god.

    The story of Saul is not an isolated incident. The prophet Isaiah rants against these same practices:

> Now if people say to you, "Consult the ghosts and the familiar spirits that chirp and mutter; should not a people consult their gods (Heb: *elohi*), the dead on behalf of the living, for teaching and for instruction?" Surely, those who speak like this will have no dawn!
>
>   (Isa 8:19–20)

Likewise in Leviticus priests are enjoined from even participating in burials except for those of close relatives:

> The Lord said to Moses: Speak to the priests, the sons of Aaron, and say to them: No one shall defile himself for a dead person among his relatives, except for his nearest kin: his mother, his father, his son, his daughter, his brother.
>
>   (Lev 21:1–2)

The high priest has even stricter standards:

> The priest who is exalted above his fellows, on whose head the anointing oil has been poured and who has been consecrated to wear the vestments, shall not dishevel his hair, nor tear his vestments. He shall not go where there is a dead body; he shall not defile himself even for his father or mother.
>
>   (Lev 21:10–11)

So powerful are the dead that the strictures to suppress this belief must be even stronger and the vigilance must be constant.

Why No Life after Death?

If Israel's neighbors have such strong and elaborate notions of the afterlife, why does Israel insist upon none? If most religions have such beliefs, why is ancient Israel such an exception, unique? If as we have just seen, there was struggle in ancient Israel over belief in the absence of a beatific afterlife, why was the struggle so important? This imagined speech of Moses to the people before they enter the promised land provides a clue.

> When you come into the land that the Lord your God is giving you, you must not learn to imitate the abhorrent practices of those nations. No one shall be found among you who makes a son or daughter pass through fire, or who practices divination, or is a soothsayer, or an augur, or a sorcerer, or one who casts spells, or who consults ghosts or spirits, or who seeks oracles from the dead. For whoever does these things is abhorrent to the Lord; it is because of such abhorrent practices that the Lord your God is driving them out before you. You must remain completely loyal to the Lord your God. Although these nations that you are about to dispossess do give heed to soothsayers and diviners, as for you, the Lord your God does not permit you to do so.
> (Deut 18:9–14)

As previously mentioned, *the* sin in Israel is idolatry, the worship of any god but Yahweh, the God of Israel. As the story of Saul and the medium of Endor indicates, the dead threaten Yahweh's uniqueness. The spirit-like, ghostly, divine nature of the dead compromises the claim of Yahweh; and so in reaction Israel, uniquely in the ancient Near East, denies life after death. This struggle against the dead begins in the pre-exilic period, and by the post-exilic period those maintaining the primacy and unique claim of Yahweh to divinity have triumphed. The price paid is to be cut off from the family of the dead.

Works Cited

Segal, Alan F. *Life after Death, a History of the Afterlife in the Religions of the West.* New York: Doubleday, 2004. The book to read—the subtitle says it all!

3 | Awakening from the Dead

We have reviewed the dominant view of life after death in Ancient Israel and Second Temple Judaism. This view was strongly established after the return of exiles from Babylon (539 BCE) and is inscribed in the Hebrew Bible. But a crisis produced a shift in that view, at least among some Jews. Given the strength of the old view, the crisis must have been severe. If Israel rejected life after death because of her abhorrence of polytheism, the crisis must have put a strain on Israel's very notion of God. This crisis was a turning point for Judaism and, as we shall see, eventually had a profound effect on early Anointed-believers.

Antiochus Epiphanes

In the second century BCE, Judaea, a small temple state, was caught between the great powers of the Ptolemies in Egypt and the Seleucids in Syria, two of the principal survivors (*diadochi*) of Alexander the Great's empire. From the west, the power of Rome was making itself felt. Judaea was a client of the larger powers, a precarious position. There were pro-Ptolemy factions as well as pro-Seleucid factions in Jerusalem. During the period of the crisis, Israel was a client state of the Seleucids.

Since Alexander the Great's establishment of his empire, the ancient Near East had been undergoing extensive hellenization, and Judaism was no exception. All parties were experiencing this and sometimes it was controversial, at other times not. In our surviving literature, hellenization plays a major role, often in a negative way. The pious are contrasted with the hellenizers.

The exact details of what happened have never been successfully reconstructed and some details make no sense. Even the bare outline of what happened is controversial, mostly because we lack the details and our witnesses are interested in telling the story from their own point of view for their own purposes or, to put it more boldly, are prejudiced. For our purposes, the exact details are not as important as the story as told. That story primarily comes down to us in two different forms: The narratives of First and Second Maccabees and the allegorical code of Daniel.

What follows is the barest outline of the events. In 175 BCE Antiochus Epiphanes ([God] Manifest) seized the throne following his father's death. He sought to expand his empire into the realm of Ptolemy VI's Egypt in two successive campaigns. In the first in 170 he conquered most of Egypt, except for Alexandria. The second one in 168 was less successful and was brought to a halt by the Romans (see Cameo on A Line in the Sand). His concerns were almost surely those of most rulers, power and money. This put Israel right in the middle and created a situation in which Antiochus needed money for his campaigns.

A Line in the Sand

When Antiochus had almost defeated Ptolemy, the Roman ambassador Caius Popilius Laenas presented Antiochus a letter from the Roman Senate. Polybius records the story:

> But when the king, after reading it, said he would like to communicate with his friends about this intelligence, Popilius acted in a manner which was thought to be offensive and exceedingly arrogant. He was carrying a stick cut from a vine, and with this he drew a circle round Antiochus and told him he must remain inside this circle until he gave his decision about the contents of the letter. The king was astonished at this authoritative proceeding, but, after a few moments' hesitation, said he would do all that the Romans demanded (Polybius 29.27.4).

The letter had demanded that Antiochus end his war with Ptolemy. It might also be worth noting that as a youth Antiochus had been a hostage in Rome.

Shortly after Antiochus assumed power, Jason made a move against his brother the high priest Onias to obtain the high priesthood for himself. Although brothers, the two names they chose by which to be remembered encode a major aspect of the problem. Onias is a Hebrew name; Jason is the Greek equivalent of Jesus. Onias is described as "a zealous defender of the laws" (2 Macc 4:2), while Jason was a leader of the pro-Greek group.

Jason offered Antiochus a sum greater than the normal tribute to buy the high priesthood, or as the author of 2 Maccabees says: "Jason the brother of Onias obtained the high priesthood by corruption" (4:7). This illustrates the point of view of the author of 2 Maccabees as well as the client nature of Judaea.

Under Jason's high priesthood hellenization accelerated. 2 Maccabees paints a graphic picture:

> He quickly established a gymnasium at the very foot of the acropolis, where he induced the noblest young men to wear the Greek hat. The craze for Hellenism and foreign customs reached such a pitch, through the outrageous wickedness of the ungodly pseudo-high-priest Jason, that the priests no longer cared about the service of the altar. Disdaining the temple and neglecting the sacrifices, they hastened, at the signal for the discus-throwing, to take part in the unlawful exercises on the athletic field.
>
> (2 Macc 4:12–14, see also 1 Macc 1:11–15. All translations from 1 and 2 Maccabees are from the New American Bible.)

Jason held the priesthood for three years until Menelaus offered Antiochus an even higher sum for the priesthood, "and secured the high priesthood for himself, outbidding Jason by three hundred talents of silver" (2 Macc 4:24). For Antiochus this was probably business as usual. He was fund raising for his treasury.

During Antiochus' second campaign in Egypt in which the line in the sand was drawn, a rumor spread that Antiochus was dead. This emboldened Jason to try to take the high priesthood back by force from Menelaus (2 Macc 2:5). Upon hearing this, Antiochus returned to Jerusalem and suppressed what he thought was a revolt and restored Menelaus.

> When these happenings were reported to the king, he thought that Judea was in revolt. Raging like a wild animal,

> he set out from Egypt and took Jerusalem by storm. He or-
> dered his soldiers to cut down without mercy those whom
> they met and to slay those who took refuge in their houses.
> There was a massacre of young and old, a killing of women
> and children, a slaughter of virgins and infants. In the space
> of three days, eighty thousand were lost, forty thousand
> meeting a violent death, and the same number being sold
> into slavery.
> (2 Macc 5:11–14)

After sacking the city, Antiochus violated the temple and Menelaus, the high priest, participated.

> Not satisfied with this, the king dared to enter the holiest
> temple in the world; Menelaus, that traitor both to the laws
> and to his country, served as guide. He laid his impure hands
> on the sacred vessels and gathered up with profane hands the
> votive offerings made by other kings for the advancement,
> the glory, and the honor of the Place.
> (2 Macc 5:15–16)

Now the confusion in the record becomes acute. For reasons that are not at all clear historically, Antiochus attempted the sup- pression of the Jewish religion. This was unprecedented in the an- cient world and went totally against Seleucid policy. The reasons for it and its goals remain unclear (see next section "Persecution").

The suppression and persecution led to a revolt led by the family of the Hasmoneans and eventually leadership fell to Judas, nicknamed Maccabee (Hammer). He waged a guerrilla war against the Syrians, who lost every opportunity to suppress the revolt. Eventually Judas was able to take Jerusalem and its temple, but not the citadel, Akra, which remained in Syrian hands until 142 BCE, when Simon gained control of it, finally establishing Jewish independence.

Eventually the Syrians attacked and Judas was decisively de- feated in the spring of 163 and the Syrians negotiated a peace. The story goes on with continued battles, Jewish success, and Syrian miscalculations until eventually the Romans intervene, but that later part of the story is beyond our concern.

Persecution

As mentioned above, what provoked the Maccabean revolt was Antiochus' attempt to prohibit the Jewish religion. This episode has long confounded historians, both ancient and modern, since it goes against the grain of religious and political policy in the ancient world. The author of 1 Maccabees simply assumed that gentiles and Antiochus in particular were wicked and arrogant (1 Macc 1:10, 24), while the author of 2 Maccabees argued that it was punishment for the people's sins: "Now I beg those who read this book not to be disheartened by these misfortunes, but to consider that these chastisements were meant not for the ruin but for the correction of our nation" (2 Macc 6:12). Tacitus maintained that "King Antiochus strove to destroy the national superstition, and to introduce Greek civilization, but was prevented by his war with the Parthians from at all improving this vilest of nations" (Tacitus, *Histories*, 5.8; written around 109–110 CE). Modern historians have offered an equal number of explanations. But for our

Books of Maccabees

There are four books of Maccabees. Only the first two concern us as they deal with events surrounding Antiochus Epiphanes. Both of these books are in the Christian apocrypha, as they are part of the Greek Septuagint. They are not part of the Hebrew canon, and were rejected by the rabbis and the reformers.

While 1 Maccabees was originally composed in Hebrew, it survives only in Greek. It deals with the events of Antiochus Epiphanes and the Hasmonean response. It concludes with John Hyrcanus succeeding his father Simon, the last of the five sons of Mattathias. It was written around 100 BCE.

2 Maccabees tells in a somewhat different fashion the same events as narrated by 1 Maccabees. It is composed of two letters and a summary (epitome) of the now lost five books of Jason. Unlike 1 Maccabees, 2 Maccabees does support the notion of resurrection. Dating is especially difficult, but probably somewhere in the first century BCE is safe.

purposes, what really happened is less important than the story told in Maccabees and Daniel, because that is the one that explains how and why Israel came to revise its rejection of life after death.

Following Antiochus Epiphanes' retaking of Jerusalem and re-installment of Menelaus, a new program that sought to abolish the Jewish religion was promulgated, although 1 and 2 Maccabees tell the story somewhat differently. Our concern is not to reconcile these two accounts or to discover what really happened. That is probably beyond our abilities. Our interest is how our sources evaluate what they thought happened. Let us first follow 1 Maccabees.

> Then the king wrote to his whole kingdom that all should be one people, each abandoning his particular customs. All the Gentiles conformed to the command of the king, and many Israelites were in favor of his religion; they sacrificed to idols and profaned the Sabbath.
> (1 Macc 1:41–43)

A universal decree is highly unlikely, as it would have violated Seleucid as well as Greek policy and would have started a general rebellion throughout the empire as it did in Judaea. For the author this universal decree demonstrates how rare virtue is.

> The king sent messengers with letters to Jerusalem and to the cities of Judah, ordering them to follow customs foreign to their land: to prohibit holocausts, sacrifices, and libations in the sanctuary, to profane the sabbaths and feast days, to desecrate the sanctuary and the sacred ministers, to build pagan altars and temples and shrines, to sacrifice swine and unclean animals, to leave their sons uncircumcised, and to let themselves be defiled with every kind of impurity and abomination, so that they might forget the law and change all their observances. Whoever refused to act according to the command of the king should be put to death.
> (1 Macc 1:44–50)

1 Maccabees begins with the forced abandonment of Jewish custom under the penalty of death and then moves to the desecration of the temple because its concern is the temple's restoration. Let us follow the temple and then return to this "putting to death."

1 Maccabees exactly records the date in the Seleucid calendar in which the temple was desecrated.

> On the fifteenth day of the month Chislev, in the year one hundred and forty-five, the king erected the horrible abomination upon the altar of holocausts, and in the surrounding cities of Judah they built pagan altars.
>
> (1 Macc 1:54)

Daniel 11:31 and 12:11 also refer to the event in its coded fashion: "They shall abolish the regular burnt offering and set up the abomination that makes desolate" (Dan 11:31). 1 Maccabees ties the desolation of the temple to putting Jews to death for following their customs.

> On the twenty-fifth day of each month they sacrificed on the altar erected over the altar of holocausts. Women who had had their children circumcised were put to death, in keeping with the decree, with the babies hung from their necks; their families also and those who had circumcised them were killed.
>
> (1 Macc 1:59–60)

When Jason took Jerusalem, he arranged for the temple's purification. 1 Maccabees has an elaborate description (see also 2 Macc 10:1–8).

> He chose blameless priests, devoted to the law; these purified the sanctuary and carried away the stones of the Abomination to an unclean place. They deliberated what ought to be done with the altar of holocausts that had been desecrated. The happy thought came to them to tear it down, lest it be a lasting shame to them that the Gentiles had defiled it; so they tore down the altar. They stored the stones in a suitable place on the temple hill, until a prophet should come and decide what to do with them. Then they took uncut stones, according to the law, and built a new altar like the former one. They also repaired the sanctuary and the interior of the temple and purified the courts. They made new sacred vessels and brought the lampstand, the altar of incense, and the table into the temple.
>
> (1 Macc 4:42–49)

Once the temple had been restored, Jason deliberately chose the date on which to celebrate sacrifice:

> Early in the morning on the twenty-fifth day of the ninth month, that is, the month of Chislev, in the year one hundred and forty-eight, they arose and offered sacrifice according to the law on the new altar of holocausts that they had made. On the anniversary of the day on which the Gentiles had defiled it, on that very day it was reconsecrated with songs, harps, flutes, and cymbals.
>
> (1 Macc 4:52–54)

The purification of the temple is commemorated every year at Hanukah. "Then Judas and his brothers and the entire congregation of Israel decreed that the days of the dedication of the altar should be observed with joy and gladness on the anniversary every year for eight days, from the twenty-fifth day of the month Chislev" (1 Macc 5:59; see also 2 Macc 10:8).

Martyrdom

2 Maccabees takes a somewhat different point of view because its interests are different. It begins with the temple's desecration.

> Not long after this the king sent an Athenian senator to force the Jews to abandon the customs of their ancestors and live no longer by the laws of God; also to profane the temple in Jerusalem and dedicate it to Olympian Zeus.
>
> (2 Macc 6:1–2)

Like 1 Maccabees, 2 Maccabees elaborated on the profanation of the temple. "They amused themselves with prostitutes and had intercourse with women even in the sacred court. They also brought into the temple things that were forbidden, so that the altar was covered with abominable offerings prohibited by the laws" (2 Macc 6:4–5). The notion of abomination occurs in Daniel, 1 Maccabees and now 2 Maccabees. Jews were forced to participate in the festival of Dionysus and even wear the ivy wreath.

But the real interest of the 2 Maccabees is that "A man could not keep the sabbath or celebrate the traditional feasts, nor even admit that he was a Jew" (2 Macc 6:6). This means that they will

Martyr

Martyr comes from the Greek word *martus*, meaning a witness, or *marturia*, meaning what is witnessed. In the second century this word was applied as a technical term to those Christians who were put to death by Rome for being Christian. The word martyr or martyrdom is used by extension for both Jews and Christians who at an earlier time died for their religion. By tradition, Abel (Gen 4:8) is the first martyr and Zechariah (2 Chr 24:20–22) is the last in the Hebrew canon. As we have seen, the pogrom of Antiochus Epiphanes brings the issue of martyrdom to a head in second temple Judaism.

Jesus is the first of a long list of martyrs within Christianity. In the second and third century CE, martyrologies become a type of literature celebrating the deeds and deaths of these martyrs.

"put to death those who would not consent to adopt the customs of the Greeks" (2 Macc 6:9). As we have noted, such an attempt to eliminate a religion is unattested in the ancient world and goes against normal policy. What is referred to here as "put to death" will later be called by Christians "martyrdom" and even later pogrom and holocaust. The author draws the obvious conclusion: "It was obvious, therefore, that disaster impended" (2 Macc 6:9).

The author narrates stories of those who continued to observe the Jewish customs:

> Thus, two women who were arrested for having circumcised their children were publicly paraded about the city with their babies hanging at their breasts and then thrown down from the top of the city wall. Others, who had assembled in nearby caves to observe the sabbath in secret, were betrayed to Philip and all burned to death. In their respect for the holiness of that day, they had scruples about defending themselves.
>
> (2 Macc 6:10–11)

The author goes on to tell the story of Eleazar and a mother and her seven sons. We will return to these stories later.

Awakening from the Dead

We now arrive at the question with which we began—where did Paul derive his notion of resurrection from the dead? The time and circumstances can be fixed exactly: the persecution of the Jews by Antiochus Epiphanes. The martyrdom of pious Jews for their very piety put a stress on the belief structure making it difficult to maintain. If God was true, living and life giving, how could these pious ones be murdered for following God's Torah without vindication? This creates a stress that leads to the unthinkable: that Yahweh is not a God who can keep God's part of the covenant. In the past, the problem had always been with Israel keeping the covenant. This situation created the opposite problem. Maybe God could not keep God's side of the covenant. But this is an unsupportable conclusion, so some way out of this problem must exist.

Writing in the very midst of the crisis, not afterwards as in the case of 1 and 2 Maccabees, the author of Daniel proposed in a vision a way out. God would raise up those dead martyrs and vindicate them. Both Daniel's writing and his solution were innovative.

Chapters 10–12 form what modern scholars call an historical apocalypse. It has three parts: the epiphany (10), angelic discourse (11), and eschatological prophecy (12:1–3). Daniel may be the first example of this type of an apocalypse. According to the convention of an apocalypse, the author writes in the name of an ancient, in this case Daniel, who is prophesying through a vision of the

---

Book of Daniel

Daniel is divided into two parts. The first part (chapters 1–6) contains the tales about Daniel who was deported to Babylon and rose within the court. The second part (chapters 7–12) is a series of apocalyptic visions of the prophet. The composition and dating of the first part is complex. The second part deals with the events of Antiochus Epiphanes and since it prophesies his death in the land of Israel, which did not happen, it must have been written before his death in 164 BCE.

future. This convention allows us to date the book with accuracy. Since chapter 11 wrongly describes the events of Antiochus' death, the apocalypse must have been composed shortly before his death. That sets up the third part of the apocalypse, the eschatological prophecy.

> At that time Michael, the great prince, the protector of your people, shall arise. There shall be a time of anguish, such as has never occurred since nations first came into existence. But at that time your people shall be delivered, everyone who is found written in the book. Many of those who sleep in the dust of the earth shall awake, some to everlasting life, and some to shame and everlasting contempt. Those who are wise shall shine like the brightness of the sky, and those who lead many to righteousness, like the stars forever and ever. But you, Daniel, keep the words secret and the book sealed until the time of the end. Many shall be running back and forth, and evil shall increase.
> (Dan 12:1–4)

The visionary sees the end time as happening now, at the death of Antiochus Epiphanes. As would so often prove to be the case with other future predictions of the end, the timing was wrong, but the vision was powerful and adaptable.

These apocalypses follow an established pattern—crisis, judgment, salvation. The crisis has been created by Antiochus Ephiphanes but it will increase, "a time of anguish, such as has never occurred." The angel Michael has been appointed prince to protect the people and render judgment. Those who are to be protected are "found written in the book." The Book of Life has a history in the Hebrew Bible and is precisely the mysterious type of reference upon which apocalyptic builds. The reference in Daniel builds on the mention of "my book" by Moses in Exodus:

> So Moses returned to the Lord and said, "Alas, this people has sinned a great sin; they have made for themselves gods of gold. But now, if you will only forgive their sin—but if not, blot me out of the book that you have written." But the Lord said to Moses, "Whoever has sinned against me I will blot out of my book."
> (Exod 32:31–33)

There is yet another reference in Psalms:

> Let them be blotted out of the book of the living;
> let them not be enrolled among the righteous.
>   (Ps 69:28)

From Daniel on, the Book of Life will have an even larger life in Judaism, eventually playing a role in Rosh Hashanah. The Book in Exodus refers to those who are in the covenant and in Daniel it serves to remind the reader that God's plan is foreordained and will happen despite the current anguish and suffering. The names are written and God will prevail. The pseudonymous author Daniel's mention of the angel Michael and the Book itself give us a hint of how the visionary author composes. He is a scribal prophet, one of the wise ones. "The wise among the people shall give understanding to many; for some days, however, they shall fall by sword and flame, and suffer captivity and plunder" (Dan 11:33). The wise one is among the group suffering persecution. The wise one has the secret revelation about the end. As a wise scribal prophet he employs the tradition in innovative ways. There is a sense of both a continuation with past tradition and a new way of understanding the present.

The dead are referred to as asleep. This is not simply a euphemism, but sleep is a natural metaphor for death and implies a metaphorical system drawn from daily life as a way to understand death. Job, for example, employs it.

> so mortals lie down and do not rise again;
> until the heavens are no more, they will not awake
> or be roused out of their sleep.
>   (Job 14:12)

A metaphorical system works by employing the everyday (the known) to understand the less understandable (the unknown). It implies that what is true of the daily activity is true of the other activity. The less known is understood in terms of the better known. What is true of A (sleep, the known) is true of B (the dead, the unknown).

> We go to sleep/we will die
> We awake from sleep/the dead will awake
> We rise up from our bed/the dead will rise up from the grave

Job uses the metaphorical system of sleep and arising from sleep to deny life after death, as is standard in the Hebrew Bible. The true innovation in Daniel is that the prophet seer envisions the dead awakening.

We have seen that this scribal prophet innovates by elaborating on the tradition, and the piece of tradition the scribe depends on is Isa 26:19:

> Your dead shall live, their corpses shall rise.
> O dwellers in the dust, awake and sing for joy!
> For your dew is a radiant dew,
> and the earth will give birth to those long dead.

"Dwellers in the dust" recalls "the dust of the earth" in Daniel, a somewhat redundant phrase.

Daniel prophesies, "Many of those who sleep in the dust of the earth shall awake" (Dan 12:3). Unlike Job, Daniel says those who are sleeping shall arise from that sleep. Unlike Isaiah, Daniel goes farther. In Isaiah the nation arises from sleep. Isaiah is one of many who prophesy that the nation of Israel shall arise. The understanding is corporate. In Daniel, for the first time in the Hebrew Bible it is not just the nation of Israel but also the individual. This is a true innovation with real consequences for the future.

Yet not all will awake, only "some to everlasting life, and some to shame and everlasting contempt" (Dan 12:2). Not all of Israel will awake, but only some: the prophecy implies judgment. Some, the wise, will awake to everlasting life, the only time this phrase is used in the Hebrew Bible. Others will awake to shame and contempt. The prophet is restrained in his innovation. There is no speculation on either life everlasting or everlasting contempt. That is left to the imagination and later times to spell out. One hint is given. In parallel phrases the vision concludes:

> Those who are wise shall shine like the brightness of the sky,
> and those who lead many to righteousness, like the stars forever and ever.
> (Dan 12:3)

Even though this is a comparative phrase, what is being described are the stars, which are often thought of as angels. Perhaps Daniel envisions the everlasting life as angelic, like the stars.

Scholars often note that Daniel 12 is the first reference to resurrection from the dead in the Hebrew Bible. We can date this idea rather precisely to period of the Seleucid Emperor Antiochus Epiphanes sometime between 167–163 BCE. Significantly the technical term "resurrection" does not appear in the passage but the traditional metaphorical system of sleep and awakening occurs. Daniel employs a metaphorical system drawn from daily life, an analogy of going to sleep and awakening to understand the situation. I in no way am denying the scholarly consensus. This is the first clear reference to "resurrection from the dead" in the Hebrew Bible. But I want to issue a word of caution. To call this resurrection imparts into Daniel a later technical term and doctrine, drawn from Christian theology, and risks ignoring that Daniel is not creating a new doctrine but employing a metaphorical system to solve a crisis. Martyrdom and awakening/raising the dead are intrinsically linked.

Daniel does NOT

- envision universal rising from the dead.
- say where the resurrection takes place.
- address the form of this awakening.

Daniel builds on the tradition of corporate restoration of Israel by employing a metaphorical system of sleep/awakening. He sees this happening soon. Finally he affirms the dead remain dead until the awakening.

Martyrdom creates the situation that demands God respond to the problem of their death. It is not death itself that demands resurrection, but how they died.

A Mother and Her Seven Sons

The prophecies in Daniel were written shortly before the death of Antiochus Epiphanes, while 1 and 2 Maccabees were written much later (see Cameo on The Books of Maccabees), yet deal with the same events. 1 Maccabees does not affirm resurrection from the dead, but remains within the tradition of the Hebrew Bible. This crisis happens for the instruction of the nation. Notably Daniel's solution did not sweep the day, but became one option within Judaism. There does not appear to be an "orthodox" or standard position on resurrection from the dead.

2 Maccabees, written sometime after 1 Maccabees, does accept the position in Daniel. In chapter 7 appears the story of a mother and her seven sons. This story has a very legendary and formulaic character. The brothers are one by one forced by the king to eat pork so as to violate the Torah. When they refuse, they are tortured. The second brother says just before he dies:

> You accursed fiend, you are depriving us of this present life, but the King of the world will raise us up to live again forever. It is for his laws that we are dying.
>
> (2 Macc 7:9)

All the brothers make similar speeches. These are interesting both in the ways in which they agree and disagree with Daniel. For example, the fourth brother addresses the king:

> It is my choice to die at the hands of men with the God-given hope of being restored to life by him; but for you, there will be no resurrection to life.
>
> (2 Macc 7:14)

Unlike Daniel the king will not be resurrected to everlasting contempt. The Greek *anastasis,* translated as "resurrection," means "standing up." The standing up to life here appears to point to a beatific view of awakening from the dead.

2 Maccabees does not see the martyrs as innocent suffers. The sixth brother clearly articulates this theme:

> We suffer these things on our own account, because we have sinned against our God; that is why such astonishing things have happened to us. Do not think, then, that you will go unpunished for having dared to fight against God.
>
> (2 Macc 7:18–19)

The youngest son points out how the death of the sons is redemptive for the people.

> Through me and my brothers, may there be an end to the wrath of the Almighty that has justly fallen on our whole nation.
>
> (2 Macc 7:38)

This view of martyrdom as benefiting the people fits into the theme of the noble death. The martyr's death is not in vain, but for the benefit of the people. Since the nation deserves to suffer, then the death of the martyr will relieve that need.

The mother's speech to her last and youngest son expands on these notions.

> Filled with a noble spirit that stirred her womanly heart with manly courage, she exhorted each of them in the language of their forefathers with these words: "I do not know how you came into existence in my womb; it was not I who gave you the breath of life, nor was it I who set in order the elements of which each of you is composed. Therefore, since it is the Creator of the universe who shapes each man's beginning, as he brings about the origin of everything, he, in his mercy, will give you back both breath and life, because you now disregard yourselves for the sake of his law."
> (2 Macc 7:21–23)

Her speech reminds us that life is connected with God as creator. God is the giver of life. In the Greek text, God gives the baby in her womb "breath and life" (*pneuma kai tēn zōēn.*) *Pneuma*, here correctly translated as "breath," is frequently in later Christian scriptures translated as "Spirit," thus obscuring it metaphorical root. The image of the breath of life comes from Gen 1:2 where it is the *rûaḥ*, the wind/breath (in the Greek LXX *pneuma*) that sweeps over the face of the waters. At the conclusion of her speech to her son, the mother returns to these same images:

> I beg you, child, to look at the heavens and the earth and see all that is in them; then you will know that God did not make them out of existing things.
> (2 Macc 7:28)

The mother articulates a logic in which just as God created the heavens and the earth out of nothing, so God can raise these faithful dead from the dust of the earth. This notion, *creatio ex nihilo* (creation from nothing), arises in connection with resurrection from the dead. They reinforce each other. The crisis created by Antiochus Epiphanes creates a revolution in Jewish thought and causes the notion of God to undergo a development. The notion of God as creator is expanded and deepened in order to resolve the crisis of pious Jews being murdered for their very observance of Torah.

4 | The Dead in the Anointed Will Rise First

We now can understand the scenario that supports Paul's Thanksgiving in 1 Thessalonians. The story involves persecution, martyrdom, raising up from the dead, God's vindication of the faithful, reclaiming of creation. This is a very Jewish story, and Paul remains very much within Judaism. His insight is that the raising up of the dead is not sometime in the future but has happened now, in his lifetime, for God has raised Jesus the martyr from the dead and so has set the whole process in motion.

Later in the letter to the Thessalonians Paul turns to a series of questions about which they have written or inquired. Ancient letters have formal conventions that govern an audience's expectations. This section occurs in a part of the letter called a *paranesis*, whose point is behavior. Paul is not concerned to present teaching but to correct behavior. He takes up two questions connected with the end times: whether the dead are disadvantaged at the end time (4:13–18) and what is the time of the end (5:1–11).

What is the behavior Paul seeks to correct? He does not want the Thessalonians to grieve at the death of fellow Anointed-believers; he wants them to encourage and comfort one another with the notion that the dead will rise. Surely the Thessalonians were not ignorant on this topic. It appears that they somehow thought the dead might be disadvantaged in comparison with the living when the lord comes. That is why Paul argues that the living "will not be given preference over those who have already fallen asleep."

> Concerning those who have fallen asleep,
> we don't want you to be uninformed:
> you shouldn't mourn as do those without hope.
> Because if we believe "Jesus died and arose,"
> so also God will bring with Jesus all those belonging to him
>   who have fallen asleep.
> We can assure you of this by these prophetic words from the
>   lord:
>   we who are still alive when Jesus comes will not be given
>   preference over those who have already fallen asleep.
>   The lord himself will descend from heaven
>   with a loud summons,
>   with an archangel's shout
>   and with the trumpet of God,
>   then those who have already died and belong to the
>   Anointed will rise first;
>   then those of us who are still living will be caught up
>   with them in the clouds to greet the lord in the air.
>   And so we will be with the lord from then on.
> So you should encourage each other with these prophetic
>   words.
>   (1 Thess 4:13–18, SV modified)

To make his point, Paul lays out the end game of the apoca-lyptic scenario, how it will play out after Jesus' resurrection. For Paul and these earliest Anointed-believers, Jesus' resurrection is one moment, a pivotal moment, in an apocalyptic scenario, God's plan. Jesus' resurrection is never an isolated event, but a moment in a plan. In a later letter Paul will refer to Jesus' resurrection from the dead as the first fruits (1 Cor 15:20, 23) because it guarantees the next step, the final resurrection of Anointed-believers.

Paul begins his argument for why the Thessalonians should not grieve by stating what he and they take to be a fact: "Jesus died and arose"; and then he draws from that the conclusion: "so also God will bring with Jesus all those belonging to him who have fallen asleep." The translation makes it clearer than the Greek.

"Arose" is a bit misleading. Paul normally uses *egeirein*, to get up or rise up (out of bed) and in the passive voice so that Jesus has been raised by God. Only in 1 Thessalonians does he employ *anastēnai*, to stand up. The noun *anastasis*, standing up, eventually comes to mean resurrection. Also he employs here the active voice, rather than the more normal passive voice. In the Thanksgiving (1 Thess 1:10) where God was the subject, Paul used the active *ēgeiren* (whom God raised, see chapter 2). The word *anastēnai* could be translated: "since we believe that Jesus died and stood up (from the grave)."

The conclusion of the "because" clause expects an indicative (a statement): "because if we believe, . . . therefore. . . ." But Paul's grammar is confusing. A literal English translation following the Greek word order reads: "so also God those who have fallen asleep through Jesus will bring with him." Part of the problem is that the subject has shifted from Jesus to God. Therefore in this second clause Jesus acts as God's agent, "through Jesus." But what does "through Jesus" go with: God, those who have fallen asleep, or "will bring"? It's not clear, although I would suggest that "will bring" makes the most sense. I would propose the following translation: "So God also will bring through Jesus those who have fallen asleep with him."

Paul then turns to the Thessalonians' concern. He declares his answer is by "these prophetic words from the lord," literally in the Greek "a word of the lord." In the Hebrew Bible this phrase is often used of a prophetic saying (thus the SV translation), so that is probably what it means here. This is Paul's prophetic word dealing with the Thessalonians' concern—that the dead are somehow at a disadvantage compared to the living at the lord's coming. He declares that they are not and that they will precede those who are alive. For this reason they are not to grieve.

The Greek for "Jesus comes" is *parousia*, which becomes a technical term in post-70 Christianity. Most of the time in Paul it simply means coming or presence. For example, "I am very pleased that Stephanas and Fortunatus and Achaicus have come because they had made up for what you were not able to do" (1 Cor 16:17). Or when arguing with the Corinthians, Paul reports: "'His letters,' they say, 'are weighty and forceful, but his physical presence is unimpressive and his speech is pathetic'" (2 Cor 10:10). Only in 1 Thessalonians (2:19; 3:13; 4:15; 5:23) and 1 Corinthians (15:23) does *parousia* refer to the coming of the lord. Its repetition in the letter indicates its importance to the Thessalonians.

Parousia

Parousia, as noted, is a Greek word for arrival, coming or presence. It is made up of two words, *para* (beside) *ousia* (being)—so being beside or present. After 70 CE in Christian circles *parousia* becomes a technical term when used in the rest of the New Testament (13 times). In the gospels only Matthew utilizes it for the coming of the son of man (Matt 24:3, 27, 37, 39). 2 Peter (3:12) refers to the coming of the Day of the Lord. 2 Thessalonians, which is probably not written by Paul, refers both to the coming of the Lord (2:1) and the coming of the lawless one (2:8, 9). Justin Martyr, writing sometime in the last half of the second century, is the first to refer to the second coming of Christ as distinguished from his first coming (*Apology* 52.3; *Dialogue* 14.8).

The notion of the coming of the Lord is rooted in the movement of early Anointed-believers, as we can see in the Aramaic phrase *marana tha* (1 Cor 16:22). But *parousia* is the official term for a visit of a king or emperor in which a town prepares for his coming as though he were a god. 3 Maccabees reports a letter from Ptolemy Philopator to his generals in which the official term occurs and Ptolemy complains about his *parousia*.

> And when we had granted very great revenues to the temples in the cities, we came on to Jerusalem also, and went up to honor the temple of those wicked people, who never cease from their folly. They accepted our presence (*parousia*) by word, but insincerely by deed, because when we proposed to enter their inner temple and honor it with magnificent and most beautiful offerings, they were carried away by their traditional arrogance, and excluded us from entering; but they were spared the exercise of our power because of the benevolence that we have toward all.
> (3 Macc 3:16–18)

Parousia can also be used for the visit of a god, and these two uses tend to converge. Paul's use derives from this Greek usage. Evidence is lacking for its use in Judaism as a reference to the end times.

Paul's actual description of the *parousia* of the Lord is full of Jewish images.

- Fallen asleep, which we have seen in Daniel
- The archangel, which does not appear in the Hebrew Bible, but there is a great deal of speculation on angels in late second temple Judaism. Unlike Daniel, Paul does not name the angel.
- God's trumpet, for example, in Joel 2:1:

  Blow the trumpet in Zion;
  sound the alarm on my holy mountain!
  Let all the inhabitants of the land tremble,
  for the day of the LORD is coming, it is near—

Those who are asleep are characterized as having "already died and belong to the Anointed," literally "dead in the Anointed." To point out the obvious, Paul remains firmly within the Jewish model. He does not opt for the Greek model of the immortality of the soul. These Anointed-believers are dead, dead in the Anointed. They have no soul that remains after death. They are in the earth, turning to dust, as in Daniel, but most importantly, they are in the Anointed. That is what guarantees their rising up from the dust, from the dead.

> Or do you not grasp the fact that all of us who were immersed in baptism as a way of identifying with the anointed Jesus were symbolically immersed into his death? What that means is that we were buried with him when we were symbolically immersed into his death so that, just as the Anointed was raised from the dead by the power and splendor of God, we also might live a new kind of life. If we have truly identified with him in a death like his, then we will certainly be united with him in rising to a new kind of life like his.
>
> (Rom 6:3–5)

Paul's cosmological model is likewise firmly Jewish. God and Jesus are in heaven (sky), and the dead and living will meet Jesus in the air—in between heaven/sky and earth. Unlike the modern Left Behind Series, Paul is silent on what then will happen.

Those who are "saved" will be caught up into the clouds. The Greek for "caught up" more literally means "snatched," which has a violent overtone. In Greek literature "death snatches" is a cliché, whereas here Paul uses "snatched" not of death but *parousia*, ironically reversing the cliché.

When will that day happen? Paul is sure it is soon, but he does not know when. It will come like a thief in the night (1 Thess 5:2). His metaphor is that the times are like a pregnant woman whose labor pains cannot be far away (1 Thess 5:3). Paul himself thinks he will be alive at that time: he speaks of "we who are still alive."

This passage from the earliest writing in the New Testament is important for our understanding of resurrection at the earliest level of the movement that is becoming Christianity—and for several reasons.

- Apocalyptic is integral to the notion of resurrection.
- Resurrection is a process that begins with Jesus' raising up and concludes with that of the Anointed-believers.
- Paul's understanding of resurrection remains firmly within the Jewish conception. The innovation is the timetable. It has happened now. The future is now.
- Resurrection is not a technical term for Paul. He is still operating with the metaphorical notion of rising up (from bed, from the earth) or standing up.
- The dead are asleep. As in traditional Judaism the dead are dead, but as Anointed-believers they are dead in Christ.
- Paul has begun to adapt the language of the apocalyptic scenario to his gentile audience. *Parousia* and "snatched" are two examples of this.

1 Thessalonians is not the normal place in which to start a study of resurrection, but we have begun there because we are following chronological order. In its Thanksgiving this letter contains our first reference to Jesus' being raised up from the dead, and its parenesis the first discussion in the New Testament of an aspect of that standing up. Not only is there no account of Jesus' rising up from the dead, no account is implied. Rather, Paul is operating with the Jewish apocalyptic scenario, not much different from that found in Daniel. In the next chapter we will turn to the earliest account of one who claims to have experienced this raised up Jesus.

Further Reading

Malherbe, Abraham J. *The Letters to the Thessalonians*, Anchor Bible. New York: Doubleday, 2000.

5 An Experience of Jesus Raised from the Dead

Introduction

In following the metaphor "raised up from the dead," we have seen how the language of getting out of bed, rising up from sleep, is applied metaphorically to understand the fate of the Jewish martyrs. This involves an apocalyptic scenario that Paul employs to understand what has happened to Jesus, to those who have confidence in Jesus as Anointed, and to the whole world. Now we turn to Paul's own experience. What convinced him that this apocalyptic scenario was in play, that now was the decisive time God had chosen to act?

Paul provides no elaborate description of his own experience. For that one has to go to the much later Acts of the Apostles (9:1–19; 22:3–16; 26:9–18). These accounts in Acts are later and do not provide primary evidence, as Paul's account does. The accounts in Acts are almost novelistic in character. This is the first of many occasions in which an apparent gap in an earlier account appears to call out for details from a later account to ease the gap, to make it go away. We should resist the temptation to fill in the gap and continue to follow chronological order.

The letter to the Galatians was written after 1 Thessalonians but before 1 and 2 Corinthians and Romans, i.e., sometime in the early 50s CE. To be more exact is not possible.

Galatians is an angry letter; it does not even include an initial Thanksgiving. Paul immediately accuses the Galatians of having turned away to follow another gospel, a charge equivalent to apostasy. "I'm amazed by how quickly you have abandoned the one who called you by the favor of God's Anointed and have embraced an entirely different message (gospel)" (Gal 1:6). Not even in 1 Corinthians 15, where Paul claims the Corinthians are denying the resurrection of the dead, does he claim they are following another gospel. Paul perceives his very apostleship to be under attack and to defend it he recounts his turn from persecuting the church of God to proclaiming Jesus among the gentiles.

> Let me make it clear, friends, the gospel I announced does not
>   conform to human expectations.
> I say this because it was not transmitted to me by anyone nor
>   did anyone teach it to me.
> Rather, it came to me as an insight [revelation] from God
>   about Jesus as God's Anointed.
> Surely you've heard of my own behavior as a practicing Jew,
> how aggressively I harassed God's new community, trying to
>   wipe it out.
> I went way beyond most of my contemporaries in my obser-
>   vance of Judaism,
> and became notably zealous about my ancestral traditions.
> But, when God, who designated me before I was born
> and commissioned me through his grace,
> was pleased to reveal his son through me with the intent that
>   I would proclaim God's world-transforming news to "the
>   nations,"
> I did not rush off to consult with anyone.
> Neither did I set out for Jerusalem to get the approval of those
>   who became envoys for God's Anointed before I did.
> Instead, I left for Arabia and afterward returned to Damascus.
>   (Gal 1:11–17, SV modified)

This sounds autobiographical and it is, but we must remember that Paul is not giving a full account. Rather he is using the account to justify his claim that he did not receive the gospel by tradition nor was he taught it, but that it came by revelation. That theme is signaled in the letter's greeting:

> Paul an apostle
> neither from humans nor through humans,
> but through Jesus the Anointed and God the Father
>   who raised him from the dead . . .
>   (Gal 1:1, BBS Trans)

Paul's apostleship and how he got to be an apostle is the issue. Paul reiterates that thesis in verse 11 and the defense runs from 1:12–2:14. The autobiography is constructed and summarized to prove his thesis that he did not receive his gospel or commission from humans but from God. Its interest is not autobiographical but rhetorical—he is trying to prove a point. This does not mean that we should discount his story as one having an agenda, but remember that he is telling his story from a particular point of view. In another discussion he might use a different way of telling the story.

Revelation

Our concern is not Paul's argument with the Galatians, but that in this argument he reports his experience of "the risen Lord." This is the earliest report by an "eyewitness" of the "risen Lord." We must try to be precise in our terminology. I have put "risen Lord" in quotes because that is not Paul's expression, but a much later expression. This is a primary example of the resurrection/ egg problem. Because Paul does not use resurrection language in this passage, we do not think of this passage as dealing with the resurrection. But Paul is describing his experience that the other apostles accept as authentic. Thus this is the earliest report we have by someone whose experience was certified by the apostles as what it means to experience Jesus the Anointed whom God raised from the dead.

The event here described is traditionally referred to as Paul's Damascus Road experience, but Damascus is mentioned only in the last line of the description and then as a place returned to, not as the place on the road to which the event happened. Acts (see Acts 9:3–13; 22:6–21; 26:12–18) draws attention to the Damascus road as the place of the event, the light, Paul being struck off his horse, and his blindness. Well, the horse is not in Acts, but in the art work. Where did that horse come from? Probably from the assumption that Paul would travel on the road by horse. We should set Acts aside and follow Paul's own account of his story. He has none of the novelistic details so prominent in Acts. He never states that his experience took place on the road, he never says where the revelation actually happened or that it was a momentary event.

Not only is Paul's account much more restrained, it is hard to reconcile Paul's account with Acts. This can be seen with two quick points. The stories in Acts make the point that Paul was taught by those in Damascus. This assumption infuriated Paul. Secondly, the picture in Acts of Paul participating in the stoning of Stephen is hard to reconcile with Paul's statement later in his autobiographical report: "I was still unknown by sight to the churches of Judea" (Gal 1:22). These are just two of several reasons why we should prefer Paul's report to Acts. One is almost tempted to wonder if the stories in Acts do not represent the type of tradition that Paul is rejecting in Galatians.

Paul prefaces his account with a report of his behavior as a Jew. Traditionally we have thought of Paul persecuting the

---

Phinehas Was Zealous

Just then one of the Israelites came and brought a Midianite woman into his family, in the sight of Moses and in the sight of the whole congregation of the Israelites, while they were weeping at the entrance of the tent of meeting. When Phinehas son of Eleazar, son of Aaron the priest, saw it, he got up and left the congregation. Taking a spear in his hand, he went after the Israelite man into the tent, and pierced the two of them, the Israelite and the woman, through the belly. So the plague was stopped among the people of Israel. Nevertheless those that died by the plague were twenty-four thousand.

The Lord spoke to Moses, saying: "Phinehas son of Eleazar, son of Aaron the priest, has turned back my wrath from the Israelites by manifesting such zeal among them on my behalf that in my jealousy I did not consume the Israelites. Therefore say, 'I hereby grant him my covenant of peace. It shall be for him and for his descendants after him a covenant of perpetual priesthood, because he was zealous for his God, and made atonement for the Israelites'" (Num 25:6–13).

early church. The image of Paul participating in the murder of Anointed-believers comes from Acts, not Paul. His language is much more circumspect. Acts has a way of constantly intruding upon this story, even in the translation of Galatians. The NRSV's "violently persecuting the church of God" is a severe over-translation. The King James by contrast has, "beyond measure I persecuted the church of God, and wasted it." "Persecute" is not a wrong translation, but it has overtones among Christians that mislead in regards to Paul's activity. Persecution conjures up the martyrdoms of Christians by the Romans and that is not what Paul was engaged in. The Greek word *diōkein* means to hasten, press on or pursue. By extension it can mean to harass or to persecute. Underlying the sense of harass or persecute is to press on or pursue. "Aggressively I harassed God's new community, trying to wipe it out" (SV). The King James translates the next phrase "and wasted it" because the primary sense of *porthein* in Greek is to plunder or pillage. The purpose of Paul's harassment is to eliminate the community.

He takes this behavior as an example of his zeal. We have a problem with zeal because of the excessiveness and fanaticism of religious zealots. In this period, however, the word does not have a negative connotation but names a virtue. Paul holds up his behavior as an example of his loyalty and faithfulness to his religious tradition, not something of which he is ashamed. The examples of Phinehas and Elijah give us a good indication of how to view zeal in this context. SV's "aggressively I harrassed" parallels NRSV's "far more zealous." Both indicate the extreme to which Paul has gone.

Zealous for the Lord

Then the word of the Lord came to him, saying, "What are you doing here, Elijah?" He answered, "I have been very zealous for the Lord, the God of hosts; for the Israelites have forsaken your covenant, thrown down your altars, and killed your prophets with the sword. I alone am left, and they are seeking my life, to take it away" (1 Kgs 19:9–10).

Paul contrasts his "before" and "now" to show that to change him was beyond human power. He makes a similar point in Philippians.

as to zeal,	a harasser of the church;
as to righteousness in the law,	blameless.
(Phil 3:6, BBS Trans)	

Here Paul employs the same language as in Galatians to make a similar point: his zeal for the Torah impelled him to harass the church of God in an attempt to eliminate it.

Paul's Call

What caused the shift from harasser to apostle?

In a brilliant and revolutionary essay, Krister Stendahl explored the language Paul used to describe his experience. He argued that Paul employed the language of call and not conversion. Paul was called to be an apostle; he did not convert to becoming a Christian.

Traditionally we have viewed this as Paul's conversion. But we must ask ourselves, in what sense is it a conversion?

- Paul already believes in the one, true God, the God of Israel.
- As yet there is no Christianity to which Paul can convert.
- Paul always self-identifies as a Jew (Phil 3:4–5; Rom 11:1).
- He is not in need of moral conversion. "As to the Torah, blameless" (Phil 3:6).

Paul's conversion has been important in Christianity for several reasons. It becomes the template for Christian conversion. Augustine is a major influence here. For the question we are considering, the resurrection of Jesus, titling Paul's revelation experience as conversion has the major advantage of distancing Paul's experience from that of the original apostles. There were the appearances to the apostles on the third day and then later was Paul's conversion. Acts of course abets this program by distancing Paul's conversion from Jesus' appearances to the apostles before the Ascension. Jesus is gone, so something else must have happened to Paul, namely his conversion. The original apostles did not need conversion because they were already followers of Jesus. This, again, is a much later imposition.

Paul himself invokes the language of the prophet Jeremiah's call:

> Before I formed you in the womb I knew you,
> and before you were born I consecrated you;
> I appointed you a prophet to the nations.
>   (Jer 1:5)

A similar description occurs in Isaiah.

> Listen to me, O coastlands,
> pay attention, you peoples from far away!
> The Lord called me before I was born,
> while I was in my mother's womb he named me.
>   (Isa 49:1)

These two quotes from the prophets indicate that Paul views his revelation as parallel to that of the prophets. Paul is being called by God. This invocation of the Jewish tradition should not surprise us. Everything we have seen to this point about Paul is that he remains firmly within that tradition. His innovation is in the timetable—the time is now—not in the scenario.

God's Son

When Paul describes his own experience, the turn of phrase is from God's point of view, not Paul's. "He [God] was pleased . . . to reveal his son in/to me" (BBS Trans). God calls Paul and reveals his son. The event is not described with a visual metaphor, but as revelation. The language of "he appeared" or "I have seen" is missing. Paul considers the prophetic call model as an adequate model for understanding an experience of the "risen son." Even more, no content is given beyond "son", the same term that we saw in 1 Thess 1:10. This revelation convinced Paul that Jesus was God's son, the Anointed.

Both in 1 Thess 1:10 and Gal 1:16 Jesus as God's son is connected to God raising Jesus from the dead. For Paul, Jesus becomes son at the resurrection. The Greeting in Romans makes this clear.

> Paul, slave of the Anointed, Jesus
>   summoned as an envoy,
> appointed to announce God's world-changing news,
>   which was anticipated by the prophets in holy scriptures,
> This news is about the "son of God,"

> who was physically descended from David
>> appointed and empowered as "son of God," in accordance with the spirit of holiness, from the time of his resurrection from the dead,
>
> Jesus, the Anointed, our lord,
>> through him I have received the gracious favor of my calling to promote in his name the obedience that comes from a confident reliance upon God among all of the world's peoples.
>>> (Rom 1:1–5)

This Greeting is a stereotyped summary of the issues we have been following. Paul is "appointed" or "set apart" as in Galatians, which invokes the language of Isaiah for the gospel ("news"). That the gospel was "anticipated" shows that God has a plan. Gospel, son, and God are tied closely together. Physically descended from David and then by the resurrection made son of God indicates a clear double step. Finally all of this results in Paul being the apostle to the gentiles. That is part of the plan of the gospel. In this Greeting we see almost the complete scenario. The only aspect missing is the apocalyptic ending.

What Rom 1:4 clearly shows is that Jesus is designated as God's son by the resurrection, a point implied in the formulae of 1 Thessalonians and Galatians.

Revelation

What then is a revelation? The Greek root *apocalyps-* means to uncover what is hidden, i.e., to reveal. There is a double aspect. Something was hidden and now is made manifest. Furthermore, for Paul the agent is God. In a revelation, God makes known something that otherwise cannot be known.

The crux of Paul's argument in Galatians is that his gospel and apostleship came through God's revelation, not through a human intermediary. Three times in his autobiography he employs the Greek root *apocalyps-*, twice as a noun, once as verb. His usage should guide us.

> **Gal 1:12**
> for I did not receive it from men,
> nor was I taught it,
> but I received it through a **revelation** of Jesus the Anointed.

Gal 1:16

But when God was pleased,

who had set me apart from my mother's womb

and called me through his grace,

to **reveal** his Son to me,

so that I might proclaim him among the Gentiles, . . .

Gal 2:2

Then after fourteen years I went up again to Jerusalem with

Barnabas,

taking Titus along with me.

I went up in response to a **revelation**.

(BBS Trans)

Verse 12 makes an explicit contrast between "from men" and "through revelation." The phrase "did not receive" is an explicit reference to the handing on of tradition. Verse 16 makes more explicit the claim of verse 12, using the prophet model. The emphasis falls on what God has done. In both of these verses "revelation" marks not only a contrast with humans and intervention by God, but also causes a shift, a shift that in Paul's mind is associated with the apocalyptic scenario. For that reason, I would suggest we refer to this use of revelation as *apocalyps*-revelation.

Galatians 2:2 deals with Paul going up to Jerusalem, to what has traditionally been called the Jerusalem Council, on analogy with the great ecumenical councils of later ages. This model is too grandiose, although surely it was important in Paul's eyes. Paul's point is that he did not go in response to those in Jerusalem, that he was not summoned but went at God's initiative. One may think of this as self-serving, but it makes clear what he means by "revelation." This too is *apocalyps*-revelation, since it is part of God's plan for vindicating the gospel.

Fifteen other times the *apocalyps*- root is used in the authentic Pauline letters. In ten of those cases it is associated with the end times and so has the same meaning as in Galatians. Romans 8:18–19 can serve as an example:

For I consider that the sufferings of the now time are not

worth comparing with the glory about to be revealed to us.

For the creation waits with eager longing for the revelation of

the sons of God.

(Rom 8:18–19, BBS Trans)

This quote indicates that *apocalyps*-revelation concerns God's activity and is associated with God's plan to redeem creation. The language is firmly situated within the apocalyptic scenario we first saw in Daniel.

Five usages in 1 and 2 Corinthians illustrate an interesting difference. These usages cluster in 1 Corinthians 14 and 2 Corinthians 12. In 1 Corinthians 14 Paul is dealing with the spiritual gifts that have caused such dissention in the Corinthian community.

> Listen, friends, if I meet with you and speak in an ecstatic language,
> how will I be of any use to you unless I offer some God-given revelation, or some piece of knowledge, or some prophecy or teaching?
> (1 Cor 14:6, SV modified)

Here he groups revelation with knowledge, prophecy, and teaching—all spiritual gifts. These four are community functions or practices that make evident what is hidden in speaking in tongues. This becomes quite clear when Paul draws his conclusion.

> So what should you do, my friends?
> When you gather together and you each have a hymn, a bit of instruction, a revelation, an ecstatic utterance, an interpretation,
> everything should be done for the benefit of the community.
> If someone breaks out in ecstatic speech
> —two or at most three at the same time—
> one of you should interpret.
> But if no interpreter is present,
> they should remain silent in the meeting
> and speak to themselves and to God.
> Two or three prophets should speak
> and the others should ponder what they say.
> If a revelation comes to someone else sitting alongside,
> the first speaker should be quiet.
> (1 Cor 14:26–30, SV modified)

Revelation here refers to a practice within the community and Paul makes this clear by coupling it with other practices. This should be distinguished from *apocalyps*-revelation which concerns the end times, the apocalyptic scenario. Not to make too fine a point, the spiritual gifts, of which revelation is one, are a sign of the end times. Paul makes clear the sense he has in mind with the words with which he associates it. For example, in the Thanksgiving to 1 Corinthians he employs *apocalyps*-revelation in association with spiritual gifts, but the difference is obvious from context.

> I thank God all the time for the generous favor God has
>   shown to you through the Anointed Jesus . . .
> so you do not lack any spiritual gift
> as you wait for the revelation of our lord Jesus the Anointed.
>   (1 Cor 1:4, 7, SV modified)

In the Thanksgiving, "revelation" means *apocalyps*-revelation, as it refers to the end time.

What and to Whom?

We now have a sense of what Paul means by *apocalyps*-revelation. The accent is on what God has accomplished, not on what Paul has experienced. It fits into the apocalyptic scenario, which means that it is part of a process that will conclude with the *apocalyps*-revelation of Jesus the Anointed at the end time. Paul does provide a hint of the content of his *apocalyps*-revelation. In Gal 1:12 he says: "but I received it [the gospel] through a revelation of Jesus the Anointed" and in verse 16: "[God] was pleased to reveal his Son to me." Now the grammar problems begin. In verse 12 what does the "of Jesus the Anointed" mean?

- The gospel was revealed by Jesus the Anointed?
- The content of the revelation was Jesus the Anointed?
- That gospel and Jesus the Anointed are identified?

Verse 16 only complicates the issue. The object of the verb "reveal" is "Son," so that is the content of the revelation. But one could take it to indicate that Jesus is God the father's son.

There is yet one more ambiguity. Literally it reads "to reveal his son in me." It is unclear whether this means that the revelation is to, or in, Paul. Verse 12 would appear to point towards "to me" but Gal 2:20 points in the other direction.

and	lives	no longer	I,
but	lives	in me	Christ.

The "in me" is the exact same Greek as in 1:16. Maybe we should allow for both possibilities at the same time. The *apocalyps-*

revelation was both to Paul and in Paul, even through Paul. Given the apocalyptic scenario with which Paul is working, such an ecstatic experience fits.

The outcome of the revelation, its purpose, is that Paul should be the apostle to the gentiles. That is why it is replayed in the letter to prove his call. Like the prophets of old, Paul's *apocalyps*-revelation results in his call. The two come together as one package. Gospel, son, Paul's call, and *apocalyps*-revelation are all part of one process.

This description reads as a rehearsed narrative which Paul tells folks when he describes how he moved from persecuting the church of God to proclaiming Jesus as God's son, the Anointed—his story of that event. This is also the earliest description of someone experiencing the "resurrection event" and it is narrated not as an appearance but an *apocalyps*-revelation. The revelation is wrapped up in a larger story, the story of Paul's call or Paul's call itself is wrapped in a revelation—the two cannot be pulled apart. Just as we saw in 1 Thessalonians, the raising up of Jesus is not a single event but always one of a chain in a total story. In 1 Thessalonians it was the apocalyptic scenario; in Galatians the story of Paul's prophetic call is also part of the same apocalyptic event. Paul's apostleship to the gentiles is the announcement of the end times.

Why persecution?

If God's revelation convinced Paul that Jesus was the Anointed, why was Paul persecuting the early Anointed-believers? Messianic belief was well within the bounds of Judaism, more varied and not as universal as Christians suppose, yet still within the bounds. During the last major Jewish revolt against the Romans in 132–135 CE, Rabbi Akiba, one of the most prominent and revered of Rabbinic figures, proclaimed the leader of the revolt (132–136 CE), Simon bar Kokhba, to be the Anointed. After bar Kokhba's defeat it was clear that Akiba was wrong. Yet Akiba was never condemned for his mistake, nor did it diminish his status as a teacher.

The bar Kokhba example contains an important clue to Paul's problem. Bar Kokhba was defeated by the Romans and so obviously was not the Anointed. His defeat was the proof. In Jesus' case, the Anointed-believers proclaimed him the Anointed *after* Rome had defeated him. They proclaimed him Anointed after there was convincing evidence he was not Anointed! If indeed Pilate condemned Jesus as a political revolutionary, his crucifixion would have reinforced his status as a loser.

Paul may refer to this issue in the elaborate discussion of the Torah in Galatians 3. We need not take up all of that debate, but only the portion that touches on our concern. Paul is dealing with the curse of the Torah by which the gentiles are excluded from the covenant. To show that the curse has been overturned he argues,

> God's Anointed freed us from the curse of subjection to the
> Law, by becoming a curse for us,
> since it is written, "Anyone who hangs on a tree is accursed."—
> This was done so that Abraham's blessing might come to the
> nations by belonging to the Anointed Jesus,
> and so that we might receive the promise of God's presence
> and power through putting our unconditional trust in God.
> (Gal 3:13–14)

For Paul before his *apocalyps*-revelation, there were two reasons why Jesus could not be the Anointed, and they are interrelated.

- The Romans crucified and defeated him.
- Anyone hung on a tree is under God's curse (Deut 21:23).

The logic derives from the conception of the Anointed. The successor of King David will defeat Israel's enemies, not be defeated by them. This is the scandal and paradox that is at the heart of Paul's gospel. This by itself would be enough to prove that Jesus was not the expected Jewish messiah. Re-enforcing

---

Crucifixion

When someone is convicted of a crime punishable by death and is executed, and you hang him on a tree, his corpse must not remain all night upon the tree; you shall bury him that same day, for anyone hung on a tree is under God's curse. You must not defile the land that the Lord your God is giving you for possession (Deut 21:22–23).

this notion is the proscription from Deuteronomy. Prior to the *apocalyps*-revelation, Paul judged the Anointed-believers as clearly heretical because their Jesus could not be the Anointed.

But the *apocalyps*-revelation from God uncovered and made known something not otherwise knowable and thus convinced Paul that Jesus was God's son, the Anointed; therefore he shifted from being a persecutor to being a proclaimer. This revelation had important consequences for Paul's thought and behavior. It led him to see how gentile sinners could be admitted to the covenant without having to observe Torah. The Anointed's acceptance of the curse of Torah ends the banishment of the gentiles.

Once we recognize that Paul's *apocalyps*-revelation is a call and not a conversion, the revelation appears in a different light. It is Paul's description of his experience of the Jesus whom God has raised from the dead and designated "his [God's] son." This is the earliest account of an experience of Jesus raised from the dead in the New Testament, and it is by an eyewitness. He is describing his own experience and he describes it as an *apocalyps*-revelation. At this early stage the language for referring to this experience is not fixed, but a variety of terms drawn from apocalyptic language can be used depending on the context. In the rhetorical context of Galatians, where Paul is defending his apostleship which he sees as under attack, he uses *apocalyps*-revelation to describe his experience. He does not stand in tradition, for it was not something handed on. God revealed his son to/in him. Furthermore, the content of the revelation is the gospel that Jesus is God's son. Paul does not describe his own subjective experience except as revelation.

Now we must turn our attention to the remaining metaphors.

Further Reading

Betz, Hans Dieter Betz. *Galatians*, Hermeneia. Philadelphia: Fortress, 1979.

Eisenbaum, Pamela. *Paul Was Not a Christian, the Original Message of a Misunderstood Apostle.* New York: HarperOne, 2009.

Martyn, J. Louis. *Galatians*, Anchor Bible. New Haven: Yale University, 1997.

Stendahl, Krister. *Paul among Jews and Gentiles.* Philadelphia: Fortress Press, 1976.

6 The Earliest Resurrection Narrative?

In chapter 2 of the letter to the Philippians Paul quotes a poem-like piece:

> [Who] Being in the form (*morphē*) of a god (or God)
> Did not consider it a thing to use for his own advantage,
> The being equal with a god,
>
> But he emptied (*ekenōsin*) himself
> Taking the form (*morphēn*) of a slave,
> Becoming in the likeness of humans
>
> And finding himself in the human schema (*schēmati*),
> He humiliated himself,
> Becoming obedient all the way to death—
> Even death by crucifixion.
>
> For this God has super-exalted him,
> Gracing him with the name,
> A name superior to all names,
>
> So that at Jesus' name
> Every knee should bow down
> In the heavens, on the earth and in the underworld,
>
> And every tongue should shout out,
> "The Lord (*kurios*) is Jesus the Anointed
> For the glory of God the father.
>   (2:6–11, BBS Trans)

This piece has generated a massive amount of research, what John Reumann has called the Mount Everest of Philippians.

Needless to say the debate has been extensive and many issues remain unresolved. Among the debated questions are:

- What is it?
- Did Paul compose it?
- Was its composition before Paul or contemporaneous with Paul?
- What do the words mean?
- How should it be translated?
- In what context should we read the passage?

Fortunately we do not have to solve all these problems to deal with the issue that concerns us, but we will need to be aware of the options in the debate. The mountain of research surely has produced an exegesis that at times is over subtle and demands of the passage a level of precision not intended at the time of composition. Furthermore, since this passage has been tremendously important in the history of Christology and Trinitarian discourse, we need to be alert to the possibility that elements of this discourse have has been inferentially read back into the exegesis of the passage. Because the lines sound like later Christology does not automatically mean that it is later Christology.

Introductory Issues

What Is It?

Since Ernest Lohmeyer's 1928 study, commentators have noticed the difference in language of Phil 2:6–11 from its surrounding material. The language readily divides into short strophes or lines, and many translations print the passage in verse. It easily divides into six stanzas of three lines each. The lone exception is stanza three, which has four lines, the last of which, "even death by crucifixion," is almost surely an addition by Paul. First proposed by Lohmeyer, this division along with the Pauline insertion commends itself. The passage does have an intensity and compactness characteristic of poetry that sets it apart from the prose of the remaining letter. Lohmeyer was also the first to identify it as a psalm or hymn, and so most scholars have assumed that it was an early Christian hymn used by the Pauline churches in their

Carmen Christi

In 111–112 CE Pliny the Younger was sent by the Emperor Trajan to serve as governor of the troubled province of Pontus and Bithynia in Asia Minor. Among the issues with which he had to deal were charges against the Christians. His letter to Trajan asking for guidance makes fascinating reading, since it gives us an upper class Roman's view of the Christian sect and illustrates how Roman imperial power operates.

He reported to the Emperor:

> They declared that the sum total of their guilt or error amounted to no more than this: they had met regularly before dawn on a fixed day to chant verses alternately among themselves in honor of Christ as if to a god, and also to bind themselves by oath, not for any criminal purpose, but to abstain from theft, robbery and adultery, to commit no breach of trust, and not to deny a deposit when called upon to restore it.
>
> After this ceremony it had been their custom to disperse and reassemble later to take food of an ordinary, harmless kind. But they had in fact given up this practice since my edict, issued on your [Trajan's] instructions, which banned all political societies.
>
> This made me decide it was all the more necessary to extract the truth by torture from two slave-women, whom they call diaconesses. I found nothing but a degenerate sort of cult carried to extravagant length.
> (Letter 10.96.7–8; tr. B. Radice)

In the English translation "to chant verses alternately among themselves in honor of Christ as if to a god," the Latin reads, "carmenque Christo quasi deo dicere secum invicem." What Pliny means by *carmen Christo* is not at all clear but it has led to the identification of the "hymn" in Philippians as *Carmen Christi*, the Hymn of Christ, and the emergence of a whole area of New Testament study on early Christian hymns. Lohmeyer, the first to call it a Psalm, thought it might represent the liturgy used by the Jerusalem community.

worship services. If so, it would be our earliest example of early Christian worship.

But in recent years its status as a hymn has been questioned. When scholars began to consider just what made these verses a hymn, it became evident that this classification was only an assumption, and that the verses did not fit what we knew about Jewish psalms/hymns or Greco-Roman music. By the 1990s the form "hymn" was increasingly questioned and categories from Greek rhetoric, especially those dealing with praise (epideictic), were being proposed, specifically the form *encomium* (Latin; *encomion*, Greek) from the rhetorical schoolbooks. An *encomium* is a speech of praise. According to Malina and Neyrey,

> The ancients not only had a specific cultural meaning for praise, but they perceived and expressed such praise in terms

---

Encomium

Sirach 44–50 is an example of this type of Greek epideictic (praise) *encomium*.

> Let us now sing the praises of famous men,
> our ancestors in their generations.
> The Lord apportioned to them great glory,
> his majesty from the beginning.
> There were those who ruled in their kingdoms,
> and made a name for themselves by their valor;
> those who gave counsel because they were intelligent;
> those who spoke in prophetic oracles;
> those who led the people by their counsels
> and by their knowledge of the people's lore;
> they were wise in their words of instruction;
> those who composed musical tunes,
> or put verses in writing;
> rich men endowed with resources,
> living peacefully in their homes—
> all these were honored in their generations,
> and were the pride of their times.
>   (Sir 44:1–7)

of stereotyped categories. When composing an *encomium*, the classical writer was advised to cover the following fixed categories: the subject's origin and birth, nurture and training, accomplishments, and outstanding qualities. (p. 23)

For our purposes settling this problem is not mandatory, but we should be on our guard about referring to it as a hymn and therefore an example of early Christian worship. The hymn assumption leads to too many untested presuppositions. The honest answer is that scholarship is in flux, probably shifting from hymn to *encomium*. But what should we call it? Hymn is convenient but not accurate, while *encomium* is both inconvenient and unfamiliar. In this section, I will refer to it as a praise piece or a praise speech. "Speech" has the virtue of reminding us that this piece is not meant to be read silently but to be heard. Reading in the ancient world means out loud. Furthermore dividing the praise speech into stanzas fits our conventions, not theirs. Since they did not print a page, typography was not a part of their world of meaning. But the division into six stanzas makes a certain sense and does have a justification in the speech's composition. Still, we must remember it is our convention, not theirs.

Did Paul Write It?

Paul is often assumed to be the author and the language does sound vaguely Pauline. Two phrases in particular stand out: "even death by crucifixion" and "for the glory of God the father." These have a strong Pauline ring. Yet other phrases do not fit so well with Paul. Three primary words in the praise speech are not Pauline.

- Form (*morphē*)
- Snatched (*harpagmos*)
- Super-exalted (*hyperpysōn*)

These words are rare in Greek and occur only here in the Pauline letters.

Two other issues raise doubts about Pauline authorship. It is very difficult to assign this language to a Jewish (LXX) background (except the last two stanzas of Isa 45:23), and we have seen that Paul's language is strongly Jewish. But by far the strongest piece of evidence against Pauline authorship is the hymn's

Philippians

The original Pauline letters have clearly been edited to form the collection of the letters we now have in the New Testament. The details of that editing are debatable and speculative. Philippians probably is made up of two or three earlier letters. At 3:1 there is a "finally" and then again in 4:8 there is another "finally." The material in between is very different in tone from the rest of the letter. It is highly polemical and harsh. Thus 3:1b–4:9 comes from a different letter. Others also think that the portion from 4:10 to the end of the letter is yet again different and may represent part of a third letter. How these two or three letters are to be arranged chronologically is anybody's guess.

If there was more than one letter to the Philippians, then we need a range of dates for their composition. Paul founded the Philippian community in the late 40s, and according to Phil 1:12–13 he is in prison under an imperial guard (*praitōrion*) and in 4:22, Paul sends greeting from those "in Caesar's household" (BBS Trans), which implies that Paul has made converts among his guard. Which imprisonment is this? Ephesus would appear the safest bet, so the letters to church at the colony of Philippi would have been written in the first half to mid 50s, during the controversy at Corinth.

non-apocalyptic character. Given the strongly apocalyptic thrust of Paul's thought, this lack of apocalyptic flavor has to be taken seriously. It could be argued that Paul is appealing to his gentile audience, but in 1 Thessalonians he made no such wholesale concession.

If not Paul, then who composed the praise piece? It is difficult to tell, but one proposal suggests that it was composed within the community of Philippi and brought to Paul for his approval and subsequent incorporation in his letter to the Philippians (Reumann). While impossible to prove, this suggestion has the advantage of locating the piece in Philippi, explains why Paul would be quoting it in his letter, and why the piece has both a Pauline as well as a strongly gentile sound. Regardless of who wrote the praise piece, its use by Paul indicates his approval.

Descent/Ascent

Traditionally the passage has been understood to exhibit the descent/ascent pattern of classical Christology, the pre-existent Christ descended to earth, suffered, and ascended to heaven. If classical Christology is in your mind (remember the egg?), the pattern is easy to see in the passage. "Being in the form of God" and then "taking the form of a slave/human" appears to imply a descent and even the two-natures theology of later Christology. But only the ascent (super-exalted) is actually expressed.

Yet is a descent really there or is it being read into the passage? Paul himself does not appear to operate with such a pattern. More recently a number of scholars (Murphy-O'Connor and Dunn) have argued that the subject of the hymn was from the beginning a human who was exalted because of his refusal to grasp at being equal to God and his obedience all the way to death. For our purposes we do not have to solve this issue or even take a stand, because our concern is with the ascent/exaltation at the passage's conclusion. I consider this issue unsettled in scholarship, so if you think pre-existence is implied in the first two stanzas, you will have many scholars on your side. But remember that there are serious arguments against it. We will pay attention to these options as we work our way through the praise speech's first part.

Adam Typology

For a considerable time now, scholars have argued that the passage alludes to the Adam myth. Form (*morphē*) of God is the equivalent to image (*eikōn*) of God: "And God made the man, in the image (*kat'eikona*) of God he made him, male and female he made them" (Gen 1:27 LXX, BBS Trans). Since *morphē* is synonymous with *eikōn*, this first line must be a reference or allusion to the Genesis creation story.

When the snake tests Eve it tells her, "You will not die; for God knows that when you eat of it your eyes will be opened, and you will be like (*hōs*, LXX) God, knowing good and evil" (3:4b–5). In the praise passage "being equal with God," the Greek uses *isos*, which means "equal" but also has the sense of "like." Once again we have the strong possibility that the Philippians passage is making an allusion to the Adam story.

For those who think that Paul composed this passage and who usually think it is a hymn, these allusions are reinforced by the prominence of the Adam typology in Paul's arguments. For example, in Rom 5:19 Paul contrasts the disobedience of Adam with the obedience of the Anointed.

> So then, just as one man's blunder led to a death sentence for all humanity,
> so one man's getting it right leads to an affirmation of life for all humanity.
> Just as through one man's rebellious mindlessness many were led to become wayward,
> so also by one man's trusting mindfulness many will be led to getting it right.
>   (Rom 5:18–19)

Here Paul explicitly contrasts the Adam story with the Christ story. In Paul's long discussion of the resurrection of the body in 1 Corinthians 15, he returns yet again to the Adam/Anointed contrast:

> For since death came through a man,
> the resurrection of the dead has also come through a man;
> for as all die in Adam,
> so also all in the Anointed will be made alive.
>   (1 Cor 15:21–22, BBS Trans)

Paul's image of "all in the Anointed" is very close to what we saw in 1 Thessalonians.

Paul is setting up a set of contraries (either/or):

Adam	Anointed
disobedience	obedience
trespass	righteous
death	resurrection
death	life

Adam and Anointed are types, two ways in which humans respond to God. It does not, by the way, demand pre-existence.

Thus the Anointed story becomes a re-telling of the Adam story: Adam had been created in God's image or form, but he failed by grasping at being equal or like God. This was the man's disobedience for which the punishment was death. The second man, the Anointed, did not consider being in the form or image of God something to take advantage of, but by contrast became willingly a human being, even a slave, and being obedient all the way to death thus accepted his status as a human being. His reward was exaltation by God.

The Adam story does make a certain sense of the passage, especially its first part. But it is hard to see how the praise speech's climax, God's exaltation of Jesus Anointed by naming him lord, fits into the Adam story. Furthermore, without quibbling about whether *morphē* is equivalent to *eikōn* or *isos* is equivalent to *hōs* (because they are certainly close enough to be an allusion), the way Paul plays out the Adam/Anointed contrast in the two quotes above is very different from the implied contrast in the Philippians passage. The language is close, the model is close, but I am less and less convinced that it is Paul. It is more *like* Paul than *actually* Paul. If you look at the contraries in the two columns, only "obedience" appears in the hymn.

Later in this letter (see Cameo on Date and Composition), Paul makes a move that follows out a similar pattern in the Philippians praise speech, but employs more strongly Pauline terms:

> . . . to know him
> > and the power of his resurrection (*anastaseōs*, standing up)
> > and the communion (*koinōnian*) of his sufferings
> > being co-formed (*summorphizomenos*) in his death,
> if somehow I may attain the resurrection-out-of (*exanastasin*, standing out from) which is from the dead.
> > (Phil 3:10–11, BBS Trans)

This is the conclusion of a long and complex sentence. It is difficult even in English to give some sense of the complexity of the sentence, and most modern English translations break the passage up into several sentences. The King James remains faithful to the complexity of the Greek (see Cameo on Philippians 3:8–11). Paul is following out a pattern similar to that in the praise passage but with important differences. First, notice the prominence of "resurrection" or "standing up" language, once even with a compound—*exanastasin*, literally, the standing up out of (the grave).

Philippians 3:8–11, King James Version

Yea doubtless, and I count all things but loss for the excellency of the knowledge of Christ Jesus my Lord: for whom I have suffered the loss of all things, and do count them but dung, that I may win Christ, and be found in him, not having mine own righteousness, which is of the law, but that which is through the faith of Christ, the righteousness which is of God by faith: That I may know him, and the power of his resurrection, and the fellowship of his sufferings, being made conformable unto his death; If by any means I might attain unto the resurrection of the dead.

Even more, this is something that Paul participates in with the Anointed. This notion of communion is missing from the hymn, although when he incorporates the praise piece into his letter, Paul adds it with his introduction: "think in the same way that the Anointed Jesus did" (Phil 2:5).

I do not think we should exclude the possibility of an allusion to the Adam typology, but it is clearly not Paul's usage. It may well have developed under Paul's influence although used in a decidedly different way.

Emperor

In recent years another option has come forward: the praise speech as anti-imperial in nature. Philippi was a Roman Colony, whose official name was *Colonia Augusta Iulia Philippensis*, named originally after Philip of Macedonia, then for Augustus. It was ruled by two military officers appointed from Rome. Situated on the *Via Egnatia*, the colony's substantial wealth came from mining, an activity strongly associated with slave labor. There was a strong imperial and Roman presence in the colony of Philippi.

The same phrases about grasping for equality with God or being in the form of God (or a god) apply to the Roman emperor as well as to the Anointed. The forum at Philippi had two temples for the worship of the imperial family, and numerous inscriptions testify to the importance of being a part of the imperial cult.

Publius Cornelius Asper Atiarius Montanus
Honored with equestrian status, also with the decorations of
a Decurion and of the duumviri, priest, flamen of the divine
Claudius in Philippi, 23 years old, lies buried here.
(Quoted in Hellerman, p. 82)

While much ink has been spilled on what "the form (*morphē*)
of God" means, those living in Philippi or anywhere in the ancient world would have seen daily graphic images of the emperor
"in the form of a god" on coins and in statues. The emperor was
widely presented in a divine image, and grasping for divine titles
was an imperial habit. We should be careful about thinking that
divine titles were not taken seriously. They were.

The praise speech's conclusion fits well with the imperial
model. To exalt (*hypsoō*) describes the status of the emperor and
the social situation of the Roman empire, a hierarchical society,
where lifting up or rising to the top was a way of life. This is viv-
idly illustrated by the Roman Triumph.

The imperial model fits especially well the situation of Paul's
converts in Philippi, a Roman colony. In their daily lives they
would have experienced the hierarchical and imperial structure of
Roman life. Praising Jesus as opposed to the emperor would have
been as appealing as it was dangerous.

We probably should not view the Adam and the imperial
models as either/or choices. They can both be alluded to as the
anti-type. The emperor is just an another version of Adam.

The Praise Speech

For convenience we will follow the traditional division of the
passage into six stanzas of three lines each. The first three have
as their subject a "who" whose identity becomes clear only in the
last two stanzas, although by incorporating the speech into his
letter, Paul makes the identity clear. The relative pronoun "who"
is the normal way in which to begin an *encomium*. The final three
stanzas have as their subject "God" and the first line of stanza 4
and the final line of stanza 6 both contain the word "God" form-
ing what the ancients called an *inclusio*, a rounding off with the
same word.

"Who"

Being in the form (*morphē*) of a god (or God)
Did not consider it a thing to be taken advantage of,
The being equal with a god,

But he emptied (*ekenōsen*) himself
Taking the form (*morphēn*) of a slave,
Becoming in the likeness of humans

And finding himself in the human schema (*schēmati*),
He humiliated himself,
Becoming obedient all the way to death—
Even death by crucifixion.

This whole passage is beset with translation problems, most of which are not easily resolved, if able to be resolved at all. Allusive, intense, compact, poetic language trades on ambiguity, a translator's, exegete's, and theologian's nightmare. The very first line is a good example of the issues.

- *hyparchō* is often translated "being" as in the senses of "to really be there, *be present, be at one's disposal*" and "to be in a state or circumstance, *be*" (Bauer, *Greek-English Lexicon*, p. 1029). It is often used in the Hellenistic Greek as synonymous with "to be."
- *morphē* is often translated "form" but it too has a range of meanings, including "form, outward appearance, shape."
- *theou* is usually translated "of God" but the capitalization is an interpretation. In English we capitalize g-o-d to signify "the God"—the God of Israel and of the Christians, the one and only true God. But Greek of this period does not distinguish between small and capital letters; it has only capitals. Either "of a god" or "of the God" is a perfectly acceptable translation, and those translations that translate "of God" have used capitalization to resolve an ambiguity in the Greek.

A number of translations are possible:
- who existing in the form of a god
- who existing in the form of God
- who having the outward appearance of a god (or God)
- who is in the shape of a god (or God)

You begin to get the idea and see the problem. Since Christian translators have traditionally assumed that the first part of the "hymn" details Jesus' pre-existence and incarnation, it was natural to translate *theou* "of God." But in the context of Philippi, no such assumption should be made.

Claiming to be equal to a god goes with being an emperor. In 2 Maccabees' imaginary view of God's afflictions upon Antiochus Epiphanes at his death, the author describes the king's pained outcry:

> When he could no longer bear his own stench, he said,
> "It is right to be subject to God, and not to think one's mortal
> self divine" (*isothea*, God-equal).
> (2 Macc 9:12)

A second-century papyrus fragment says:

> What is a god? Exercising power.
> What is a king? Equal to God (*isotheos*, see Hellerman, p. 133).

In the colony of Philippi, which had a strong cult of the emperor, some imperial overtone is highly likely. The first stanza then describes a "who" who has the outward appearance of a god and is equal to a god, but does not consider eminence a thing to hold onto tenaciously, "as something to take advantage of" or "as something to use for his own advantage" (Hoover, p. 118). This equally references imperial power, divine pretentions, and ruthlessness.

The second stanza contrasts with the first. Having resisted the temptation to divine attributes, the being moves in the opposite direction. Opposition is the point of this stanza. He moves from the form of a god (God) to the form of a slave—a true emptying out. He chooses full humanity, not some halfway house between divine and human. To be sure, a downward descent is implied, but not necessarily from heaven to earth (although that is possible), but downward in status, from the highest to the lowest.

The third stanza continues the humiliation. In contrast with Adam who was disobedient or the emperor who demands obedience, this one is obedient to the point of death. In total compliance with the human condition, Paul appears to have added to the praise speech the clarifying remark, "even death by crucifixion."

Slaves and Mining

Mining was an important source of wealth in the Colony of Philippi. Slaves used for mining were particularly low and despised in the ancient world and their life expectancy was short. Diodorus Siculus' remarks are well known:

> The slaves who are engaged in the working of them [mines] produce for their masters revenues in sums defying belief, but they themselves wear out their bodies both by day and night in the diggings under the earth, dying in large numbers because of the exceptional hardships they endure.

This not only refers to the explicit form of Jesus' death, but in a Roman colony signals the additional shame of being a form of death used by Rome to humiliate its enemies.

God Acts

"Super-exalted"

> For this God has super-exalted him,
> Gracing him with the name,
> A name superior to all names

In the final three stanzas, as noted, the subject shifts to God. The first line of the fourth stanza begins with *dio* which is an emphatic marker of conclusion—therefore, for this reason. The praise speech draws a direct connection between this person's death and God's action. This action is not a *deus ex machina,* a rescue from death. This is not God stepping in at the last minute and rescuing the hero. Rather because the person has taken this action, has been humiliated, has died even on a cross, God has acted.

Super-exalt is a made up word in English much like *hyperypsōsen* is in Greek. Greek frequently compounds a verb (*hypseroō*) and a preposition (*hyper*). In this case the preposition intensifies the verb.

The root sense of the word group has to do with height. Paul in 2 Cor 11:7 uses the verb (without intensifying preposition) in a secular sense.

> Did I commit a sin by humbling myself so that you might be
> exalted,
> because I proclaimed God's good news to you free of charge?

Paul uses the verb "humble" (*tapeinōn*) which is also employed in the Philippians praise speech. But the verb "exalted" only means to raise the Corinthians above him.

The verb is somewhat rare in secular Greek but frequent in the Septuagint. The word *hyperypsoō* occurs 50 times in the LXX, almost always without a Hebrew equivalent. Psalm 96:9 (LXX) is a good example:

> Because you are the lord most high (*hypsistos*) over all the
> earth;
> You are greatly super-exalted (*hyperypsōthēs*) above (*hyper*)
> all the gods.
> (BBS Trans)

This quote is interesting for a number of reasons. It exhibits the use of the adjective as a substantive noun for "the most high" God and uses the word "lord" which will come into play later in the praise piece. In the second line the compound verb used in the Philippians passage also occurs but with an adverb "greatly" and a repetition of the *hyper*. The last line, with its exaggeration of exaltation, has the purpose of insisting that the lord most high is the most high over all the gods. This reminds us of the ambiguous use of god in the praise piece.

Psalm 9:13 also provides an interesting parallel.

> Have mercy on me, Lord.
> See my humiliation from my enemies,
> you who lift me up from the gates of death.
> (LXX BBS Trans)

Once again we see the combination of humiliation and lifting up (exaltation).

The Septuagint also applies the verb to the servant of Isa 52:

> Behold, my servant (*pais*) shall understand
> and shall be exalted (*hypsōthēsetai*)
> and shall be glorified.
> (LXX Isa 52:13, BBS Trans)

Here the verb without the preposition is used and *pais* (servant), not *doulos* (slave) as in the praise speech. *Pais* and *doulos* are not interchangeable. *Pais* means a young boy and by extension a servant or slave, often with the sense of a favorite slave. *Doulos* always means a slave.

In the praise speech in Philippians the person is super-exalted, that is, exalted to the most high God, to heaven. It gives body to the super-exaltation that God will grace him with a name above (*hyper*) all names. This phrase is parallel to Ps 96:9 (LXX). Instead of "above all gods" in the praise piece it is "a name above all names."

Name

> So that at Jesus' name
> Every knee should bow down
> In the heavens, on the earth and in the underworld

Now the name of the "who" is finally mentioned, Jesus—the historical person whom the Romans crucified. But in the praise speech the name with which God graces Jesus is not Jesus, but another name signifying his God-given status.

"Name" rings out in stanzas four and five, reverberating over and over three times.

> Therefore even God has him <u>super</u>-exalted
> and graced upon him the **name**
> which is <u>super</u> every **name**
> so that at the **name** of Jesus

Hyper (super) and *onoma* (name) organize this section of the praise speech. That names were more important in the ancient world than the modern is a truism, but one that is important to remember. A name denotes and demarcates something real. Even more, "name" is part of the honor aspect of the ancient world. One's name has to be defended.

At this name every knee shall bow. The second line of stanza 5 and the first line of stanza 6 refer to Isa 45:23 (LXX). While the reference is not verbatim, the immediate context in Isa 45:22 indicates why the reference might be important. It refers to God's singleness and the whole earth being saved, turning to God and submitting to God. These are themes that would appeal to the Anointed-believers in the colony of Philippi. Paul in his letter to the Romans (14:11) quotes Isa 45:23 in a context which reminds the Roman audience that it too shall be judged.

Turn to me and you will be saved,
Who are from the ends of the earth.
I am God, and there is no other.
By myself I have sworn,
righteousness will come from my mouth,
my words will not be turned away:
To me every knee shall bow,
every tongue shall swear by God.
      (Isa 45:22–23 LXX, BBS Trans)

In the Philippians praise speech these concluding stanzas take a universal point of view. All will be subjugated to him: the Greek literally translates, "Every knee of the heavenly beings, of the earthly beings, and the underworld beings should bend." This depicts the classic three-storey universe—the abodes of angels, humans, and the dead. This explicit universal subjection to Jesus as God's agent is moving beyond what we have seen in 1 Thessalonians and Galatians. There Paul was concerned with those "in Christ" with no mention of other humans, much less the whole of reality envisioned as a three-storey universe.

Lord

And every tongue should shout out,
"The lord (*kurios*) is Jesus anointed"
For the glory of God the father.

Now the praise piece concludes with the continuing reference to Isa 45:23 (LXX). The second line of the final stanza is a quote that should be shouted out. Supposing the setting of this praise piece in the Roman colony of Philippi, a Roman triumphal procession may well lie in the background. The triumph was shot through Roman culture, a dominant metaphor in an imperial world. Originally, a triumph was voted to a conquering general by the Roman senate, but since the time of Augustus triumphs had been reserved for the emperor. The triumph also has divine overtones. The conquering hero (the emperor) rides in a chariot pulled by four horses (*quadriga*), echoing Jupiter's chariot, with a globe symbolizing the whole world being subject to the Romans. The triumph ended at the temple of Jupiter. In the arch of Titus, which celebrates the conquering of Jerusalem, the interior panels depict the triumph accorded the emperor Titus. On one side

soldiers are carrying the booty in triumph, with the huge me-
norah and table of the showbread prominent. On the opposite
panel Titus is riding in the *quadriga* with the winged goddess
of victory at his side and another partially nude goddess, probably Roma, seated on one of the horses. It is hardly an historical
reminiscence. In the actual triumph these places would have been
occupied by family members, the most likely being Titus' younger
brother Domitian, who constructed the arch. In the ceiling of the
arch overlooking this scene of triumph, Titus is being carried into
heaven by Jupiter's eagle. This is Titus' apotheosis. The dedicatory
inscription on the arch summarizes its theology:

> The Senate
> and the Roman people
> (dedicate this) to the divine Titus Vespasianus Augustus, son
> of the divine Vespasian.

The praise piece invokes the model of the Roman triumphal
procession and has the crowd shout out: "The lord is Jesus the
Anointed."

Kurios (lord) presents another of those ambiguous translation
problems. In Greek it means "master" as distinguished from slave,
so it is inherently hierarchical in nature. It can mean "sir" as a way
of denoting someone higher in the hierarchical scale. It is also an
important imperial title, in Latin *dominus*. In an imperial colony
with two temples dedicated to the imperial family dominating its
forum, we cannot doubt that the primary overtone in the praise
speech's use of "lord" is anti-imperial. After all, the imperial cult
was the fastest growing religion in the empire. Finally in the LXX
kurios can translate the tetragrammaton, the untranslatable and
unspoken name of God. God has given Jesus not only the emperor's title but God's own name.

For a Roman this praise speech asserts the unthinkable: the
Jewish messiah whom the Romans had crucified is now exalted
as the lord and master of the universe. The contradiction, almost
an obscenity in its betrayal of the Roman praise speech, is beyond
comprehension.

Next to "even death by crucifixion," "for the glory of God the
father" has the strongest Pauline ring in the passage. In his impor-

Tetragrammaton

The Hebrew Bible uses a number of different words for God—chiefly *Elohim, Adonai,* and *Yahweh.* By far the most common is Yahweh (6,828 times). As a sign of reverence for the sacred name, Jews do not pronounce it. Where the manuscripts read *YHWH,* they pronounce *"Adonai,"* "my Lord." Since Hebrew does not employ vowels in its script, but only consonants, Yahweh in Hebrew has 4 letters, *YHWH.* In Greek this was referred to as the tetragammaton (four letters). The equivalent to *Adonai* in Greek is *kurios* (lord), so Greek translators of the LXX translated the four characters into Greek as *kurios* (lord). The Vulgate in Latin followed suit with *Dominus* and English translators have continued the tradition with "Lord." Sometime in the late middle ages, Latin transcriptions merged the consonants *YHWH* with the vowels from *Adonai* and got *Iahovah* or *Jehovah.* Yahweh is a modern guess at the pronunciation of the ancient name. We do not really know how it was pronounced or exactly what it means.

tant 1952 essay, Käsemann suggested that it too is an addition by Paul the letter writer. The strongest argument for its inclusion is that, as we noted, it does round off the mention of God in line one in stanza four. This rounding would signal closure. Also given the anti-imperial thrust of the last part of the praise speech, is it only accidental that "father of the country" is an imperial title? Naming God as father could be the final sneer at imperial pretentions. For these reasons I suspect it is original. It should not be surprising that converts made by Paul would employ his language.

"Father" language points out the strangeness of "lord" as the primary title. Paul does employ lord as a primary title for Jesus Anointed, but as we have seen in 1 Thessalonians and Galatians, in the context of resurrection, he prefers "son." But this praise speech was most likely constructed by gentile Annointed-believers and as such they are exploring their own language and models to make sense of what Paul has told them. While the last three stanzas deal with what is traditionally referred to as resurrection, they make no mention of it. They employ the model of exaltation.

The use of exaltation in Philippians is not just an isolated occurrence. Paul himself implies it in the Thanksgiving from 1 Thess 1:10: "to wait for God's 'son' from heaven" (see also Rom 8:34). Later in the late first century both Hebrews and the fourth gospel will employ the exaltation model. Both have much more highly developed Christologies, but they indicate that the exaltation model remains viable.

> But in these last days he has spoken to us by a Son,
>> whom he appointed heir of all things,
>> through whom he also created the world.
> He is the reflection of God's glory and the exact imprint of
>> God's very being,
>> and he sustains all things by his powerful word.
> When he had made purification for sins,
>> he sat down at the right hand of the Majesty on high (*en hypsēlois*),
>> having become as much superior to angels as the name
>> he has inherited is more excellent than theirs.
>> (Heb 1:2–4)

Here Jesus' death is referred to as "he had made purification for sins" and his exaltation is "he sat down at the right hand of the Majesty on high."

John also employs "exalt" but in an ironic sense. The son of man's lifting up refers to his death (e.g., John 8:28).

Conclusion

In 1 Thessalonians Paul employed the model of "raised up from the dead" and in Galatians the model of "revelation." Now the Philippians praise speech has used "exaltation." Paul drew one model from Jewish apocalyptic and the other from the prophets; the Philippians praise hymn draws primarily from the Adam story and imperial propaganda. This indicates that both are using metaphorical systems to understand what they are experiencing and judging to be happening in reality. Thus the experience is primary and they are seeking language in which to express it.

What are our gains?

- The move away from apocalyptic. The Philippians praise speech is the first step in a long process of disengagement from apocalyptic that will have important consequences for the emergence of resurrection.
- The use of gentile categories. Paul has been strongly bound to the categories of second temple Judaism. The Philippians are beginning the development of a gentile view expressed in gentile categories.
- The fact that Paul quotes the praise speech in his letter indicates that he approves of the effort. It may not be fully his language, but he does not reject it. Therefore he can see that experience can be separated from language.
- The Adam metaphor implies two ages or two types. Paul understands this metaphor apocalyptically; the Philippians understand it typologically.
- Exaltation introduces a new metaphor drawn from the LXX and imperial propaganda. Exaltation has implications for all of reality, for all those in heaven, on the earth and in the underworld. It concerns the *oikoumenē*, as befits a Roman colony. Still, Paul seems primarily concerned about the community built up around the resurrection. These interests are not necessarily in opposition, but they at least represent different emphases.

Further Reading

Attridge, Harold W. *The Epistle to the Hebrews*, Hermeneia. Philadelphia: Fortress Press, 1989.

Beard, Mary. *The Roman Triumph*. Cambridge: Harvard, 2007.

Dunn, James D. G. *Christology in the Making, a New Testament Inquiry into the Origins of the Doctrine of the Incarnation*. London: SCM, 1980, rev. ed. 1989.

Georgi, Dieter. *Theodicy in Paul's Praxis and Theology*. Translated by David E. Green. Minneapolis: Fortress Press, 1991. See esp. "Philippians: A Disguised Affront," pp. 72–78.

Hellerman, Joseph H. *Reconstructing Honor in Roman Philippi, Carmen Christi as Cursus Pudorum*, Society for New Testament Studies Monograph Series. Cambridge: Cambridge University, 2005.

Hoover, Roy W. "The Harpagmos Enigma: A Philological Solution." *Harvard Theological Review* 64 (1971): 95–119.

Käsemann, Ernst. "A Critical Analysis of Philippians 2:5–11." In *God and Existence*, edited by Herbert Braun, 45–88. New York: Harper and Row, 1968.

Lohmeyer, Ernst. *Kyrios Jesus: Eine Untersuchung zu Phil 2,5–11.* 2nd edition, 1961 ed, Sitzungsberichte Der Heidelberger Akademie Der Wissenschaften, Philosophisch-Historische Klasse, Jahrgang 1927/28, 4. Abhandlung. Heidelberg: Carl Winter, 1928. Brown, Colin. "Ernst Lohmeyer's *Kyrios Jesus.*" In *Where Christology Began*, edited by Ralph P. Martin and Brian J. Dodd, 6–42. Louisville, KY: Westminster John Knox, 1998. A very good study of Lohmeyer's contribution.

Malina, Bruce J., and Jerome H. Neyrey. *Portraits of Paul, an Archaeology of Ancient Personality.* Lousiville, KY: Westminster John Knox, 1996. See pages 23–33 for an excellent discussion of *encomium*.

Martin, Ralph P. *Carmen Christi, Philippians II. 5–11 in Recent Interpretation and in the Setting of Early Christian Worship.* 2nd edition 1983, 3rd edition (InterVarsity Press, 1997). Cambridge: Cambridge University, 1967.

Oakes, Peter. *Philippians, from People to Letter.* Edited by Richard Bauckham, Society for New Testament Studies Monograph Series. Cambridge: Cambridge University, 2001.

Reumann, John. *Philippians*, Anchor Yale Bible. New Haven: Yale University Press, 2008.

Works Cited

Bauer, Walter. *A Greek-English Lexicon of the New Testament and Other Early Christian Literature.* Edited by Frederick William Danker. 3rd ed. Chicago: University of Chicago Press, 2000.

Hellerman, Joseph H. *Reconstructing Honor in Roman Philippi, Carmen Christi as Cursus Pudorum*, SNTS Monograph Series. Cambridge: Cambridge University, 2005.

Hoover, Roy W. "The Harpagmos Enigma: A Philological Solution." *Harvard Theological Review* 64 (1971): 95–119.

Malina, Bruce J., and Jerome H. Neyrey. *Portraits of Paul, an Archaeology of Ancient Personality.* Lousiville, KY: Westminster John Knox, 1996.

7 | The List

The Corinthian Situation

1 Corinthians 15 is the most extensive and arguably the most important passage in the New Testament on the topic of resurrection from the dead. In this chapter the telling words "he appeared" occur for the first time in a Pauline letter and for the first time in the New Testament. You might well wonder why we did not start with this passage. It was for two reasons:

- We are following chronological order as strictly and carefully as we can, trying not to read later developments back into earlier passages or to assume that what appears later had to be there earlier.
- We needed to explore how Paul had dealt with the "metaphor of "getting up from the dead" and where his language came from.

So important is 1 Corinthians 15 for our topic that we will spend the next three chapters on it. First we will consider Paul's report of the common preaching of the resurrection of Jesus, and then the list of those to whom Jesus has appeared. Finally, we will turn to the knotty problem that besets Paul in chapter 15: "How are the dead raised? With what kind of body do they come?"(1 Cor 15:35).

Why is Paul so central to this question? Or to put it another way it, Why does the popular imagination ignore Paul in this discussion? Why do scholars start with Paul while lay folks and churches start with one of the gospels? There are several reasons:

- Canonical order
- Liturgy
- The visual imagination

These three conspire to discount Paul. In canonical order the gospels come first, then Acts, and then Paul (and the other letters), and finally Revelation. Canon implies a narrative—Jesus, then the church, and finally the end. This arrangement assumes the primacy of the gospel stories and views Paul as secondary and later. A canon arranged chronologically would look very different from the one we have. Since the Easter liturgy begins with the gospel of John, one of the latest gospels becomes the liturgical focus. Finally, only two gospels have vivid images of the resurrected Jesus, those of Luke and John, both written towards the end of the first century. The vivid stories—On the Road to Emmaus, Mary Magdalene being told not to touch (*Noli Me Tangere*), Doubting Thomas—these vivid stories make for vivid images that have dominated Christians' imagination of resurrection.

Paul, on the other hand, has no such vivid stories. Actually, he is a minimalist who constantly tempts us to fill in the blanks with the vivid images in Acts, Luke, and John. But Paul's letter writing took place from the late 40s to the mid 50s. In terms of evidence, we do not get any closer. Despite the controversy that surrounded Paul in his own time, I suggest that we should take Paul at his word, and examine what he has to say with an open mind. He is, after all, as close as we come to an eyewitness to raising up Jesus from the dead. Furthermore, when the apostles extended the right hand of fellowship to Paul, I assume they accepted his claim to be an apostle because God had revealed to him that Jesus was God's son and he, Paul, was the apostle to the gentiles. This is why the argument and testimony of Galatians is so important. Now let us turn to 1 Corinthians.

Paul's relationship with the community he founded at Corinth was tortured, frequently heated, at times almost broken, and the final outcome not really known. The Corinthian correspondence took place in the early 50s, and the two extant letters clearly have been edited. The real "1 Corinthians" is missing (see 1 Cor 5:9: "When I said in the letter I wrote to you") and debate rages on the unity of 1 Corinthians, while 2 Corinthians obviously consists of several letters. An early scribe more in sympathy with the views of the 1 and 2 Timothy and Titus than those of the apostle Paul added the note about women being silent in church (1 Cor

14:33b–36). For our purposes, we can assume that 1 Corinthians 15 is part of a response by Paul to a series of questions posed by the community in Corinth: "Now concerning the matters about which you wrote" (1 Cor 7:1). The Corinthian community is comprised of gentiles who have recently been converted. They take great pride in "spiritual gifts" and demonstrations of their power in the spirit. These issues will become paramount, especially when we turn to the issue of "what kind of body?"

The Gospel

Before turning to the most controversial issue (denial of the resurrection of the dead), Paul begins with what he and the Corinthians agree upon by recapping the gospel.

> I made known to you, brothers, the *gospel*
> > which I *gospelized* to you
> > which also you received,
> > in which you also stand,
> > through which you are being saved
> > in the very message I *gospelized* to you, if you hold fast,
> > unless you have had confidence in vain.
> For I deliver to you as the most important
> > what I also received.
> > (1 Cor 15:1–3a, BBS Trans)

The initial sentence, built around a series of relative clauses, reminds the Corinthians of the gospel that binds Paul and the Corinthians together. In the Greek the sound *euaggeli-* (gospel-) rings through the sentence, thrice repeated to make his point. This is Paul's account of the early community's preaching, its *kerygma*. We will refer to this with the term, "gospel-statement" to denote its special, traditional character.

"In what message" or "in what word" appears to be reference to the very words in which Paul evangelized the Corinthians. The grammar is difficult and so the meaning is less than clear.

In the second sentence Paul employs the technical Greek terms for the handing on a tradition "for I have delivered (*paredōka*) . . . what I also received (*parelabon*)." This, of course, raises some problems since in Galatians Paul swore that he did not receive the gospel from humans. Is this a contradiction? Did Paul

Gospel/*euaggelion*

The Greek word *euaggelion* means "good news." Probably the closest parallel to Christian use of the word is in the imperial cult. An inscription from Priene dated to the time of Augustus deals with the new calendar and birthday of the emperor.

> Since the providence that has divinely ordered our existence has applied her energy and zeal and has brought to life the most perfect good in Augustus, whom she filled with virtues for the benefit of mankind, bestowing him upon us and our descendents as a savior—he who put an end to war and will order peace, Caesar, who by his epiphany exceeded the hopes of those who prophesied good tidings (*euaggelia*), not only outdoing benefactors of the past, but also allowing no hope of greater benefactors in the future; and since the birthday of the god first brought to the world the good tidings (*euaggelia*) residing in him (Trans. David C. Braund, *Augustus to Nero*, p. 122).

change his mind? Or is he trying to have it both ways, to have his cake and eat it, so to speak?

The difference is in what is claimed in each letter. In Galatians Paul is claiming that *how* he received his conviction (*pistis*, faith) in the gospel is through God's revelation. In 1 Corinthians he is dealing with the *what* (in what message or with what words) that was handed on. Those words were the same for Cephas as for Paul. Perhaps this distinction is too subtle and self-serving, but it does explain the odd grammar of the first sentence.

Traditional or from Paul?

Furthermore, there are clear indications that the language is not Paul's but traditional. The following three phrases found in 1 Cor 15:3–5 are not typically Pauline:

- for our sins
- according to the writings
- the twelve

The Greeting in the letter to the Galatians contains the only other occurrence of the phrase "for our sins" in Paul's letters.

> Grace to you and peace from God our Father and the lord
>   Jesus Anointed,
>   who gave himself for our sins to set us free from the
>   present evil age,
>   according to the will of our God and Father.
>   (Gal 1:3–4, BBS Trans)

This Greeting has a structural similarity to the gospel-statement from 1 Corinthians, but it has "gave himself" instead of "died" and "according to the will of our God and Father" instead of "according to the writings." There is also a clear apocalyptic reference in "the present evil age." God is referred to as "God and Father," a strongly Pauline usage. The title for Jesus is lord, just as in the Philippians praise speech, and Jesus Anointed is his name. For Paul the notion that Jesus "died for (*hyper*) us" is important, but he does not usually employ the formula "for our sins." 1 Thessalonians 5:10 is a representative Pauline formulation:

> For God has not set us up for condemnation,
> but intends for us to be liberated through our lord Jesus, God's
>   Anointed,
> who died for us so that
> —whether we have died or are still alive—
> we might live together with him.
>   (1 Thess 5:9–10)

Not only does "according to the writings" occur nowhere else in the Pauline letters, but he normally uses the singular when quoting a specific verse ("the scripture says," Rom 4:3 is typical) and the plural when referring to scripture in general (Rom 15:4). This particular usage occurs only in the gospel-statement.

In the list of those to whom the Anointed has been revealed, the Twelve immediately follow Cephas. This is the only occurrence of "the Twelve" in a Pauline letter. He refers to apostles often, but not to the Twelve. This is yet another indication that this formulation of the gospel does not come from Paul, but is traditional.

If it is traditional, where does it come from? Since "according to the writings" has no clear parallel in Hebrew or Aramaic, this formulation of the gospel is surely Greek, as we will see even more clearly as we move forward. It may go back to an Aramaic archetype, but so far no convincing reconstruction has been offered.

The statement is traditional, formulaic and concise. It is not an eyewitness report but a traditional formulation.

Gospel

Paul now quotes what he claims to be the gospel that he delivered and they received:

> that Anointed died for our sins   in accordance with the writings
>
> that he was buried
> that he was raised up on the third day   in accordance with the writings
> that he has been seen for Cephas.
>
> (15:3b–5a BBS Trans; on this rendering, see p. 109)

In Greek a marker (*hoti*, that) signaling a quote or statement introduces each of these four clauses. The first and third statements are parallel, both ending with a reference to "in accordance with the writings," i.e., the scriptures of Israel. The fourth line, also introduced by *hoti* (that), begins a series of listings that then are introduced by a temporal or series marker, not *hoti* (that).

No particular scriptures are noted and one should probably understand this phrase to represent that it is willed by God and is the outcome of the plan implicit in Israel's scriptures. We saw a similar move in the composition of Daniel. This understanding of Israel's scriptures results from their experience, from their understanding of what God is accomplishing, not the other way around. For example, Isaiah 53 refers to Israel's corporate understanding. In a Jewish context it is never applied to the Anointed. Once early believers had identified Jesus as the Anointed, then Isaiah 53 can be taken to be about Jesus. But there is no evidence that Isaiah 53 was being applied to Jesus in the Pauline communities; that does not occur in Paul, although it does occur later in Matthew (8:17). Their experience and conviction is used as a lens to read the scriptures, a fact that in turn helps interpret their situation. The result is an interpenetrating, mutually interpretive scheme: experience and conviction interpret scripture, which in turn interprets situation. This makes available the language and metaphors of Israel's writings for understanding the Anointed-believers' experience and convictions.

In the Greek "Anointed" occurs without an article; this usually means for Paul that it is Jesus' name and not a title. But as a piece of tradition, that may not be the case. Therefore it is unclear how we should understand it—as Jesus' name or as a title? The manner of his death is not noted, and here Paul does not add "crucifixion" as he did in the Philippians praise speech. "For our sins"—on our behalf—recalls the martyr language of 4 Maccabees (17:22). That would suggest that since the Corinthians see the Anointed's death as that of a martyr, crucifixion is presupposed.

The burial is simply stated with no elaboration. No mention of a tomb or the manner of burial. In the martyr tradition burial in the earth is an important aspect of the martyr's being raised up from the earth, from the dead. It demonstrates that God's enemies will not triumph by killing the martyr. The amount of time in the earth is unimportant; having been in the earth, among the dead, is what counts. Burial in the earth accents God's creative power, the ability to create from nothing, a notion that, as we saw, arose in Judaism in connection with being raised from the dead.

The lack of any mention of a tomb does not warrant conclusions one way or another about the tomb itself—there may have been a tomb or there may not. This is part of our conservative methodology. This gospel-statement is uninterested in that issue, although that very lack of interest in itself is interesting.

The raising up language is from Daniel. "He was raised up" in the passive implies that the agent of the raising up is God. The verb in Greek is *egēgertai*, the perfect passive. Only in 1 Corinthians 15 does Paul employ this tense of the verb. Normally he uses the aorist passive *ēgerth-* form (e.g., Rom 4:25). While a small point of grammar, this further suggests that the gospel-statement is not Paul's composition.

"Was raised up" implies from the dead, from the earth. That is the significance of the metaphor (was raised **from** [bed]) as employed in Daniel and other places in Paul. That is why it immediately follows "was buried." This is the third verb in a row and it subtly shifts tense in a way that is almost impossible to translate. The first two verbs, "he died, he was buried," are in the Greek aorist tense, a tense that indicates past, completed action. "He was raised up," by using the Greek perfect tense, indicates a past action with continuing effect.

"On the third day" in line three parallels "for our sins" in the first line. To what does it refer? If one has the gospel accounts in mind, then it clearly points to finding the tomb empty. But once again, that is using later writings to fill in gaps in earlier ones. Just as likely the formula "on the third day" determined the timing of the finding of the tomb empty in the later gospel stories. The phrase becomes a stereotyped formula by the last part of the first century. The phrase does not appear in Mark, the first gospel, but Matthew and Luke employ the phrase in the three "son of man" sayings that foretell his suffering and rising "**on** the third day" (Matt 16:21; 17:23; 20:19; Luke 9:22; 18:33; 24:7). In the parallel passages Mark used "**after** three days" (Mark 8:31; 9:31; 10:34). Luke also uses the phrase "on the third day" twice in his resurrection account. "In three days" occurs in the fourth gospel in connection with the prophecy of the destruction of the temple, which will be rebuilt in three days. But here it has a double meaning—not the temple of Jerusalem but the temple of his body (John 2:19–21). Thus only after the composition of Mark's gospel late in the first century does the phrase becomes standard.

Does "according to the writings" refer to "on the third day" or does it refer more generally to the raising up as according to the writings, as did the same phrase in the first line? If it is referring to a particular scripture, which one? The most common suggestion is Hosea.

> Let us come and return to the lord our god;
> for he has torn and will heal us;
> he has struck and will bind us up.
> He will make us healthy after two days;
> on the third day we will be made to stand up,
> and we will be made to live before him.
> (Hos 6:1–2 LXX, BBS Trans)

In Hosea this quote is in the mouth of Israel understood as a corporate reality, and represents the people/nation. The Greek for "made to stand up" is *anistēmi*, whose noun form *anastasis* means "standing up" or "resurrection." The Hebrew employs *qvm*, to rise or stand up. If Hosea is the allusion, then the corporate understanding of Israel has now been applied to the Anointed. Daniel had already begun this move by using corporate references to the people of Israel and applying them to those who were to be raised up from the dead, the sleepers. Hosea 6:2 is the most likely reference, and raises the question of whether it was selected because the standing up of Jesus took place on the third day or because those around Jesus became convinced of his standing up from the dead. Did this Hosea passage become available as a reference to the third day and thus lead to stories of the tomb being constructed around this reference? From the gospel-statement and its use in Paul it is impossible to resolve this issue. Paul never refers to a tomb and uses the formula "on the third day" only in the gospel-statement.

There are other candidates for the source of "on the third day." Jonah was in the belly of the fish for three days and three nights.

> And the lord commanded a great sea monster to swallow up Jonah,
> and Jonah was in the belly of the sea monster for three days and three nights.
> (Jonah 2:1 LXX, BBS Trans)

While the reference to Jonah is not as close as Hosea, yet the extensive use of the Jonah allusion in early Christianity recommends it. Certainly it is one of the most common themes in early Christian art, although admittedly that is from a later period. Jonah is also employed in the Q-gospel, a very early composition (see Q 11:29; Matt 12:40).

The phrase is not uncommon in the Septuagint, although not in contexts that would suggest their applicability to the gospel-statement. Last but not least, traditionally female funerary rites began on the third day. Exactly what the phrase refers to and what it means is not as clear as might appear at first glance.

The List

The last line of the gospel-statement is: "that he was seen for Cephas," which is followed by a list of the others by whom he was seen. There are two issues here that we will deal with separately.

- The list
- What is meant by "he was seen"?

While interest is probably stronger in "he was seen," we will proceed first to the list itself before taking up what happened to those on the list and what they saw. The reason for this procedure is that the context of the list, its purpose, and its structure all need to be clear before tackling "he was seen."

Structure

The list has a clear structure, which can be laid out in an A-B-C pattern:

> **A** and that he was seen to/for/by Cephas,
> **B** then to/for/by the twelve,
> **C** then he was seen to/for/by more than five hundred brothers at one time,
>> (most of whom are still alive, though some have fallen asleep)
>
> **A** then he was seen to/for/by James,
> **B** then to/for/by all the apostles,
> **C** last of all, as to one in whose birth God's purpose seemed to have miscarried, he was seen to/for/by me as well.
>> (1 Cor 15:5–8, SV modified)

The "that" (*hoti*) in the first line is the last of four "thats" and the remaining names on the list are introduced with "then" (twice *eita* and twice *epeita*). These are temporal connectives that indicate a sequential order. This shift to a temporal sequence has indicated to many scholars that the original gospel-statement concluded with the reference to Cephas and that the others were added later. Surely Paul has added to this list both the reference to himself as "last of all" and also the comment about the 500, "most of whom are still alive, though some have fallen asleep." That is why I put it in parentheses: the use of "fallen asleep" for death is typically Pauline. If the gospel-statement originally ended with Cephas, there is no indication of who added the others to the list. Other than these obviously Pauline additions, it is not likely that Paul is the source of the additions, because "twelve" occurs nowhere else in his letters.

The A-B-C pattern indicates that, although temporal, the list also envisions two groups—one centered around Cephas and the other around James. The A-B groups share a single verb, drawing them together. There is also a movement from an individual (Cephas and James) to a group (twelve and apostles). Thus the sequential order is formalized.

The list raises a number of important questions.

Cephas and the Twelve

Paul normally employs Cephas, whereas the gospels use Peter, and only once Cephas. Cephas is an Aramaic name meaning "rock," and Peter is a transliteration of the Greek *petros*, which plays on *petra*, "rock." The later tradition has always assumed that Cephas and Peter are the same person. When Jesus meets Peter for the first time, the fourth gospel explains the wordplay.

> When Jesus laid eyes on him, he said,
> "You're Simon, John's son; you're going to be called Kephas"
>   (which means Peter <or Rock>).
>   (John 1:42)

The gospel of Matthew represents another version of the wordplay without employing Cephas.

> Let me tell you,
> you are Peter (*petros*),
> and on this very rock (*petra*) I will build my congregation,
> and the gates of Hades will not be able to overpower it.
>   (Matt 16:18, SV modified)

Only in Galatians does Paul employ both Cephas and Peter and they appear in close proximity. While defending his reception of the gospel, he reports his dealing with those pillars of Jerusalem.

> On the contrary, they recognized that God had entrusted me
>   with the task of announcing God's world-transforming
>   message to the uncircumcised,
> just as Peter had been entrusted with taking it to the circum-
>   cised.
> For it was evident that the God who worked through Peter as
>   envoy to the circumcised worked through me as envoy to
>   the rest of the world.
> When they realized that God had given me this special role,
> James, Cephas, and John, the reputed pillars <of the
>   Movement> extended the right hand of fellowship to
>   Barnabas and me
> and agreed that we should go to "the nations" and they to the
>   circumcised.
>   (Gal 2:7–9)

The shift in names is difficult to explain without the later explanation of John and Matthew. Without that explanation we might assume that Peter and Cephas are two different people, for Peter as an apostle is associated with the grouping around James, while Cephas is associated with the Twelve. However this may be resolved, for Paul it is Cephas who is first on the list.

As mentioned before, the Twelve appear only here in Paul's letters. In the gospels they remain a somewhat shadowy group, but clearly associated with Peter, James, and John. Why the number twelve? Perhaps it represents the twelve tribes of Israel, and if so it could be part of an apocalyptic restoration ideology. The gospel of Luke joins the Twelve with the apostles and creates the powerful fiction of twelve apostles (Luke 6:13). Paul appears uninterested in the group, but is clearly concerned with the supposed pillars, James, Cephas, and John.

A major question, of course, is why does Paul say "the Twelve" and not the Eleven? Matthew 28:16 and Luke 11:33 correct this problem—a problem only if the betrayal by Judas, one of the Twelve, is an historical account. Paul apparently knows no such story.

The Five Hundred

In the middle of the list occurs a real anomaly, the 500 brothers. The number is rather large, to put it mildly, and no such story concerning a group this large occurs in the tradition. Some have suggested that this group reflects the Pentecost event, but that suggestion has not found general support because Pentecost is not an "appearance" story, but rather the visitation of the Holy Spirit upon a crowd. Besides it is most likely a construction of the author of Acts.

"Brothers" does not here mean "males," for in Greek the plural can include both males and females. This usage is well attested.

Even more remarkable, the event happened to this whole group "at one time." This is not a series of events but a single event.

Some have suggested that Paul added both the note about some being still alive and others having fallen asleep for apologetic reasons: he is trying to provide proof. I find this unlikely because here his argument is not about Jesus' resurrection, but the general resurrection of the dead, and specifically the promise of the Corinthians rising up from the dead.

There is no note about where such an event took place. Was it in Jerusalem? Judaea? the Galilee? Furthermore, given the number it would almost have to have taken place outdoors. You could not rent the local theater for such an event.

Finally, Paul's note about some being alive, while others have fallen asleep, indicates that he knows some of the members of this group, at least to the extent that he knows whether they are dead or alive.

All in all, this reference is puzzling. But I propose to take Paul at his word, that this is part of the gospel-statement that he had handed on to the Corinthians and that they had accepted.

James

Next in the list comes James. Besides here in the gospel-statement, this name occurs only in Paul's letters in Galatians. In defending the independence of his apostleship, he recounts his first visit to Jerusalem after his revelation and notes that he stayed with Cephas and "did not meet any of the Anointed's other envoys (apostles) except James, our lord's brother" (Gal 1:19). One assumes that the James in the statement is the same James mentioned in Galatians. That James is identified as the brother of the lord, the brother of Jesus. Furthermore he is called an apostle, at least that is the natural way to read the Greek. Likewise the list's structure groups him with the apostles. In Galatians Paul associates him with the pillars—James, Cephas, and John—and his name comes first. Finally the representatives of James provoke Cephas' withdrawal after the confrontation with Paul over Cephas' refusal to eat with gentiles in celebrating the Lord's supper. Perhaps listing James' name first among the pillars has real significance.

In the synoptic gospels James is the son of Zebedee and his brother is John (Mark 1:19). He is listed among the apostles (Mark 3:17). James and John are always mentioned together and the triad is not James, Cephas and John (Paul's pillars) but Peter, James and John. James and John make no appearance in the fourth gospel.

Nowhere else in the New Testament do we find a resurrection appearance to James, the brother of the lord, although the gospel of the Hebrews, now lost, recorded such an event. Jerome in his "On Illustrious Men" (written 392 CE) preserves the passage.

I recently translated into Greek and Latin the gospel called the "Gospel of the Hebrews," the one that Origen (circa 185–254) also frequently uses. After the resurrection of the Savior, it says,

> The Lord, after he had given the linen cloth to the priest's slave, went to James and appeared to him. (Now James had sworn not to eat bread from the time that he drank from the Lord's cup until he would see him raised from among those who sleep.)

Shortly after this the Lord said,

> "Bring a table and some bread."

And immediately it is added:

> He took the bread, blessed it, broke it, and gave it to James the Just and said to him, "My brother, eat your bread, for the Son of Adam has been raised from among those who sleep."
>
> (Gospel of the Hebrews 9)

The oath ascribed to James, not to eat bread until "he would see him raised from among those who sleep," is ascribed to Jesus in a different form in Luke 22:16. The story concludes with a eucharistic blessing similar to that found in the Emmaus story (Luke 24:30).

In the gospel of the Hebrews, James has the place of priority, not Cephas. The gospel of Thomas also contains a saying giving priority to James:

> The disciples said to Jesus, "We know that you are going to leave us. Who will be our leader?"
>
> Jesus said to them, "No matter where you are, you are to go to James the Just, for whose sake heaven and earth came into being."
>
> (Thomas 12)

This saying comes from a stage before Thomas had become the chief apostle of this gospel (see Thomas 13).

The absence of James the brother of the Lord in the canonical gospels almost cries out for explanation. The traditional answer is that the family of Jesus were not followers during his ministry and did not become believers until after his resurrection. This may well be the case. James makes a sudden appearance in the Acts of the Apostles, but only after Herod "had James, the brother of

> ## Gospel of the Hebrews
>
> This gospel survives only in nine fragments quoted by others, and it is not always clear whether we are dealing with quotes or summaries. Because of the fragmentary character, it is difficult to be precise about the gospel. It appears to know the synoptics, and so was probably written in the early part of the second century. Because those quoting it are connected to Egypt, that has been assumed to be the place of composition. For a translation of the extant fragments, see *The Complete Gospels*.

John, killed with the sword" (Acts 12:2). Herod then arrests and imprisons Peter, but when an angel delivers Peter from prison, Peter says, "Announce to James and the brothers these things" (Acts 12:17). The assumption is that this is James, the brother of the lord. But "brother of the lord" is never applied to James and we make the assumption that this James is James the brother of the lord only because Herod has just killed James, the brother of John. Again, this sudden appearance of James in Acts cries out for explanation. When did he become one of the followers? This is even more puzzling, when a little later in Acts, at the so-called Jerusalem council, James appears to speak with authority for the whole group (Acts 15:13–31). He addresses the assembly, "Men [meaning males], brothers, listen to me" (BBS Trans), and he concludes with "Therefore I have reached the decision that we should not trouble those gentiles who are turning to God." He is speaking for the whole group.

We are not in a position to untangle the web surrounding James the brother of the lord, but a few observations are in order. I again would insist on the priority of Paul. He is our earliest witness. Reading between the lines in the letter to the Galatians, we learn that James is someone to deal with concerning both Paul and Cephas. Cephas may be first in the list, but James appears to command respect in Jerusalem. For Paul the pillars are James, Cephas, and John. That is the order in which he lists them, and it probably is not accidental.

The synoptic tradition replaces James, Cephas and John with Peter, James and John. Probably the only person on the list who changes is James: from James, the brother of the lord, to James, the brother of John. I am assuming that Cephas and Peter are the same person, although one cannot be sure that is the case. James' appearance in the later part of Acts as very prominent among the brothers in Jerusalem, if not their leader, is better explained by Paul's list than it is by his sudden and unexplained appearance in Acts. Paul probably has it right. James the brother of the lord is prominent in Jerusalem because he is on the list of those the risen Jesus "has been seen for." That Acts never mentions that James is indeed the brother of the lord is very interesting.

This indicates competition for leadership among the Anointed-believers was intense and continued well into the late first century and beyond. Paul's list is the first attempt to establish that authority, but it will by no means be the last.

The Apostles

Because the synoptic gospels have lists of the Twelve and Luke notes they are twelve apostles, the tradition has identified the Twelve and the apostles. But Paul's list makes it clear that originally they were two separate groups.

The Greek noun *apostolos* (apostle) derives from the verb *apostellō*, meaning to send, especially to send as a representative, and this is why the SV translation uses "envoy." The English "apostle" is not a translation, but a transliteration. It simply takes over the Greek characters and creates a made up word. In secular Greek the noun has a range of meanings, primarily connected with maritime activities, and only occasionally meaning "persons dispatched for specific purpose" (Bauer, *A Greek-English Lexicon*). The New Testament employs the noun in this narrow sense.

Paul never explicitly names Cephas among the apostles, although Gal 1:17–19 could be read that way:

> Neither did I set out for Jerusalem to get the approval of those who became envoys [apostles] for God's Anointed before I did. . . .
>
> Then, three years later I went up to Jerusalem to get acquainted with Cephas, and I stayed with him for two full weeks. I did not meet any of the Anointed's other envoys except James, our lord's brother.

In my reading this indicates that both Cephas and James are among the apostles and that the apostles are a larger group somehow associated with Jerusalem.

Among those whom Paul refers to as apostles are some surprising names. At the conclusion of the letter to the Romans , Paul greets a variety of folks:

> Greet Andronicus and Junia, my compatriots and fellow-prisoners.
> They are persons of distinction among [the Anointed's] emissaries [apostles]
> and they identified themselves with the Anointed before I did.
> (Rom 16:7)

Andronicus and Junia are mentioned only here. Furthermore, Junia is a female name—she is a woman. Given Paul's description

---

The Apostle Junia

Junia has had to struggle to take her rightful place among the apostles. The history of her transformation into a male and rediscovery as a female reads almost like a detective novel with denial of her existence, the invention of a phony Latin male name, and other convoluted grammatical contortions.

In early Christianity there was no real challenge to her status as an apostle. The oft quoted words of John Chrysostom (c. 347–407) clearly make the point.

> "Salute Andronicus and Junia my kinsmen . . . who are of note among the Apostles." And indeed to be apostles at all is a great thing. But to be even amongst these of note, just consider what a great encomium this is! But they were of note owing to their works, to their achievements. Oh! how great is the devotion of this woman that she should be even counted worthy of the appellation of apostle! (*On the Epistle of St. Paul the Apostle to the Romans*, 31.2).

The quote makes it clear that Chrysostom considered Junia a full-fledged apostle. As far as we can tell, Chrysostom represents the standard position in Christianity until the late

Continued on next page

medieval period. Although the first identification of the name as male occurs in the late thirteenth century, the decisive influence is Luther's translation. He identifies the name as masculine.

Despite Luther's influence, the *textus receptus* as well as all Greek printed editions of the New Testament save one take the name as feminine until the 1927 edition of Nestle. Early, English translations, including the King James, likewise take the name as Junia, female. In the nineteenth century translations suddenly began to move to a masculine interpretation of the name.

Bernadette Brouton's 1977 article changed the situation by producing a mass of evidence that a female Junia was the correct reading, and that there was no evidence of the supposed male name that scholars had proposed to avoid the certification of a female apostle. The 1998 Nestle-Aland (27th edition) and UBS (4th edition) restored Junia as a female. English translations also have begun shifting. Beginning in 1970 with the New American Bible (a Catholic translation) more and more English translations have interpreted the name as female. The REB and NRSV made the shift in 1989, while the NIV has retained the male name.

Works Cited

Brooten, Bernadette J. "'Junia . . . Outstanding among the Apostles' (Romans 16,7)." In *Women Priests: A Catholic Commentary on the Vatican Declaration*, edited by L. S. and A Swidler, 148–51. New York: Paulist, 1977. Written in the wake of the Vatican's document rejecting the ordination of women, this essay amassed the evidence for Junia, a woman, as an apostle.

Chrysostom, John. *Homilies of St. John Chrysostom, on the Epistle of St. Paul the Apostle to the Romans*. Translated by J. B. Morris and W. H. Simcox. Edited by Philip Schaff, *Nicene and Post-Nicene Fathers*: T&T Clark, 1889.

Epp, Eldon Jay. *Junia, the First Woman Apostle*. Minneapolis: Fortress, 2005. Epp's little book brings together the whole history of Junia's transformation and rediscovery.

of these two as "persons of distinction among the apostles," they surely have the same rank as himself.

When Paul complains to the Corinthians about how he is being treated, he refers to a group of unnamed apostles.

> Am I not entitled to be provided with food and drink?
> Do I not have the right to be accompanied by a wife as do the other envoys and the brothers of the lord and Cephas?
> Or are Barnabas and I the only ones who are supposed to pay their own way?
> (1 Cor 9:4–6)

Here the apostles appear to be travelling missionaries like Barnabas and Paul, but they get support and have their wives travelling with them. In this statement does Paul imply that Barnabas also is an apostle? In Acts 14:4 and 14:14 Barnabas and Paul are referred to as apostles, although that is contrary to normal usage in Acts, where apostles are limited to those who were present with Jesus from the baptism to his death (Acts 1:22). This reference in Acts to Barnabas and Paul as apostles may reflect a tradition earlier than the composition of Acts itself.

The reference to "apostles, brothers of the lord and Cephas" is interesting. Who are these brothers of lord? Is this an otherwise unknown honorary group or does it refer to physical brothers of the lord? Once again, Cephas stands out.

In 2 Corinthians Paul uses apostle in a somewhat difference sense. This composite letter is made up of a number of other letters Paul had most likely addressed to Corinth. Since exactly how many letters are involved and how they should be arranged is a matter for debate, using evidence from this edited letter is tricky. But 2 Corinthians 8 appears to be the conclusion of a letter in which Paul recommends Titus and notes that he is sending him with a famous brother who otherwise remains unidentified. He concludes this section with:

> As for Titus, he is my partner and co-worker in your service;
> as for our brothers, they are apostles of the churches, the glory of Christ.
> (2 Cor 8:23, BBS Trans)

Here "apostles" has the distinctive sense of one sent for a purpose, but does the "of the churches" denote on Paul's part a distinction between them and himself as an apostle of the lord? We will return to this issue when we return to the last name on the list, the apostle Paul.

Finally in 2 Corinthians Paul wages a fierce contest over the loyalty of the Corinthian community with a group whom he calls "super-apostles."

> As I see it, I'm in no way inferior to the "super-envoys"!
> Although I'm not a polished speaker, I'm not without knowledge.
> In all kinds of ways I've made it clear to you that I know what I am talking about.
> (2 Cor 11:5–6)

A group of apostles has come to Corinth, and from Paul's point of view they are preaching "another gospel." These apostles exhibit powerful signs, work wonders, and are impressive speakers. In the judgment of the Corinthians, Paul does not measure up. In addition they accept payment, but "I robbed other gatherings of the Anointed, as it were, and took my pay from them to serve you" (2 Cor 11:8). For Paul these super-apostles are "phony envoys, specialists in deceit, who disguise themselves as envoys of the Anointed" (2 Cor 11:13).

Paul's contrast with them is interesting:

> Are they "Hebrews?" Me too!
> "Israelites?" Me too!
> "Descendents of Abraham?" Me too!
> Are they "servants (*diakonoi*) of the Anointed?"
> I'm babbling like I'm out of my mind—my service far surpasses theirs!
> With so many more troubles, so many more arrests, even more lashes, often in danger of death.
> (2 Cor 11:22–23)

These folks are claiming to be apostles and among their signs of an apostle, honors of which they boast, is their Jewish heritage, which, of course, Paul can match. This raises two interesting questions.

- Were all the apostles Jewish?
- Did all apostles see the risen lord?

If we consider only Paul's evidence, the folks he lists as apostles are Jewish—in the case of Andronicus and Junia he mentions that they are fellow Jews. In this debate with the super-apostles, being Jewish is apparently an important criterion for being an apostle.

The list states, "He was seen . . . to all the apostles," suggesting that seeing the risen lord is one of the criteria for being an apostle. (But all who have seen the lord are not necessarily apostles, e.g., the 500.) Since visions and revelations are part of the claim of the super-apostles (2 Cor 12:1), one must assume that they were claiming such as authentication of their claim to apostleship.

This consideration of what apostle might mean in the gospel-statement's list has shown that the view of the synoptics, which are much later, is too restricting for Paul's pre-70 CE period. The twelve must not be confused with the apostles, even though the two groups may have overlapping membership. The apostles were Jewish missionaries, with Greek names, operating in the diaspora, the gentile world. Even in the case of Peter, whose mission is "to the circumcised," a Greek name is used. How large this group was, we have no way of knowing, but it was surely larger than twelve and made up both women and men.

Paul

The last name on the list is Paul's. We have seen that Paul could not take for granted that others would accept his claim of apostleship. Since we know it was contested in Galatia and in Corinth, putting his name last on the list is yet another claim for his equality among the apostles.

The statement is carefully constructed.

> Last of all, as it were to an aborted one, he has been seen even to me.
> (BBS Trans)

Does Paul suggest that the call to apostleship ends with him or is he simply the last on this list? Either reading is possible. He goes on to consider himself an abortion. Since he views himself as set apart from his mother's womb, he considers his life before his call as an abortion of what God called him to. Finally in Greek the statement emphasizes, "even to me" or "to me also" (*kamoi*).

As though he cannot help himself he launches into a defense of his apostleship in language reminiscent of Galatians. This is Paul's story. He is "the least of the apostles, unfit to be called an apostle," because he harassed the church of God. But then God acted and "the generous favor of God has made me what I am." Paul "worked harder than any of them" and then almost as an afterthought he remembers that it is by God's grace that he is an apostle. Finally he remembers his point: "So it doesn't make any difference whether it was I or they; this is what we present and this is what you embraced," namely, the gospel-statement and the list that he received and handed on. It is, he affirms, the common affirmation of the Anointed-believers.

We have often seen, in examining the gospel-statement and the list, the importance of maintaining its independence and not reading the assumptions of later documents and writings into it. It is a pre-70 document, while all the gospels are post-70. Paul's gospel-statement and list should be given a chance to stand on their own two feet and guide us into the world of pre-70 Anointed-believers.

Paul's inclusion of himself on the list calls for comment. Commentators often note that Paul added himself to the list, and that is surely correct. But that does not mean the inclusion is arbitrary or self-serving. The rehearsal of Paul's call in the letter to the Galatians significantly indicates that the pillars in Jerusalem—James, Cephas, and John—accepted the authenticity of Paul's call and extended to him the right hand of fellowship, even though he had persecuted the church of God. While his apostleship was controversial, it was accepted by the pillars. We should take Paul at his word, unless we have compelling evidence to the contrary. Paul cannot simply be set aside in favor of later evidence, because without Paul we lose any connection to the earliest level. He is our connection to Cephas, the Twelve, James, and the apostles.

If we accept Paul's place on the list as legitimate, then the construction of Luke/Acts collapses. Acts wants to limit apostleship to those who were with Jesus from his baptism to his death. This excludes Paul, and was probably meant to do so. Paul's list indicates that in the pre-70 period, apostleship was much wider in scope. Luke/Acts limits the appearances to the period between the resurrection on the third day and the ascension forty days later. This, of course, would exclude not only Paul but also Andronicus and Junia and who knows who else. By including himself on the list Paul indicates that these appearances went on for much longer than forty days, indeed for at least several years, depending on how one dates Paul's call. This wholesale disagreement with Paul calls into question the entire Luke/Acts construction in this matter. It does not mean that Acts is always wrong, but that one should be very suspicious.

Further Reading

Chilton, Bruce, and Jacob Neusner, eds. *The Brother of Jesus, James the Just and His Mission*. Louisville: Westminster John Knox, 2001.

Fitzmyer, Joseph A. *First Corinthians*, Yale Anchor Bible. New Haven: Yale University, 2008.

Freyne, Sean. *Retrieving James/Yakov, the Brother of Jesus, from Legend to History*. Annandale-on-Hudson, NY: Institute of Advanced Theology, Bard College, 2008.

Koester, Helmut. *Ancient Christian Gospels*. Philadelphia: Trinity Press International, 1990.

Painter, John. *Just James, the Brother of Jesus in History and Tradition*. Edited by D. Moody Smith, Studies on Personalities of the New Testament. Minneapolis: Fortress, 1999.

Pervo, Richard L. *Acts*, Hermeneia. Minneapolis: Fortress, 2009.

Works Cited

Augustus to Nero, a Sourcebook on Roman History 31 BC–AD 68. Translated by David C. Braund. Totowa, NJ: Barnes and Noble, 1985.

Bauer, Walter. *A Greek-English Lexicon of the New Testament and Other Early Christian Literature*. Edited by Frederick William Danker. 3rd ed. Chicago: University of Chicago Press, 2000.

Chrysostom, John. *Homilies of St. John Chrysostom, on the Epistle of St. Paul the Apostle to the Romans*. Translated by J. B. Morris and W. H. Simcox. *Nicene and Post-Nicene Fathers*. Edited by Philip Schaff. T. & T. Clark, 1889.

8 He Has Been Seen

We have been following Paul's usage and have seen that he employs several metaphors when writing about what happened to Jesus following his crucifixion:

- he was raised up
- the standing up
- super-exalted

The first two of these have their source in the writings coming out of the attempt of Antiochus Epiphanes to destroy Judaism as seen in Daniel and 2 Maccabees. The third term, "super-exalted," comes from the praise statement of the Philippians and has as its milieu both the LXX and Roman imperial propaganda.

When in Galatians Paul speaks of his own experience of Jesus as raised up from the dead, he uses "revelation of Jesus anointed" or "he [God] revealed his son in/to me."

1 Corinthians 15 uses yet another Greek verb, *ōphthē,* which the King James version translated literally: "And that he was seen of Cephas." Modern translations have translated the verb "he appeared to Cephas" (ESV, RSV, NRSV, NIV [which has Peter instead of Cephas], REB, NAB, JB). "He appeared" as a translation is not incorrect but can misdirect.

- "Appeared" in English implies visions.
- It tempts a reader to insert the appearance stories in the later gospels, especially those in Luke and John.
- The passive sense is lost.

The first and second reasons go together. The verb "to appear" in English is intransitive, i.e., does not take a direct object. It has as its primary sense "to become visible" (*American Heritage Dictionary*) and tempts us to think it is referring to visions or something of the sort. That in turn begs for an explanation, and the tradition has been only too quick to fill the gap with the stories from the gospels, even though those stories do not match up well with Paul's list. In fact, one could almost say that those stories include what is not on Paul's list (see Comparison chart).

Or to take a contrasting example, James appears on Paul's list, yet no one wants to fill that in with the account found in the gospel of the Hebrews. Shouldn't we wonder why?

A Comparison of Paul and Gospel Resurrection Stories				
Paul	**Mark**	**Matthew**	**Luke**	**John**
Cephas				
	3 Women but no appearance	2 Women	A group of women	Mary Magdalene
			Emmaus	
			Has appeared to Simon	
Twelve		Eleven on the Mountain in Galilee	Eleven in Jerusalem	Disciples in Jerusalem
				Thomas
500				
James				
Apostles				
				Disciples at Sea of Tiberias; Peter
			Ascension	
Paul				

Now to the grammar. The Greek verb *ōphthē* is an aorist (past tense), passive voice of *horaō*, to see. This indicates the real problem with "he appeared" as a translation—it is active rather than passive. The Anointed does the acting, making himself appear or become visible.

Let us take a moment to consider how the passive voice operates. In the following two examples notice the relationship.

> Cephas saw the Anointed.
> The Anointed has been seen by Cephas.

The example points out how to convert an active verb into a passive one. Normally in Greek the person "by whom" the activity is done (the seeing is done **by** Cephas) is indicated by the preposition *hypo*, just as "by" indicates agency in English. But here there is no *hypo* in the Greek; instead a dative of advantage indicates **for** whom the action is performed, not **by** whom. Literally the sentence reads: "The Anointed has been seen for the advantage of Cephas." While "for" is not idiomatic in English it has the advantage that this formula stresses that the seeing is being done for Cephas' advantage, not by Cephas. In the case of Paul, for example, the advantage of the seeing was his call to be an apostle. The dative "for" ties seeing with purpose, just as in Galatians the revelation was for the purpose of certifying Paul's apostleship.

In the translation "he has been seen" the passive suggests that the agency is God—God is causing the Anointed to be seen, made manifest, revealed. Three of the verbs in the gospel-statement stress this passivity:

> The Anointed died,
> was buried
> was raised from the dead
> has been seen for

Likewise in Galatians, where Paul first explains his experience, he writes, "when God . . . was pleased to reveal his son in/to me" (Gal 1:15–16). The description in Galatians stresses God as the active agent. God is revealing Jesus, God is making Jesus visible.

Verbs of Seeing in Greek

Greek has three main verbs for seeing, often used synonymously, but having important shades of meaning:

horaō—to see or to perceive, often with less emphasis on physical seeing.

blepō—to see, to become aware of or take notice of something. Frequently in a strong physical sense.

theōreō—to see, perceive, to discover, investigate, contemplate. In koine Greek it largely replaces *horaō*.

The verb *ōphthē* is unusual in koine Greek (the "common" Greek of the New Testament), but it does have an important usage in the Septuagint. Of the 40 occurrences of *ōphthē* in the LXX, the vast majority (32) announce a theophany, an appearance of God, frequently in the formulaic phrase, "the lord [or God or an angel of the lord or the glory of the lord] has been seen for. . . . The following examples are from the Septuagint.

> And the Lord was seen for Abram, and said,
> "To your seed I will give this land."
> And Abram built there an altar to the Lord who had been seen
>   for him.
>   (Gen 12:7, BBS Trans)

> And God has been seen for Jacob again in Louza when he
>   came out of Mesopotamia of Syria
> and God blessed him and said to him,
> "Your name is Jacob;
> no longer will you still be called Jacob, but Israel is your
>   name."
>   (Gen 35:9–10, BBS Trans)

> And when Aaron was speaking to the whole congregation of
>   the sons of Israel,
> and they turned toward the desert,
> and the glory of the Lord has been seen in a cloud.
> The Lord spoke to Moses saying,
> "I have heard the murmuring of the sons of Israel."
>   (Exod 16:10–12, BBS Trans)

And the angel of the lord has been seen for him and said to
    him,
"The lord is with you, you mighty in strength."
    (Judg 6:12, BBS Trans)

In most of these cases "he has been seen for" is followed by a
verb of saying and what follows is a speech indicating the advantage. God never physically appears. There is no hint of physically
seeing God. The classic example is God's appearing to Moses in
the burning bush.

And Moses was shepherding the sheep of Jothor his father-in-
    law, the priest of Madiam;
and he led the sheep from the desert
and came to the mountain of Choreb.
And an angel of the Lord has been seen for him in a flaming
    fire out of a bush;
and he sees that the bush is burning
and the bush is not burning up.
And Moses said,
"Drawing near I will see this great sight, why the bush is not
    burning up."
And when the Lord saw that he was drawing near to see,
the Lord called to him out of the bush, saying, "Moses,
    Moses!"
And he said, "What is it?"
And he said, "Do not come near!
"Take the sandals from your feet, for the place on which you
    are standing is holy ground."
And He said to him,
"I am the God of your father, God of Abraham, God of Isaac,
    and God of Jacob."
And Moses hid his face, for he was afraid to look at God face
    to face.
    (Exod 3:1–6, BBS Trans)

When the angel of the lord shifts into the lord, it becomes
clear that "angel of the lord" is simply another way of saying "lord"
or "God." An angel of the lord is a manifestation of the lord. Never
in this story is God or the lord seen, but only the burning bush.

This leads us to conclude that in the LXX *ōphthē*, "he has been
seen for" is a stereotyped or formulaic way of expressing a mani-

festation, experience or revelation of God's revealing power. There is no indication of seeing in a physical sense. Most of the time, the "seeing" is followed up by God speaking. This, of course, coheres perfectly with Paul's *apocalyps*-revelation in Galatians.

Furthermore this use of *ōphthē*, "he has been seen for," is clearly recognized in Jewish commentary on the LXX. Philo of Alexandria (20 BCE to 50 CE) in his "On Abraham" remarks on this usage. Because of its importance I am quoting the passage in its entirety.

> We have a very clear proof of the mind's migration from astrology and the Chaldean creed in the words which follow at once the story of the departure of the Sage. "God," it says "was seen (*ōphthē*) by Abraham." This shews that God was not manifested to him before, when in his Chaldean way he was fixing his thoughts on the choric movement of the stars with no apprehension at all of the harmonious and intelligible order of things outside the world and the sphere of sense. But when he had departed and changed his habitation he could not help but know that the world is not sovereign but dependent, not governing but governed by its Maker and First Cause. And his mind then saw for the first time with its recovered sight. For before a great mist had been shed upon it by the things of sense, and only with difficulty could it dispel this mist and so be able as in clear open sky to receive the vision (*phantasian*) of Him Who so long lay hidden and invisible. He in His love for mankind, when the soul came into His presence, did not turn away His face, but came forward to meet him and revealed His nature, so far as the beholder's power of sight allowed. That is why we are told not that the Sage saw (*eide*) God, but that God was seen (*ōphthē*) by him. For it were impossible that anyone should by himself apprehend the truly Existent, did not he reveal and manifest Himself.
>
> (Philo, *On Abraham*, 17.77–80)

Philo was a Jewish philosopher who interpreted Judaism by means of Plato. Since as this passage demonstrates his method was allegorical, he interprets Abraham's movements (migrations) in an allegorical or double sense. They are both physical journeys and also migrations of the soul. Thus he interprets Gen 12:7

as a migration or shift of the soul from the false system of the Chaldeans to a true harmonious system.

Important for our consideration is the way Philo employs visual metaphors throughout the passage. Abraham before the migration is described as in a mist, but afterwards it is as though he is under a clear sky. He receives a vision *(phantasian)* of the one who had been hidden and invisible: "his mind then saw again for the first time with its recovered sight," literally in Greek, "he saw as seeing again *(anablepsasa)*." Visual metaphors dominate the passage. Yet Philo draws from Genesis the conclusion that Abraham, now a sage, did not "see God" *(eide theon)* but that "God was seen" *(ōphthē)*. God is in charge, not the sage, "For it were impossible that anyone should by himself apprehend the truly Existent, did not He reveal and manifest Himself."

Despite the dominance of the visual metaphors, there is no physical seeing in the passage. That is the point of using the verb of seeing in the passive voice. One might describe Philo's account as "mental" seeing, but it is clear that for Philo this is real seeing: God has made himself visible, but it is not physical seeing. One might describe it as insight.

The evidence from the Septuagint and from Philo indicates that *ōphthē* is a Hellenistic Jewish formula for God revealing God's self for someone's advantage. Paul's description in Gal 1:15–16 of his own experience as revelation confirms this understanding of *ōphthē* as a formula. From this we can draw two conclusions.

1. The whole passage (1 Cor 15:1–8) is formulaic. It is not the account of eyewitnesses, but a community's experience expressed in formulae borrowed mostly from Hellenistic Judaism. The formulaic character of the whole passage explains phrases like "died for our sins according to the scripture." This is a formula, not a reference to a specific scripture. The use of *ōphthē* in the list of 1 Cor 15:5–9 fits into this same formulaic scheme. It does not describe physical seeing, but rather a revelation of what God has accomplished by raising the Anointed up from the dead.

2. This is why in Paul's writings no stories of resurrection appearances occur. It is an experience described by the Septuagintal formulaic phrase "He has been seen for." Paul

has given us his story: "God revealed his son in/to/for me."
That is Paul's appearance story.

In two other passages in the Corinthian correspondence Paul refers to seeing the lord and visions and revelations. We must now try to discover what these add to our inquiry.

Have I Not Seen the Lord?

In 1 Cor 9:1 Paul is once again defending his apostleship, and once again he calls on his experience:

> I'm a free man, am I not?
> I'm an envoy, am I not?
> I have seen Jesus our lord, haven't I?
> You are the result of my work in the lord's service, aren't you?
> (1 Cor 9:1–2)

The first line indicates what the issue is. Paul's freedom has been challenged because he has not accepted payment for his services. To defend himself he appeals to his apostleship. Seeing the lord appears to be a requirement for apostleship. In this case Paul uses the active voice, "I have seen Jesus our lord," instead of the passive, and his use of the perfect tense indicates the ongoing influence of that past action. Thus the accent does not fall on the past act of seeing, but on its continuing influence, and Paul immediately points to the outcome of that seeing: "You are the result of my work in the lord's service." In both cases the foundation of his apostleship is the revelation or the seeing of Jesus. For Paul these are interchangeable terms referring to the same event.

While the active does deviate from the passive pattern we have seen, Paul makes no claim here beyond what he has asserted before. He goes into no detail, he reports no vision or apparition. The object of the seeing is "our lord" and its outcome is the Corinthian church, "my work in the lord's service."

Visions and Revelations

The Corinthian community was a difficult experience for Paul. He met challenges of many different types, some of which were painful and tearful. As we have mentioned, Paul also faced in

> ### Editing the Corinthian Correspondence
>
> 1 and 2 Corinthians as they appear in the New Testament are the result of an editing process. While scholars agree on this, they disagree on what is edited and how many letters or parts of letters are contained in the correspondence. For our purposes, we need only recognize that 2 Corinthians is made up of two or more letters and those letters were written after 1 Corinthians, probably in the mid 50s CE.

Corinth a group of Jewish missionaries he called "super-apostles" because they exhibited all kinds of marvelous "signs." They were great preachers, they worked wonders and did healings, they had visions and revelations, and they were paid for their ministry. Paul had to face this challenge.

Paul's strategy in resisting the super-apostles was never to deal directly with them, but only with the Corinthian believers, and never to boast. He contrasts the boasts of the super-apostles with his own weaknesses. Only of his weaknesses will he boast.

Paul is engaging in what the ancients called a fool's speech (2 Cor 11:1–12:10). He even refers to his foolishness several times in the speech (2 Cor 11:1, 16–17, 19, 21; 12:6, 11), and he concludes the speech with an appeal to his foolishness.

> I've played the fool! You forced me into it!
> I should have been recommended by you.
> I'm in no way outranked by the "super-envoys," even though I'm nothing.
> The marks of an authentic envoy were brought out with full sustaining power in your midst with signs, wonders, and miracles.
> What is it that makes you feel that I treated the other gatherings of the Anointed better than you, except for the fact that I didn't press you for financial support?
> Forgive me that slight!
>   (2 Cor 12:11–13)

The speech drips with irony and sarcasm, as this conclusion indicates.

Apparently one of the boasts of the super-apostles is that they have had "visions and revelations," and in 2 Cor 12:1–5 Paul responds.

> I have to brag. Although it's pointless,
> I'll move on to visions (*optasias*) and special insights (*apokalypseis*) about the lord.
> I know a man who belongs to the Anointed who fourteen years ago was carried away
> —whether in the body, I don't know, or out of the body, I don't know, God knows—
> carried off to heaven's third level.
> I know that this man
> —whether in the body or out of the body I don't know, God knows—
> was carried off to Paradise
> and heard indescribable words which no one may speak.
> I am willing to brag about that one,
> but I'll not brag about "yours truly" except for my limitations.

Paul's Heavenly Vision in Acts

Acts 26:19 has Paul use "visions" in his speech before King Agrippa to describe his Damascus experience:

> After that, King Agrippa, I was not disobedient to the heavenly visions (*ouraniōi optasiai*), but declared first to those in Damascus, then in Jerusalem and throughout the countryside of Judea, and also to the Gentiles, that they should repent and turn to God and do deeds consistent with repentance (Acts 26:19–20, NRSV modified).

For the author of Acts, Paul's Damascus experience does not count as an appearance of the resurrected Jesus because it does not take place between the resurrection and ascension of Jesus. By describing Paul's experience as a heavenly vision Acts disassociates Paul's experience from that of the twelve apostles, another fiction of this author.

This speech is clearly not Paul's, not only because of the use of *optasaia* but because Paul never uses "repentance" as a topic. That belongs to the theological program of the author of Luke/Acts.

The phrase "visions and revelations" apparently comes from the super-apostles. This is the only place in Paul's writings where we find the word "visions" (*optasiai*) and "revelations" (*apokalypseis*, "special insights" in SV) in the plural (vss 1 and 7). Since Paul uses "revelation" in the singular a number of times in other passages that we examined above, this unique usage would suggest that the phrase is not Paul's.

Paul is describing a phenomenon frequently reported in Judaism, a journey into the heavens. 1 Enoch 39 contains a good example.

> In those days, whirlwinds carried me off from the earth,
> and set me down into the ultimate ends of the heavens.
> There I saw other dwelling places of the holy ones and their
> resting places too.
> (1 Enoch 39:3–4)

In comparison with other visions and revelations about journeys to the heavens, Paul shows remarkable restraint. The third heaven and Paradise are normal configurations of such journeys. But Paul confesses to be unaware whether he is in or out of the body—twice he notes this. Jewish apocalypses normally involved an in-body experience, while Greeks opted for an out-of-body or soul experience. In the Testament of Abraham, Abraham requests of God through an intermediary, the angel Michael, "Master Lord, heed my plea: While I am yet in this body I wish to see all the inhabited world and all the created things which you established." God responds to Michael, "Take a cloud of light, and the angels who have authority over the chariots, and go down and take the righteous Abraham on a chariot of cherubim and lift him up into the air of heaven so that he may see all the inhabited world" (Testament of Abraham 9:6–8).

The final book of Plato's *Republic* contains the Myth of Er, which is a story of the warrior Er's journey through the underworld and the heavens. This story had great influence on the Western conception of the afterlife, the heavens, and underworld. Its influence in later Christianity has also been considerable. Having been killed in battle, Er's body did not decay, and on the twelfth day after his death, when placed on the funeral pyre, he came alive.

> After coming to life he related what, he said, he had seen
> in the world beyond. He said that when his soul went forth
> from his body he journeyed with a great company and that
> they came to a mysterious region where there were two
> openings side by side in the earth, and judges were sitting
> between these, and that after every judgment they bade
> the righteous journey to the right and upward through the
> heaven with tokens attached to them in front of the judg-
> ment passed upon them, and the unjust to take the road to
> the left and downward, they too wearing behind signs of all
> that had befallen them, and that when he himself drew near
> they told him that he must be the messenger to mankind to
> tell them of that other world, and they charged him to give
> ear and to observe everything in the place.
>
>   (*Republic*, X)

Plato's story is clearly the journey of a soul, not of a body as was
the case in the Testament of Abraham. Paul's uncertainty as to
whether he is in the body or not only makes his report that much
more of a problem for his audience. Since he must boast, as he
says, the way he boasts ends up making the boast almost useless.
And that, of course, is Paul's point. He will boast only of his weaknesses.

Not only does Paul show restraint, but concerning his "vision" he reports nothing that he has seen and moreover describes
what he heard as "unutterable words" (literal translation) that no
one is permitted to speak. The phrase "unutterable words" (*arrēta
rēmata*) is a contradiction in terms, for the whole point of words
(*rēmata*) is that they be utterable. For Paul this is a private revelation, not "open to the public," and he gives no real hint about its
content.

Despite our pride in modernity, we should not be too quick
to cast aside these descriptions of journey's into the heavens or
underworld. It is never clear whether they are about the cosmos or
the future. Probably both. These are descriptions of mystical ex-
periences that employ the conventions of their culture to explain
the experience.

Some scholars have argued that in 2 Cor 12:1–5 Paul is describing his "resurrection experience," but this is hardly likely for
three major reasons:

- Sarcasm and irony flows through the passage. Paul was too defensive about and protective of his apostleship to treat his revelation of the son in such a fashion (see, e.g., Galatians).

The Apocalypse of Paul

Paul's restrained description of his visions and revelations in 2 Cor 12:1–5 gave rise to at least two Apocalypses of Paul. The major one, written in Greek in the fourth century and then translated into many different languages including Latin, has had a strong influence in the West on the view of heaven and hell. Dante's Inferno (11.28) reflects scenes taken directly from The Apocalypse of Paul. This Apocalypse is highly dependent on the Apocalypse of Peter. It is a syncretic composition drawing upon both Jewish apocalypses and Greek categories.

Among the scrolls found at Nag Hammadi was a composition entitled The Apocalypse of Paul. It is considerably shorter than the Greek Apocalypse of Paul, but no less unrestrained. It too is highly syncretic, borrowing from both Jewish and Greek traditions. Furthermore it is easily situated within gnosticism, especially that of the Valentinian school. It is probably dated sometime in the late second century. The heavenly journey is most commonly set in the sixth and seventh heavens, even though Paul says he went only to the third heaven.

Further Reading

For the Greek Apocalypse of Paul see Edgar Hennecke and
    Wilhelm Schneemelcher. *New Testament Apocrypha*,
    Vol 2, *Writings Relating to the Apostles; Apocalypses*
    and Related Subjects. Translated by R. McL. Wilson.
    Philadelphia: Westminster, 1965, pp. 755–98.
For a translation of the Latin text see J. K. Elliott, *The*
    Apocryphal New Testament. Oxford: Clarendon Press,
    2005, pp. 616–44.
For the Nag Hammadi Apocalypse of Paul see James M.
    Robinson, *The Nag Hammadi Library in English*. San
    Francisco: Harper and Row, 1978, pp. 256–59.

- He specifically says this experience took place fourteen years ago. Since the letters in 2 Corinthians were written in the mid 50s, that would date this experience to the early 40s, about ten years after Paul's call in the early to mid 30s.
- Paul clearly differentiates this experience as "visions and revelations," a phrase that, as we have seen, is unique in Paul's letters.

The specific content of the experience described in 2 Cor 12:1–5 is something that Paul is reluctant to describe because he does not want to be drawn into the boasting game with the super-apostles. That content no doubt derives from the Jewish heavenly journey tradition.

Conclusion

We have now surveyed Paul's language about his experience of God's son raised up from the dead. This language stems largely from Jewish tradition. He uses:

- "God revealed his son to/in me."
- "The Anointed has been seen for . . ."—a phrase that employs the LXX phrase, "God has been seen for . . ." (ōphthē) to indicate that God manifested the Anointed as raised up from the dead.
- "I have seen the Lord"—again using a perfect tense that accents a past act with continuing outcome.
- "Super-exalted" in the Philippians praise piece.

In none of these does Paul describe an appearance of the Lord. An appearance story is not even implied in Paul. The content of his experience (his revelation, "he has been seen for") is the conviction that God has raised Jesus from the dead, and has made Jesus his son by raising him from the dead. Therefore the final apocalyptic scenario is underway. For Paul the end times are dawning and to be in the Anointed is to participate in those end times. We can best describe Paul's experience as revelation or revelatory insight.

Paul has a definite list of those for whom the Anointed has been seen and he puts himself on that list. That placement was clearly controversial and, since it was not accepted by some, Paul had to defend it. But the point of the Galatians account of the meeting in Jerusalem is that Cephas and the others extended the right hand of fellowship to Paul and so accepted his place on the list. Despite the controversial character of Paul's apostleship, my judgment is that he is telling the truth. As an historian, I give priority to his account. Where other accounts disagree, they are suspect.

Further Reading

Fuller, Reginald H. *The Formation of the Resurrection Narratives.* Philadelphia: Fortress Press, 1980.

Furnish, Victor Paul. *II Corinthians*, Anchor Bible. New York: Doubleday, 1984.

Works Cited

For 1 Enoch and Testament of Abraham, see Charlesworth, James H., ed. *The Old Testament Pseudepigrapha*, Vol 1, *Apocalyptic Literature and Testaments.* Garden City, NJ: Doubleday, 1983.*)*

Philo. *On Abraham.* Loeb Classical Library, 1935.

9 With What Kind of Body?

There is yet another way to ascertain what Paul means when he writes "the Anointed has been seen for me" or "Have I not seen the Lord?" In 1 Corinthians 15 Paul responds to the question, "How are the dead raised? With what kind of body do they come back?" (1 Cor 15:35). By following his response to this question we can gain yet another vantage point in our quest.

To follow Paul's argument we must be clear about what the discussion is about. The two questions (How are the dead raised? With what kind of body do they come back?) result from some in Corinth denying the resurrection from the dead. That is made clear in verse 12: "How can some of you possibly be saying that there is no such thing as the resurrection of the dead?" We must be clear about this point. They are not denying the resurrection itself. That is why Paul begins with the gospel-statement—in effect saying, "This is what we agree on." The Corinthians are not denying resurrection itself, but resurrection *from the dead*.

What then is the difference and what does it mean? Paul thinks this distinction is nonsense because immediately after posing the two questions, he responds, "Stupid man" (15:36), indicating what he thinks of those who separate resurrection from resurrection from the dead.

The Corinthians' Position

What might be motivating the Corinthians to take up such a position? Since Paul does not explain their position, we must reconstruct it. Our situation is like overhearing one side of a telephone conversation. Since one can easily mistake what is happening on the other end, we need to be careful in our reconstruction. We have Paul's reply, which apparently restates the two questions that provoked the answer, but we do not have their reasoning.

Several possibilities suggest themselves as explanations for the Corinthians' position.

- Greeks rejected the idea of coming back from the dead.
- Belief in the immortality of the soul is incompatible with resurrection from the dead.
- They think the resurrection has already begun.

Let's consider each of these possibilities.

No Coming Back

Greeks found the notion of coming back from the dead ridiculous. As is so often the case, Homer can speak for the tradition. When in the last book of the Iliad Achilleus comforts Priam over the death of his son, Achilleus concludes his speech:

> "But bear up, nor mourn endlessly in your heart, for there is not
> anything to be gained from grief for your son; you will never bring him back (*anstēseis*); sooner you must go through yet another sorrow."
> (Homer, *Iliad*, Book 24. 549–51)

The verb *anistēmi* means "to stand up or raise up" and the noun *anastasis*, "standing up" or "resurrection," is the noun form of this verb used by Paul in 1 Cor 15:12. In 1 Thess 4:14, 16, Paul uses this verb for Jesus' standing up.

In *Electra* by Sophocles the chorus confronts Electra with these words:

> But never by weeping nor by prayer will you resurrect (*anstaseis*) your father from the pool of Hades which receives all men. No, by grieving without end and beyond due limits you will find cureless misery and your own ruin; in these actions there is no deliverance from evils. Tell us, why do you pursue such suffering?
> (*Electra*, 137–44)

Jebb's translation Christianizes the translation by rendering *anstaseis* as "resurrect." This is the same verb used in Homer and so a more correct translation would be "nor by prayer will you raise up your father."

Apollo's speech in Aeschulus' *Eumenides* forcibly drives home that after death no one returns to life:

> Oh, monsters utterly loathed and detested by the gods! Zeus could undo fetters, there is a remedy for that, and many means of release. But when the dust has drawn up the blood of a man, once he is dead, there is no return to life. For this, my father has made no magic spells, although he arranges all other things, turning them up and down; nor does his exercise of force cost him a breath.
> (*Eumenides*, 644–50)

Given this rejection of coming back after death in Greek thought and Judaism's traditional rejection of life after death, Paul's raising up of the body from the dead is probably a hard sell in Corinth.

Immortality of the Soul

The classic argument for the immortality of the soul is in Plato's *Phaedo* (428–347 BCE; the *Phaedo* is usually placed in the middle group of dialogues), a dialogue between Socrates and Cebes.

> "Now," said he [Socrates], "shall we assume two kinds of existences, one visible, the other invisible?"
> "Let us assume them," said Cebes.
> "And that the invisible is always the same and the visible constantly changing?"
> "Let us assume that also," said he.
> "Well then," said Socrates, "are we not made up of two parts, body and soul?"
> "Yes," he replied.
> "Now to which class should we say the body is more similar and more closely akin?"
> "To the visible," said he; "that is clear to everyone."
> "And the soul? Is it visible or invisible?"
> "Invisible, to man, at least, Socrates."
> . . .

"And now again, in view of what we said before and of what has just been said, to which class do you think the soul has greater likeness and kinship?"

"I think, Socrates," said he, "that anyone, even the dullest, would agree, after this argument that the soul is infinitely more like that which is always the same than that which is not."

"And the body?"

"Is more like the other."

"Consider, then, the matter in another way. When the soul and the body are joined together, nature directs the one to serve and be ruled, and the other to rule and be master. Now this being the case, which seems to you like the divine, and which like the mortal? Or do you not think that the divine is by nature fitted to rule and lead, and the mortal to obey and serve?"

"Yes, I think so."

"Which, then, does the soul resemble?"

"Clearly, Socrates, the soul is like the divine and the body like the mortal."

"Then see, Cebes, if this is not the conclusion from all that we have said: that the soul is most like the divine and immortal and intellectual and uniform and indissoluble and ever unchanging, and the body, on the contrary, most like the human and mortal and multiform and unintellectual and dissoluble and ever changing. Can we say anything, my dear Cebes, to show that this is not so?"

"No, we cannot."

"Well then, since this is the case, is it not natural for the body to meet with speedy dissolution and for the soul, on the contrary, to be entirely indissoluble, or nearly so?"

"Of course."

"Observe," he went on, "that when a man dies, the visible part of him, the body, which lies in the visible world and which we call the corpse, which is naturally subject to dissolution and decomposition, does not undergo these processes at once, but remains for a considerable time, and even for a very long time, if death takes place when the body is in good condition, and at a favorable time of the year.

. . .

"But the soul, the invisible, which departs into another place which is, like itself, noble and pure and invisible, to the realm of the god of the other world in truth, to the good and wise god, whither, if God will, my soul is soon to go,— is this soul, which has such qualities and such a nature, straightway scattered and destroyed when it departs from the body, as most men say? Far from it, dear Cebes and Simmias, but the truth is much rather this—if it departs pure, dragging with it nothing of the body, because it never willingly associated with the body in life, but avoided it and gathered itself into itself alone, since this has always been its constant study—but this means nothing else than that it pursued philosophy rightly and really practiced being in a state of death: or is not this the practice of death?"

"By all means."

"Then if it is in such a condition, it goes away into that which is like itself, into the invisible, divine, immortal, and wise, and when it arrives there it is happy, freed from error and folly and fear and fierce loves and all the other human ills, and as the initiated say, lives in truth through all after time with the gods. Is this our belief, Cebes, or not?"

"Assuredly," said Cebes.

(Plato, *Phaedo*, 79a–81a)

Plato's *Phaedo* had an enormous influence on the belief in the immortality of the soul in the West, and it lays out a vision of the human as a body and soul in which the body is impermanent, unruly, and at war with the soul. In *Gorgias* Socrates says, "in fact I once heard sages say that we are now dead, and the body is our tomb" (493a). This saying is based on the wordplay *sōma* (body) *sēma* (tomb).

The soul, on the other hand, is the divine part that breaks free of the body at death and joins the divine realm. When Plato's doctrine of the soul was propounded in the fifth century BCE, it was surely not the majority position, but it quickly became the dominant viewpoint in the Hellenistic and then Greco-Roman worlds.

Given this understanding of the human as a body and soul, a resurrection of the dead, i.e., of the body, is superfluous. From the Corinthians' point of view, raising up the body to reunite it with the soul would only recreate the original problem. For them the solution is to separate the soul (the divine part) from the body (the material part). Therefore they could accept resurrection (separation of the soul from the body) and deny the resurrection of dead (reuniting the body and soul).

Resurrection Has Begun

Some Corinthians may have thought that the resurrection had already begun. At baptism they died with the Anointed and are now raised with him, the soul and body having separated or being in the process of separating. The signs of this are their spiritual powers of which they are so proud (1 Corinthians 12).

In the later Pauline tradition this becomes an explicit position. The author of the Letter to the Colossians attributes this position to Paul.

> When you were buried with him in baptism,
> you were also raised with him through faith in the power of
>   God,
>   who raised him from the dead.
>   (Col 2:12–13; see also Col 3:1)

Even later the author of 1 Timothy has Paul attribute this position to two other men.

> Among them are Hymenaeus and Philetus,
> who have swerved from the truth by claiming that the resur-
>   rection has already taken place.
> They are upsetting the faith of some.
>   (1 Tim 2:18–19)

This indicates that the issue of when the resurrection of Anointed-believers began remained a debated issue within Pauline communities well into the second century.

What Is a Body?

Before turning to Paul's immediate response to the Corinthians, we should consider what Paul means by body, especially in light of its importance in 1 Corinthians.

Argument has raged concerning exactly what Paul means by body (*sōma*). Rudolf Bultmann's (1884–1976) position has been dominant, but is not without problems. Bultmann rejects the traditional understanding of body as a form which takes different shapes, i.e., a corruptible shape or an incorruptible shape. Such an understanding follows upon Christianity's adoption of Neo-Platonism and the immortality of the soul.

Because Bultmann recognizes that Paul rejects the body/soul dualism so characteristic of Hellenistic thought, his method is driven by the commendable effort to understand and translate Paul into categories compatible with modern thinking, and for Bultmann this meant existential categories. In his view, by body Paul "means the whole person" (*Theology of the New Testament*, 1:192). "*Man, his person as a whole,* can be denoted by *soma*" (p. 195). "[T]he *soma* is not something that outwardly clings to a man's real *self* (to his soul, for instance), but belongs to its very essence, so that we can say man does not *have a soma*; he *is a soma*, for in not a few cases *soma* can be translated 'I'" (p. 194). Philippians 1:20 offers a fine example. Paul is detailing his problems as a prisoner and he writes:

> This is in keeping with my keen anticipation and hope that I am not going to be ashamed about anything. On the contrary, I am completely confident that now as always the Anointed will be exalted by my life whether I live or die.

The SV translators have translated *sōma* as "my life," or as the KJ puts it more literally, "Christ shall be magnified in my body, whether *it be* by life, or by death."

In many ways, Bultmann's understanding of body has proven powerful and helpful, but it has two major problems.

- The existential interpretation renders Paul too individualistic.
- This understanding does not really fit well in 1 Corinthians 15.

Bultmann actually admits this later point when he argues, "Paul lets himself be misled into adopting his opponents' method of argumentation, and in so doing he uses the *soma*-concept in a way not characteristic of him elsewhere" (p. 192).

The way forward is to not give up Bultmann's achievements, but correct his mistakes. The *sōma*/body is a unity for Paul, not part of body/soul division, and at times it can mean simply "I" (or whatever the pronoun demanded by the context). But body is more than the individual. While body is an important topic in Paul's letter to the Corinthians, his use of body is rich, varied, and polyvalent.

In 1 Cor 6:12 Paul is dealing with a series of slogans from the Corinthian community. He first quotes the slogan and then comments on it.

> \<Some of you say,\> "I am free to do anything I want;"
> but not everything is good for me.
> "I am free to do anything I want";
> but I am not going to let anything dominate me.

These slogans then lead to a commentary by Paul on the body.

> In any case, the body is not intended for sexual indulgence,
> but is intended for the lord, and the lord is intended for the
>   body.
> God raised up the lord and God will raise us up by divine
>   power.
>   (1 Cor 6:13b–14)

"Body" is not something separate from "I" or "soul" but is the person. This is clear when "us" is substituted in the next-to-last line for "the body." This is a clear instance of where body equals the person. Body is also understood as physical: body is the whole person existing in a physical environment. Even more, the body is for the lord and the lord is for the body. The reason for this mutual intending of body and lord is that God has raised up the lord and will raise the believer up so that the body is not intended for death or enslavement (the literal meaning of the Greek verb translated "dominate").

Paul pushes the language even further.

> Don't you know that your bodies are parts of the body of the
>   Anointed?
>   (1 Cor 6:15)

"Body of the Anointed" takes on a sense different from "your bodies." The parts (Greek *melē*, a body part) of the body are those who are Anointed-believers. "Body of the Anointed" has a metaphorical or perhaps even a mythical sense. If metaphorical, for what is it a metaphor? The body of the Anointed could be a metaphor for the community or even the church, and this is the traditional understanding. But something more appears to be at stake.

> So then, shall I take members of the Anointed's body and join
>   them with the body of a prostitute?
> Certainly not!
> Don't you understand that the one who unites with a prosti-
>   tute becomes one body with her?
> Scripture says, "The two of them will become one flesh."
> On the other hand, the one who is united with the lord has
>   completely identified with him.
>   (1 Cor 6:15–17)

If the body of the Anointed is a metaphor for the community, then uniting with a prostitute is about boundary breaking and polluting the community's purity. The Greek for what is translated "who unites with" (*kollōmenos*) means to cling or to stick to and by extension to join or unite with. The phrase about the prostitute is set in parallel to that of the Anointed.

> Do you not know that one who
>   clings to a prostitute   is one body?
> and one who clings to the lord   is one breath (spirit).

The SV translation renders the Greek *pneuma* as "has completely identified with him" in an effort to give some sense of what the Greek is conveying. The Greek word *pneuma* means "breath" and often is translated into English as "spirit" or "Spirit," meaning the Holy Spirit. (You can see how quickly presuppositions become involved in the supposedly neutral act of translation.) The SV has correctly conveyed the sense. Paul is saying that the interpenetration occurring in sexual intercourse makes the two one, and clinging to the lord makes one animated by the same breath, God's breath, as the Anointed is. "Cling to" is a metaphor for a way of living and so he contrasts two different ways of living—the way of sexual immorality and living as the Anointed lives. This is why Paul can say in Gal 2:19–20:

> I was crucified with the Anointed.
> The person I used to be no longer lives.
> God's Anointed lives in me;
> and the bodily [lit. fleshly] life I now live,

I live by the same confident trust in God that the "son of God" had.

He loved me and gave up his life for my benefit.

What characterizes the body of the Anointed is its crucifixion, so to be in the body of the Anointed is to live as the Anointed did, as crucified. The body of one who is a part of the body of the Anointed is already crucified and awaiting God's raising up from the dead.

Paul's Response

First Fruits

Now that we have some sense of why and what the Corinthians are thinking, we can turn again to Paul's response. Paul argues that since we agree that Anointed was raised, then "If there is no such thing as the resurrection of the dead, then the Anointed has not been raised either" (1 Cor 15:13). Paul assumes that Jesus has been raised from the dead as the gospel-statement proclaims: "he died, was buried, and was raised up." For Paul, died and buried means buried in the ground, and so raised up means from the ground. Paul's model, as we have seen, ultimately derives from Daniel, while the Corinthians' model comes from the Greek world.

Paul draws the further conclusion that what is true of the Anointed is true of the believer. "If the Anointed has not been raised, your faith is worthless and you are still not free from the seductive power of corruption, and in that case those who have died believing that they belonged to the Anointed have perished" (1 Cor 15:17–18). Because the Anointed's having been raised up from the dead is connected to the believer's being raised up, he says that the Anointed is "the first fruits of the harvest of the dead" (1 Cor 15:20). The Anointed's having been raised up from the dead is the necessary preliminary to the believer's being raised up from the dead. This is all part of Paul's apocalyptic scenario.

The Anointed the first fruits,
afterwards at the Anointed's coming, those who have become his people.
Then comes the end of all things,
the time when the Anointed hands the sovereignty back to God our father,

after he has put down every ruler and every authority and
  power.
    (1 Cor 15:23–24, SV modified)

Paul's fundamental distinctions are not metaphysical, as in
Plato, but temporal, i.e., apocalyptic. This difference must be
borne in mind or we will put Paul in the wrong categories.

Sowing

Paul argues from the analogy of planting a seed. In understanding
his analogy it is important not to read into it a modern understanding of biology. His is the ancient view, a common sense view
of what happens.

> What you sow does not come to life unless it dies.
> And what you sow is not the body which it will be;
> what you sow is a bare seed, it could be of wheat or one of the
>   other grains.
> God gives it the body God intended,
> and to each kind of seed God gives its own kind of body.
>   (1 Cor 15:36–38)

This analogy makes several important points.

- The planted seed must die.
- Plant a seed; get a plant.
- God gives the plant its body.

This is not modern biology. Paul assumes the seed dies in the
ground and hence the analogy to burying the dead in the ground.
"What you sow [the seed] is not the body which will be [the
plant]." Thus in this analogy Paul envisions two bodies—one for
the seed, one for the plant. And in the final step, God creates the
new body (the plant). By analogy, it is God who raises up, gives
life (*zōopoieō*, literally to make alive).

Paul now expands his metaphor.

> Not all flesh is the same,
> but there is one kind of flesh for humans,
> another for animals,
> another for birds,
> and another for fish.
>   (1 Cor 15:39)

Paul's sequence follows that of the creation story in Gen 1:20–27 (but in reverse order), and thus indicates he has that story in mind during this discussion. He has already referred to it with the first Adam and Anointed reference (1 Cor 15:22). He also employs a new term "flesh" (*sarx*), but here in a neutral, not negative sense. Bodies on earth are flesh.

Then he introduces yet another distinction: "There are also heavenly bodies and earthly bodies" (1 Cor 15:40a). Here he reverts to "body" language, indicating that body is the more general term and flesh the more specific one; and he draws a distinction between earthly and heavenly bodies that is very reminiscent of Plato.

Paul's final distinction has to do with splendor or glory (*doxa*). Each thing has its own splendor.

> The splendor of the sun is of one kind
> and the splendor of the moon of a different kind,
> and that of the stars yet another.
> In fact, one star differs from another in its splendor.
>   (1 Cor 15:41)

In Judaism the stars are often thought of as animate objects, heavenly beings, or angels, and in the Greco-Roman world the sun and moon are also divinities. Paul is describing the way he thinks God has created everything, giving to everything its own body and splendor.

We need to make two points about Paul's analogy:

- He is employing a Jewish and Hellenistic common sense view of nature, and maintains that this is a natural arrangement.
- This is part of God's creative, life-making process.

Since this is an analogy, we should not expect it to explain all details. We should follow Paul's usage and not raise questions it was not designed to answer. Some commentators and readers always ask what happens between death and resurrection? Is something left over, some element that connects the body as seed planted in the ground and the plant that grows? We should be honest and say that Paul's analogy does not really entertain that question, regardless of how logical or important we might consider it. Probably the most we can say is that Paul's understanding of death in 1 Thess 4:17 leads to the conclusion that he thinks nothing subsists. A body planted in the earth would turn to dust, and God would raise up another body. God can bring life from nothing.

Paul sees death and raising up from the dead by God as part of God's natural, creative process. The need for raising up from the dead flows out of God's creative drive. God is life-making (*zōopoieō*).

Body Raised Up

In setting up his argument about the kind of body they will come back with, Paul first reminded the Corinthians in the gospel-statement of the common ground on which they all stand and then argued that what was true for the Anointed was the case for all who trusted in the Anointed. Since the Anointed was buried in the ground and was raised up from the ground, he was raised from the dead; therefore there must be a standing up from the dead. Having laid that groundwork, Paul raises the questions, "How are the dead raised? With what kind of body do they come back?" His first answer uses the seed analogy implying that death and raising up are a natural part of God's creative process.

With the analogy in place, Paul lays out a series of parallels:

sown in corruption,	raised incorruptible;
sown in a condition of humiliation,	raised in a state of splendor;
sown in a condition of weakness,	raised in a state of power.
Sown with a body fit for earthly life,	they are raised with a body fit for life in God's new world,

(1 Cor 15:42–43)

All the phrases are in the present tense and not, as we might expect, in the present and future tenses. Paul normally describes the raising up as a future activity, but here the present tense accents the normal, natural course of events that follows upon the analogy of the seed.

The first column can be described as the before and the second as the after, and we might also describe them as earthly and heavenly; but we should be careful not to make primary the two storey universe rather than the apocalyptic scenario. This before/ after distinction is much closer to that made in the Address of Romans:

> This news is about the "son of God"—who was physically descended from David,
> appointed and empowered as "son of God," in accordance with the spirit of holiness, from the time of his resurrection from the dead
> —Jesus, the Anointed, our lord.
> (Rom 1:3–4)

The point of the first column is obvious. It is the human condition, impermanent, transitory, the natural state of things, what Plato would see as characteristics of the body. The second column represents the raised up person, what Plato would have seen as characteristics of the soul. The meaning of two of the Greek words in the last line is debatable, and so also are English translations. Literally the last line reads:

It is sown a *psychikon*   body; it is raised a *pneumatikon*   body.
It is sown a   natural   body; it is raised a   spiritual   body.
         (1 Cor 15:44, KJ)

Both Greek words are difficult to translate. We will take each word separately.

Psychikon

Psychē is the Greek word for soul, and so the first part of the last phrase could be translated: "it is sown an ensouled body" or "a body with a soul." Following normal Greek usage for the period, this would be the proper translation. But such has not been the case.

Bauer's *Greek-English Lexicon*, the standard in scholarship, notes the normal meaning of *psychikon* as "of the soul/life." It is a common Greek word. But then the Lexicon notes:

> [I]n our lit. pert. To the life of the natural world and whatever belongs to it, in contrast to the realm of experience whose central characteristic is πνεῦμα [spirit], natural, unspiritual, worldly.

This strikes me as special pleading and I am always suspicious of special meaning for New Testament literature. I prefer standard Greek meaning, or at least to see first if the standard meanings will work. I find it hard to understand how Paul could have developed such a special meaning so early in the movement. The development of technical in-group language is to be expected only later. Paul would have had to send a dictionary to the Corinthians along with the letter. I am not alone in this suspicion, and a number of scholars have questioned the traditional translation.

The steps to the traditional translation are apparent. By the time Jerome translated the Vulgate Latin (commissioned 382, finished 405), the doctrine of the immortality of the soul was firmly in place in Christianity—a Platonic doctrine that, as we have seen, was rejected by Paul. That being so, Jerome is unlikely to have seen that Paul is rejecting the doctrine, and apparently deduced from the first column that *psychikos* must mean the normal "unsaved" state of humans in contrast to "spiritual." Accordingly, he translates it "*animale*." The rest is history.

Luther translated it "natürlicher" and the King James "natural," as do most modern English translations. The NRSV translates it "physical."

If Paul had wanted to contrast natural/physical with spiritual, he could have written *sōma sarkikon* (fleshly body) or *sōma physikon* (physical body). But he wrote *sōma psychikon*. From the Platonic point of view this represents the whole person as made up of a body and soul. The bottom line is that in the first column Paul is accepting the Corinthians' Platonic description of the human being.

Pneumatikon

From the Corinthians' point of view, the real problem is the final term in the second column—it is raised *sōma pneumatikon*, a spiritual body. The word they would have expected here is *psychikon*/soul—it characterizes the second column. The unwanted word is *sōma*/body, which does not belong in the second column and certainly does not fit with *pneumatikon*/spiritual. Even for us moderns it does not fit. We intuitively contrast body and spirit.

Some modern scholars have even described "spiritual body" as an oxymoron (Hays, Fitzmyer).

What does Paul mean? Part of the problem is that in this last line he shifts from a Platonic worldview to a Jewish apocalyptic worldview. Paul justifies his last line by an appeal to Gen 2:7, which in the LXX reads:

> And God formed the man, dust of the ground,
> and breathed upon his face the breath of life,
> and the man became a living soul (*psychēn zōsan*).
> (BBS Trans)

Paul reinterprets this verse:

> Even as it is written:
> **the first man** Adam **became a living soul,**
> the last man a life-making spirit.
> (1 Cor 15:45, BBS Trans)

The words in bold are from Gen 2:7. Paul is following in a tradition represented by Philo of Alexandria's exegesis of Gen 2:7.

Philo is caught between Plato, for whom the soul is naturally immortal, and Judaism, where such an idea would imply that the human is divine and so conflict with monotheism. He solves this problem through Gen 2:7.

> For that which is holy among things that have come into being is, in the universe, the heavens, and in man, the mind, since it is a divine fragment, as Moses, especially says: "He breathed into his face a breath of life, and man became a living soul."
> (Philo, *On Dreams*, 1:34)

This use of Genesis allows Philo to see the living soul as God's creation and destined for immortality; and some such exegesis allowed those in Corinth to deny the resurrection of the body: it was the living soul that was resurrected. But for Paul, the living soul is Adamic, the first man. The second man is a life-making spirit.

Spirit

"Spiritual" is likewise a confusing translation. The primary sense of *pneuma* in Greek (as well as *rûᵃḥ* in Hebrew) is breath or wind. Paul once again is drawing on the creation story in Genesis. God the life-maker creates the world. The LXX reads, "In the beginning God made (*epoiēsen*) the heaven and the earth" (Gen 1:1). God's creating activity is described as "the breath/wind (*pneuma*) of God lay upon the water" (Gen 1:2). This is the sense of *pneuma* that Paul has in mind. The *sōma pneumatikon* is a body in which God has breathed life. In that sense it is a new creation, part of the second man, the new Adam.

We can translate the difficult line as follows:

> It is sown a soul-body; it is raised up a body whose breath is God's.
>
> (1 Cor 15:44)

Although it is not as felicitous or simple as the Greek, this expansive translation gets at the sense of what Paul is arguing. The SV translation, "Sown with a body fit for earthly life, they are raised with a body fit for life in God's new world," is likewise expansive and makes the same point.

Paul is rejecting the Greek solution to immortality in which the soul as the divine spark survives the death of the body. For him, the raised up body is a new body given by God, one that has God's breath in it. Its chief characteristic is that it is "of God." Paul ultimately understands God's raising up of Jesus and those who are Anointed-believers as a new beginning of creation itself.

Paul's Conclusion

Having made his case, Paul draws out the conclusion in another series of parallels.

> The first human was a lump of earth, an earthly man;
> > the second human is from heaven.
> As was the earthly man, so are those who are earthly,
> > and as is heavenly man, so are those who are heavenly.
> Just as we have borne the likeness of the earthly man,
> > so we will also bear the likeness of the heavenly man.
> > (1 Cor 15:47–49)

In the last line, "so we will also bear" could be subjunctive: "Let us also bear." The evidence for whether to prefer a future or a subjunctive is unclear, and exegetically one could make a good argument for either. Paul tends to refer to the raising up in the future, but he has also been concerned in the letter to the Corinthians to draw ethical conclusions from theological positions.

Adam and the Anointed function as archetypes of humanity—two different ways of being human. Adam is from the earth;
the Anointed is from heaven, which is a euphemism for God.

Paul drives home his conclusion with an emphatic statement.

> What I am saying, my friends, is this:
> flesh and blood is not capable of inheriting the coming Empire
>   of God,
> no more than the corruptible can inherit the incorruptible.
> (1 Cor 15:50)

"Flesh and blood" is a Jewish phrase denoting the human. Sirach
14:18 catches the sense exactly:

> Like green leaves on a bushy tree,
> some fall but others grow,
> so is a generation of flesh and blood,
> one is finished and another is born.
> (LXX, BBS Trans)

Flesh and blood contrasts humanity's impermanence with God's
permanence. Paul emphatically denies a physical resurrection—it
is not raised up flesh and blood.

Paul concludes his discussion of the resurrection by revealing a mystery. It should be no surprise that the mystery reflects
the playing out of his apocalyptic scenario. This has always been
Paul's final step.

> We are not all going to fall asleep;
> rather, we are all going to be transformed
>   in an instant,
>   in the blink of an eye,
>   at the sound of the last trumpet-signal.
> The trumpet will sound
> and the dead will be raised incorruptible
> and we <too> will be transformed.
> Because this perishable man must be clothed with the imper-
>   ishable,
> and this mortal man must be clothed with immortality.
> And when the perishable is clothed with the imperishable
> and the mortal is clothed with immortality, then the saying
>   that is written will come true.
> (1 Cor 15:51–54, SV modified)

Hebrew Version of Hosea 13:14

Shall I ransom them from the power of Sheol?
Shall I redeem them from Death?
O Death, where are your plagues?
O Sheol, where is your destruction?
Compassion is hidden from my eyes.

The language is strongly reminiscent of 1 Thess 4:14–18. He uses two metaphors to describe what happens to those who are alive—transformed and clothed. The clothing metaphor could imply a body clothed with immortality and therefore the body remains unchanged; these attributes are only laid over a body. That is why the primary metaphor is transformation. Paul consistently has argued for a new body to replace the old body.

Paul concludes by reframing a quote from Hos 13:14. This section of Hosea deals with Israel, and as we saw in chapter 2 points to the inevitability of death and lack of rescue beyond the grave. As is often noted, the LXX version of Hos 13:14 is different from that of the Hebrew (Masoretic) text and Paul even modifies the LXX. The Septuagint reads:

> Where is your penalty, o death?
> Where is your sting, Hades?
> (LXX, BBS Trans)

Paul rearranges the word order of the LXX and substitutes "victory" (*nikos*) for "penalty" (*dikē*). In the process he gives the quote a quite different meaning.

> Death has been engulfed by victory.
> Where, O Death, has your victory gone?
> What's happened, O Death, to your fatal sting?
> (1 Cor 15:56)

Conclusion

Paul's view of the body raised up from the dead is critical to an understanding of his view on resurrection. From this discussion we can draw a number of conclusions:

- God raises up the dead.
- Paul rejects the immortality of the soul.
- Humans (and animals, etc., for that matter) are bodies.
- The body that God raises up or transforms is not a soul-body, is not flesh and blood.
- The body that God raises up is a new body that has God's breath as the principle of life.

Beyond this Paul does not speculate. He does not answer some of the questions that we may have. Paul thinks in terms of an apocalyptic model. The basics of that model did not change from when he was a Pharisee to when he was an Anointed-believer. What changed was the timetable. God had acted now by making the crucified Jesus his son and his anointed. This was demonstrated by God's raising him from the dead. This resurrection is the first step, the first fruits, in a scenario that will result not only in the raising up or transformation of all those who are Anointed-believers, but also in the reclaiming of creation—all will be made subject to God. This explains the first and second Adam language, as well as the language of a new creation.

What Paul says about the body God will raise up also applies to the body of the Anointed. It is a *sōma pneumatikon*, a body in which God has breathed God's life. This description of the body coheres with how Paul has employed "he has been seen for/by" and "God revealed his son to/in me." As a body in which God has breathed life, it cannot be seen by the eyes of flesh and blood, but can be seen only as made manifest by God. When Paul says, "I have seen the lord," that is what he means. The lord is a *sōma pneumatikon*, a body in which God has breathed God's life. For Paul a flesh and blood Jesus would not be addressed as "lord" or "son of God." Only as raised up from the dead is he Anointed, lord, and son of God. This explains why there are no appearance stories in Paul. For Paul it is not an event that can be shaped in that way.

Further Reading

Bultmann, Rudolf. *Theology of the New Testament.* Translated by Kendrick Grobel. Vol. I and II in one volume, Scribner Studies in Contemporary Theology. New York: Charles Scribner's Sons, 1951, 1955.

Fitzmyer, Joseph A. *The Acts of the Apostles*, Anchor Bible. New York: Doubleday, 1998.

Hays, Richard B. *First Corinthians*, Interpretation. Louisville: John Knox, 1997.

Horsley, Richard A. *1 Corinthians*, Abingdon New Testament Commentaries. Nashville: Abingdon, 1998.

Kim, Yung Suk. *Christ's Body in Corinth, the Politics of a Metaphor*, Paul in Critical Contexts. Minneapolis: Fortress, 2008. An important work that convincingly reconceives Paul's use of body language in 1 Corinthians.

Martin, Dale B. *The Corinthian Body*. New Haven: Yale University, 1995.

Pearson, Birger Albert. *The* Pneumatikos-Psychikos *Terminology in 1 Corinthians. A Study in the Theology of the Corinthian Opponents of Paul and Its Relation to Gnosticism*, SBLDiss 12. Missoula, MT: Scholars Press, 1973.

Segal, Alan F. *Life after Death, a History of the Afterlife in the Religions of the West*. New York: Doubleday, 2004.

Works Cited

Aeschulus. *Eumenides*. Loeb Classical Library, 1926.

Bauer, Walter. *A Greek-English Lexicon of the New Testament and Other Early Christian Literature*. Edited by Frederick William Danker. 3rd ed. Chicago: University of Chicago Press, 2000.

Bultmann, Rudolf. *Theology of the New Testament*. Translated by Kendrick Grobel. Vol. I and II in one volume, Scribner Studies in Contemporary Theology. New York: Charles Scribner's Sons, 1951, 1955.

Homer. *Iliad*. Translated with an introduction by Richmond Lattimore. Chicago: University of Chicago Press, 1951.

Plato. *Gorgias*. Loeb Classical Library, 1967.

Plato. *Phaedo*. Loeb Classical Library, 1966.

Sophocles, *Electra*. Translated by Richard Jebb. Cambridge: Cambridge University Press, 1894.

10 Assumption

The Q-Gospel

What is the Q-gospel doing in a book on resurrection? After all it is just a hypothesis, for no manuscript of the document is extant, and it contains no mention of resurrection.

"Just" is a devious little word. We can easily dismiss something by simply saying "it's just a hypothesis." A hypothesis is a tested solution to a known problem. The known problem is this: How are the three synoptic gospels related? A major part of the tested solution is the Q-gospel.

Not to use the Q-gospel in understanding the pre-70 movement that emerged around Jesus is like not using Darwin's hypothesis of natural selection to understand the development of species.

Scholarly thinking is by its very nature hypothetical. Even the printed text of the New Testament, itself the result of centuries of scholarship, is a hypothesis. We do not possess the original manuscript of any writing in the New Testament. Nestle-Aland[27] is a hypothetical text, a scholarly reconstruction, and indicates only what the New Testament looked like at the end of the second century.

By far the more serious issue is that the Q-gospel contains no mention of Jesus' resurrection. Not only is there no resurrection narrative, but there is no mention of resurrection. This poses a problem for any reconstruction of the communities of Jesus' early followers. Is it possible there was a Christian group that did not know of the resurrection? If so, what are the implications of that?

Synoptic Problem

Traditionally, the four canonical gospels were taken as independent, eyewitness reports. But that tradition fell in the face of critical scholarship. If not independent, then how are they related? By far the best solution to that problem is the so-called two document hypothesis. Mark is the first gospel and provides the narrative outline for both Matthew and Luke. After accounting for the material from Mark in Matthew and Luke, there remains a large group of sayings that are common only to Matthew and Luke. The common group of sayings is the Q-gospel, which scholars have reconstructed and studied.

In referring to verses in the Q-gospel the convention is to use the abbreviation Q + chapter and verse numbers from Luke.

Any way you look at it, the Q-gospel is an important element of our effort to understand the emergence of resurrection in early Christianity.

A Starting Point

Paul's starting point is his apocalyptic orientation, his initial understanding of crucifixion as incompatible with Jesus being the Anointed, with his revelation that God has designated the crucified Anointed as his son by raising him from dead, and with Paul's call to be an apostle. The apocalyptic scenario undergirds both Paul's position and his use of the metaphor "raised up from the dead."

The Q-gospel's starting point is a Deuteronomic view, a dominant position in the Hebrew Bible and Second Temple Judaism. In this view a recurring pattern asserts itself. The people are sinful, God sends prophets to preach repentance, the prophets are rejected, or even killed, and God inflicts judgment on his disobedient children. Then the cycle starts all over again. The word of the lord in Jer 7:22–34 provides a good summary of the Deuteronomic position.

> But this command I gave them, "Obey my voice, and I will be
> your God, and you shall be my people; and walk only in the

Q-Gospel

Since it is a hypothetical reconstruction, there is no copy of Q. "Q" is an abbreviation of the German word *Quelle* which means "source," i.e., one of the two sources for the synoptic gospels. It is a sayings gospel similar in form to the gospel of Thomas. It appears somewhat primitive inasmuch as Jesus is not called Anointed, and no disciples are named. It was surely composed in Greek, probably in Galilee, beginning sometime in the 50s CE, although being a sayings document, it clearly underwent expansion.

way that I command you, so that it may be well with you." Yet they did not obey or incline their ear, but, in the stubbornness of their evil will, they walked in their own counsels, and looked backward rather than forward. From the day that your ancestors came out of the land of Egypt until this day, I have persistently sent all my servants the prophets to them, day after day; yet they did not listen to me, or pay attention, but they stiffened their necks. They did worse than their ancestors did.

So you shall speak all these words to them, but they will not listen to you. You shall call to them, but they will not answer you. You shall say to them: This is the nation that did not obey the voice of the Lord their God, and did not accept discipline; truth has perished; it is cut off from their lips.

. . .

Therefore, the days are surely coming, says the Lord, when . . . The corpses of this people will be food for the birds of the air, and for the animals of the earth; and no one will frighten them away. And I will bring to an end the sound of mirth and gladness, the voice of the bride and bridegroom in the cities of Judah and in the streets of Jerusalem; for the land shall become a waste.

The pattern is clearly present. The people have not obeyed, God has sent prophets but the people have remained stiffed necked. In the end will come judgment "And I will bring to an end the sound of mirth and gladness."

Jesus' Death

In Q, John the Baptist is a preacher of repentance:

> You spawn of Satan!
> Who warned you to flee from the impending doom?
> Well then, start producing fruit suitable for a change of heart,
> and don't even think of saying to yourselves,
> "We have Abraham for our father."
> Let me tell you, God can raise up children for Abraham right
>   out of these rocks!
> Even now the axe is aimed at the root of the trees.
> So every tree not producing choice fruit gets cut down and
>   tossed into the fire.
>   (Q 3:7–9)

The people have sinned and failed to repent. In the phrase "God can raise up children" the Greek word is *egeirai*, the same word Paul uses for "raise up" from the dead. Here, of course, it does not apply to resurrection, but only indicates God's power to create new children.

John and Jesus are both contrasted and compared. John appears as an ascetic, not eating and drinking, and is rejected as having a demon, but the "The Human One appeared on the scene both eating and drinking, and you say, 'There's a glutton and a drunk, a crony of toll collectors and sinners!'" (Q 7:33–34). But in the Q-gospel, both John and Jesus fit within the Deuteronomic pattern. They are prophets from God rejected by the people.

The Q-gospel knows of Jesus' death by crucifixion but it has no passion account and does not understand Jesus' death as salvific. Once again it employs the Deuteronomic pattern to understand his death when it quotes Jesus as saying:

> Damn you! You build the tombs of the prophets whom your
>   ancestors murdered.
> So, you witness against yourselves: you are descendants of
>   your ancestors.
> That's why Wisdom has said,
> "I will send them prophets and sages, and some of them they
>   are always going to kill and persecute."
> So, this generation will have to answer for the blood of all the
>   prophets that has been shed since the world was founded,

> from the blood of Abel to the blood of Zechariah, who per-
> ished between the altar and the sanctuary.
> Yes, I'm telling you, this generation will have to answer for it.
> (Q 11:47–51)

In this speech Jesus applies the Deuteronomic pattern explicitly
and implies that he too fits within it. He will be another in a line of
rejected and murdered prophets and the people will have to pay for
it. The final beatitude in Q invokes yet again this pattern and implies that what is true of Jesus will be true of those who follow him.

> Congratulations to you when they denounce you and perse-
> cute you and spread malicious gossip about you because of
> the Human One.
> Rejoice and be glad!
> In heaven you'll be more than rewarded.
> Remember, this is how they persecuted the prophets who pre-
> ceded you.
> (Q 6:22–23)

Among those "who preceded you" is, of course, Jesus. Q clearly
aligns Jesus with the fate of the prophets and the community with
the fate of Jesus: "Unless you carry your own cross and follow
after me, you cannot be my disciple" (Q 14:27). Here the cross is
explicitly mentioned, so Q knows of Jesus' crucifixion; but for the
Q-gospel the cross becomes simply another sign of the people's
rejection of Jesus; in no way is it elaborated as in Paul's theology,
nor developed into a passion account as in Mark and the other
canonical gospels.

Jesus' Assumption

In one speech in Q Jesus is made to take on the voice of wisdom
and makes a prediction about Jerusalem. Jerusalem is accused
of murdering the prophets sent to her, and the voice of wisdom
(Jesus) speaks for God. The final line is interesting in regards to
our issue.

> Jerusalem, Jerusalem, you murder the prophets and stone
> those sent to you!
> How often I wanted to gather your children as a hen gathers
> her chicks under her wings, but you wouldn't let me.

Can't you see, your house is being abandoned?
I'm telling you, you certainly won't see me until the time
    comes when you say,
"Blessed is the one who comes in the name of the Lord."
    (Q 13:34–35)

Daniel A. Smith has recently suggested that the last two lines invoke a model of assumption and predict the assumption of Jesus after his death. To test this suggestion we must detour through a brief history of assumption stories.

Assumption Stories

Greco-Roman

Assumption stories are widespread in the Greco-Roman world. These stories have a stereotyped character. The three storey worldview undergirds the experience of the ancients, and they express their experience in its assumptions. It does no good to poke fun at it—for them it is reality and conditions how they experience and explain reality. Moreover, the boundary between heaven and earth is fluid, not as fixed as we might imagine. They are, after all, thinking literally. They can look up and see the firmament that separates the sky/heaven from earth. It's a large dome right up there! They literally do not see what we see, or rather they see what we see, but see it differently.

Assumption stories involve passing from the world of humans to that of the gods. In the Greco-Roman tradition, the person being assumed is either a god returning to the abode of the gods or a human being made into a god, an apotheosis. The assumption can take place either before or after death. The disappearance of the body is a major theme. We can take as an example of this type of story the disappearance of Romulus, the legendary founder and first king of Rome. Many versions of this story survive, but we will use Plutarch's as representative. A confrontation with the senate occurred, during which they thought their prerogatives had been violated;

> Wherefore suspicion and calumny fell upon that body when
> he [Romulus] disappeared unaccountably a short time after.
> He disappeared on the Nones of July, as they now call the

month, then Quintilis, leaving no certain account nor even any generally accepted tradition of his death, aside from the date of it, which I have just given. For on that day many ceremonies are still performed which bear a likeness to what then came to pass. Nor need we wonder at this uncertainty, since although Scipio Africanus died at home after dinner, there is no convincing proof of the manner of his end, but some say that he passed away naturally, being of a sickly habit, some that he died of poison administered by his own hand, and some that his enemies broke into his house at night and smothered him. And yet Scipio's dead body lay exposed for all to see, and all who beheld it formed therefrom some suspicion and conjecture of what had happened to it; whereas Romulus disappeared suddenly, and no portion of his body or fragment of his clothing remained to be seen. But some conjectured that the senators, convened in the temple of Vulcan, fell upon him and slew him, then cut his body in pieces, put each a portion into the folds of his robe, and so carried it away. Others think that it was neither in the temple of Vulcan nor when the senators alone were present that he disappeared, but that he was holding an assembly of the people outside the city near the so-called Goat's Marsh, when suddenly strange and unaccountable disorders with incredible changes filled the air; the light of the sun failed, and night came down upon them, not with peace and quiet, but with awful peals of thunder and furious blasts driving rain from every quarter, during which the multitude dispersed and fled, but the nobles gathered closely together; and when the storm had ceased, and the sun shone out, and the multitude, now gathered together again in the same place as before, anxiously sought for their king, the nobles would not suffer them to inquire into his disappearance nor busy themselves about it, but exhorted them all to honour and revere Romulus, since he had been caught up into heaven, and was to be a benevolent god for them instead of a good king. The multitude, accordingly, believing this and rejoicing in it, went away to worship him with good hopes of his favour; but there were some, it is said, who tested the matter in a bitter and hostile spirit, and confounded the patricians with the accusation of imposing a silly tale upon the people, and of being themselves the murderers of the king.

(Plutarch, *Romulus*, 27.8)

In Plutarch's account we see all the classic tropes for an assumption story. The body has disappeared, in contrast to that of Scipio Africanus. There are various reports about what has happened, and a ritual begins in which Romulus is caught up into heaven to become a god.

Judaism

Stories of assumptions are much less frequent in Judaism. A tractate of the Talmud lists only nine people who have "entered the garden of Eden alive" with Enoch and Elijah heading the list. Interestingly, the Anointed also makes the list. To avoid conflict with monotheism the motif of the one being taken up becoming a god is absent, and normally assumption takes place *before* death. Otherwise, Judaism shares similar motifs with the Greco-Roman world.

As the Talmud indicates, Enoch and Elijah are the two classic figures in Judaism who are taken up into heaven. An extensive story tradition develops out of their mention in the Hebrew Bible.

Enoch

Enoch appears in a very suggestive and understated listing in a genealogy in the Hebrew Bible:

> When Enoch had lived sixty-five years, he became the father of Methuselah. Enoch walked with God after the birth of Methuselah three hundred years, and had other sons and daughters. Thus all the days of Enoch were three hundred sixty-five years. Enoch walked with God; then he was no more, because God took him.
>   (Gen 5:21–24)

From this small note an elaborate tradition about Enoch develops. Even the LXX translation of this note shows development. Instead of the "Enoch walked with God" in both cases the LXX reads "He was pleasing to God," a theme from the Hellenistic assumption literature. The rest of the last verse in the LXX likewise shows conformity to the Hellenistic model: "and Enoch was pleasing to God and was not found, because God had taken him." Besides being pleasing to God, another theme is invoked in the last line: "he was not found." Not finding the body is a major aspect of the type, but the Hebrew is more circumspect, saying, "then he was no more." The LXX accents the earthly point of view. Those here could not find the body of Enoch. Finally the LXX translates the Hebrew *lqh* with *metatithemi* (literally "to take with"), one of the technical terms in Greek for assumption. In the LXX translation, Enoch's assumption tradition was already well underway.

Elijah

The second classic figure in this tradition is Elijah, whose assumption story is told in 2 Kgs 2:1–12. It begins with the narrator saying, "Now when the Lord was about to take Elijah up to heaven by a whirlwind . . ." (2:1). This announcement appears with no preparation and both Elijah and the group of prophets know that he is to be taken up into heaven. The story proceeds with a threefold test, standard in oral storytelling technique. Elijah tells his disciple Elisha to stay put while he goes on and Elisha replies three times: "As the Lord lives, and as you yourself live, I will not leave you." Finally Elijah says to Elisha,

> "Tell me what I may do for you, before I am taken from you." Elisha said, "Please let me inherit a double share of your spirit." He responded, "You have asked a hard thing; yet, if you see me as I am being taken from you, it will be granted you; if not, it will not." As they continued walking and talking, a chariot of fire and horses of fire separated the two of them, and Elijah ascended in a whirlwind into heaven. Elisha kept watching and crying out, "Father, father! The chariots of Israel and its horsemen!" But when he could no longer see him, he grasped his own clothes and tore them in two pieces."
> (2 Kgs 2:9–12)

Seeing and not seeing are important aspects of assumption stories. In the LXX it translates "if you will see me as I am taken from you" (LXX 4 Kgs 2:10, BBS Trans). Elijah "saw and cried" and "he did not see him still" (LXX 2:12, BBS Trans). When Elijah ascends, the LXX employs *analambanein* (literally "to take up"), another technical term for assumption. Because of the significance of the Enoch and Elijah stories, the verbs *metatithemi* and *analambanō* become the standard terms in Jewish assumption stories.

The Righteous One

The Wisdom of Solomon implies a tale of the "righteous one." Its outline is easily epitomized: the righteous one is opposed by the ungodly in a pattern that is similar to the Q-gospel's Deuteronomic perspective.

> Let us lie in wait for the righteous one,
> because he is inconvenient to us and opposes our actions;
> he reproaches us for sins against the law,
> and accuses us of sins against our training.
> He professes to have knowledge of God,
> and calls himself a child of the Lord.
>
> . . .
>
> For if the righteous one is God's child, he will help him,
> and will deliver him from the hand of his adversaries.
> Let us test him with insult and torture,
> so that we may find out how gentle he is,
> and make trial of his forbearance.
> Let us condemn him to a shameful death,
> for according to what he says, he will be protected.
>   (Wis 2:12–20, NRSV modified)

The ungodly plot the death of the righteous one, who, for his own protection, will die young: "But the righteous, though they die early, will be at rest" (Wis 4:7). The righteous one is pleasing to God as was Enoch and to preserve that one, God takes him up (*metatithemi*). The language clearly draws on the LXX of Gen 5:21.

> There were some who pleased God and were loved by him,
> and while living among sinners were taken up.
>
> . . .
>
> Being perfected in a short time, they fulfilled long years;
> for their souls were pleasing to the Lord,
> therefore he took them quickly from the midst of wickedness.
>   (Wis 4:10–14)

Finally, the righteous one will judge those who oppressed him.

> Then the righteous will stand with great confidence
> in the presence of those who have oppressed them
> and those who make light of their labors.

When the unrighteous see them, they will be shaken with
   dreadful fear,
and they will be amazed at the unexpected salvation of the
   righteous.
They will speak to one another in repentance,
and in anguish of spirit they will groan, and say,
"These are persons whom we once held in derision
and made a byword of reproach—fools that we were!
We thought that their lives were madness
and that their end was without honor.
Why have they been numbered among the children of God?
And why is their lot among the saints?
   (Wis 5:1–5)

The righteous one now becomes the eschatological judge of those
who oppressed him.

Assumption of Jesus in Q

As part of the wisdom tradition, the Q-gospel views Jesus as the
righteous one who was God's prophet, was rejected and murdered
by his enemies, was taken up, and will stand in judgment at the
end. The pattern is remarkably similar to that of the righteous
one in the Wisdom of Solomon. With this pattern in mind, the
Q prophecy of judgment against Jerusalem begins to make sense.

Jerusalem, Jerusalem, you murder the prophets and stone
   those sent to you!
How often I wanted to gather your children as a hen gathers
   her chicks under her wings, but you wouldn't let me.
Can't you see, your house is being abandoned?
I'm telling you, you certainly won't see me until the time
   comes when you say,
"Blessed is the one who comes in the name of the Lord."
   (Q 13:34–35)

Seeing him as the one coming in the name of the Lord implies his
disappearance, his being taken up, and his coming in judgment.

The assumption model helps explain why the death of Jesus
receives such minimal attention in the Q-gospel. Since in most
though not all Jewish assumption stories the righteous person
does not die, Q tends to pass over Jesus' death rather than make

it central as does Paul. As the Elijah tradition demonstrates, the expectation grew up that Elijah would return as an eschatological figure. This folk belief is well attested in the synoptic gospels, although not in the Q-gospel. Because Jesus is now the one to return, that may also explain why Elijah does not occur in the Q-gospel.

Note also that the assumption model bears some similarity to the exaltation model found in the Philippians praise speech. Both are searching for models from the tradition to explain their experience that the death of Jesus was not final. While the Philippians praise speech is a more complete model, both employ a type of exaltation and end with an acclamation. The Philippians praise speech explores exaltation with models from the LXX and Roman imperial theology, while the Q-gospel understands exaltation as assumption, within the model of the righteous one in the Wisdom of Solomon. It remains firmly within Judaism. In each case, the acclamation itself indicates the differences and similarities between these two approaches. In the Q passage there is a quote from Ps 118:26, which prophesies the return of the one assumed into heaven, the one they cannot see. In the Philippians praise speech the acclamation "Jesus the Anointed is lord!" draws from both the LXX and the imperial model.

Gospel of Peter

The gospel of Peter is strange, to the point of being a bit weird, and yet an intriguing writing. Even the manner of its discovery is unusual. It was found in 1886 in a monk's grave at Akhmin in Egypt, where it had been buried in the eighth or ninth century.

For some scholars it is so strange that it appears to be simply a pastiche of snippets from the canonical gospels. For others it is not only independent of the canonical gospels, but a source for those gospels and perhaps one of the earliest accounts of faith in a vindicated Jesus.

A cursory reading of the gospel of Peter will quickly confirm its strangeness, but perhaps we should not be too surprised; might not our accustomed gospels appear strange if two millennia of reading and translation had not domesticated them?

I must confess that I have studied these issues for some time and have not arrived at a firm conclusion. I remain in some doubt and confusion, a condition that may not be of much help to the reader, but is an honest position. Nonetheless, I have reached some firm conclusions.

- Those who reject the gospel of Peter as simply a late document, a paste-up assembled from the canonical gospels, are driven by what can only be called a canonical prejudice. Their (theological?) prejudice in favor of the gospels in the New Testament is so strong that they will not see any non-canonical gospels as independent.
- We are aware of no compositional procedure used in the ancient world that can explain the gospel of Peter as a pasting together from the canonical gospels.
- The gospel of Peter is an edited composition that contains earlier sources. The reconstruction of earlier sources underlying the gospel of Peter is confusing, and how they may relate to the canonical gospels is even more subject to debate.

Helmut Koester, John Dominic Crossan and Arthur Dewey have put forward proposals which, while having merit, have not found wide acceptance among scholars. Although I sometimes think most scholars would prefer that the gospel of Peter would just go away, these three are serious scholars and their arguments cannot be dismissed as eccentric.

My discussion is highly dependent on the reconstruction of Dewey, because as the latest it has the advantage of responding to the positions of Koester and Crossan. I find myself intrigued but not fully convinced by his arguments.

Dewey has reconstructed a primitive passion account that was incorporated into the gospel of Peter. His reconstruction is based on the same methods that scholars use to reconstruct sources used by the synoptic gospel writers. In such cases, we always work with two options:

- They made it up.
- They had sources.

Yet the situation is not either/or, but both/and. We have to test each document to discover what sources, if any, the author employed, and what the author created. We have to discover an author's editing and writing procedure. For example, we have seen that Paul employed such sources as the gospel-statement in 1 Corinthians and the praise piece in Philippians.

Part of Dewey's reconstructed passion source, which is also part of Crossan's, pertains to our investigation:

> And one of them said, "Give him vinegar mixed with something bitter to drink." And they mixed it and gave it to him to drink. And they fulfilled all things and brought to completion the sins on their head. Now many went about with lamps, and, thinking that it was night, they lay down. And the Lord cried out, saying, "My power, <my> power, you have abandoned me." When he said this, he was taken up. And at that moment, the veil of the Jerusalem temple was torn in two.
>
> (Pet 5:2–5)

Both Dewey and Crossan see the reconstructed passion account as employing the pattern of the suffering and vindicated righteous one. This pattern, as we have seen, clearly appears in the Wisdom of Solomon 2–5 and is also used in the Q-gospel. In Q

Death of Jesus in Peter and Canonical Gospels

Peter	Mark	Luke	Matthew	John
And the Lord cried out, saying, "My power, power, you have abandoned me."	And Jesus giving a great cry	Father, into your hands I commend my spirit (breath).	Jesus again crying in a great voice	He bowed his head
When he said this, he was taken up.	breathed out	Saying this, he breathed out	gave up his spirit (breath)	and handed over his spirit (breath)

the full pattern is not so obvious , for since the Q-gospel is not a narrative, the assumption is in the form of a prediction.

If we compare Jesus' death in the gospel of Peter with that in the canonical gospels, we immediately notice the difference.

In the canonical gospels, following Jesus' outcry, he quits breathing or gives up his spirit, which are the same thing in Greek. In the gospel of Peter "he was taken up." Dewey has maintained that this is the exaltation or assumption of the righteous one into heaven. The Greek (*anelēphthē*, the aorist passive of *analambanō*) is the same word used of Elijah in 4 Kingdoms (LXX), one of the two words that, as we noted earlier, became technical terms for assumption in Jewish accounts. Given the model of the righteous one, Dewey's contention is convincing.

How to date this reconstructed fragment in the gospel of Peter and how it relates to the canonical gospels remains unsolved. But Dewey's reconstruction offers strong evidence that it is pre-70 and independent of the canonical gospels.

Both the Q-gospel and the gospel of Peter fragment employ the model of the righteous sufferer whom God vindicates by taking him up. In Q, that assumption is embedded in a prediction; in the gospel of Peter it is imaginatively narrated as the death of Jesus. Q and the gospel of Peter have employed the same mythic pattern to understand what has happened in Jesus, and in both cases they are responding to Jesus' death and the conviction that God has vindicated Jesus. Both express that conviction with the metaphor of taking up, of assumption into heaven. The Wisdom of Solomon has pioneered the way with a model for the death and assumption of the righteous one.

The assumption model, along with the exaltation model from the Philippians praise piece, indicates that the early Anointed-believers employed models and metaphors other than "raised from the dead." From the Jewish tradition they borrowed models and metaphors to explain their conviction that God had vindicated Jesus, that his death by crucifixion was not final. Conviction drives the use of varied metaphors and sends them to their Jewish tradition for an explanation. The available models were raising up from the dead, assumption, and exaltation.

Further Reading

Crossan, John Dominic. *The Cross That Spoke, the Origins of the Passion Narrative*. San Francisco: Harper & Row, 1988.

Dewey, Arthur J. "Resurrection Texts in the Gospel of Peter." Pp. 61–74 in *The Resurrection of Jesus, A Sourcebook*. Edited by Bernard Brandon Scott. Santa Rosa: Polebridge, 2008.

Kloppenborg, John S. *Q the Earliest Gospel, an Introduction to the Original Stories and Sayings of Jesus*. Louisville: Westminster John Knox, 2008.

Koester, Helmut. *Ancient Christian Gospels*. Philadelphia: Trinity Press International, 1990.

Smith, Daniel A. *The Post-Mortem Vindication of Jesus in the Sayings Gospel Q*. Library of New Testament Studies. London: T&T Clark, 2006.

Works Cited

Dewey, Arthur J. "Resurrection Texts in the Gospel of Peter." Pp. 61–74 in *The Resurrection of Jesus, A Sourcebook*. Edited by Bernard Brandon Scott. Santa Rosa: Polebridge, 2008.

Plutarch. *Lives*. Loeb Classical Library, 1914.

11 | Empty Tomb

Gospel of Mark

The gospel of Mark is the first written narrative of the "life" of Jesus. As a "life" of Jesus it is somewhat truncated. Unlike Matthew and Luke, for which it provides a source, it has no birth narrative, but begins *in medias res* with John the Baptist and has a strange and puzzling ending in which the tomb is empty and women flee in fear and say nothing.

The first written life of Jesus ends with no resurrection appearance, but only the young man's promise, ". . . go and tell his disciples, including 'Rock,' 'He is going ahead of you to Galilee. There you will see him, just as he told you'" (Mark 16:7).

So unsatisfactory is this ending that both Matthew and Luke follow Mark to 16:8 and then create their own independent and

---

Gospel of Mark

We do not know who wrote this gospel, even though traditionally it has been ascribed to Mark, a disciple of Peter. That ascription has been rejected by modern scholarship. The author remains anonymous. We also do not know where the gospel was written, although northern Galilee or Syria are good guesses, since much of the tradition of the gospel apparently comes from Galilee. It was written shortly after the trauma of the sacking of Jerusalem and destruction of the temple in 70 CE by Titus. How soon after is hard to tell. Along with the Q-gospel, this gospel also served as a source for Matthew and Luke in the construction of their gospels.

incompatible appearance stories. Somewhat later a scribe added a longer ending to Mark made up of a mishmash of other traditions (Mark 16:9–19). Whether the fourth gospel knows Mark's ending is debated, and scholars have even tried to suppose a lost ending for Mark. Although it is not common today, scholars of previous generations assumed that the gospel's original ending had been lost in antiquity.

Let's settle that problem first. Most translations print two additional endings, a longer one and a shorter one. The best manuscripts (Sinaiticus and Vaticanus, both fourth century) end at 16:8, and Clement of Alexandria (about 150–215) and Origen (about 185–254) do not know a different ending. Furthermore Eusebius (about 263–339) and Jerome (347–420) note that most of the copies of the Greek New Testament that they know lack the longer ending. The textual evidence is compelling. Not only that, but the language of the longer ending is decidedly non-Markan in character. Finally, as we noted, the copy of Mark that the authors of Matthew and Luke were following undoubtedly ended at 16:8. For all these reasons, it is clear that neither the longer nor the shorter endings is original, but both are compositions of the second century.

Still, it could be that the ending was lost before Matthew and Luke made use of Mark. Are there convincing reasons to see the empty tomb as the original ending of the first gospel? The women have already been mentioned in 15:40 and 15:47. "There you will see him, just as he told you" (16:7) looks back to 14:28. Whether the young man in 14:51 is related in some way to the young man in the tomb is undecided, but the descriptions are remarkably similar. The words in bold are the same.

> And a **young man** was following him, **wearing** a shroud over his nude body, and they grab him (14:51).
> They saw a **young man** sitting on the right, **wearing** a white robe (16:5).

Finally the language is Markan even down to the doubling of which he is so fond, exhibited in the redundant mention of time in verses 1 and 2 of chapter 16. All in all, it seems best to assume that Mark's gospel, the first gospel, originally ended at 16:8. Let me suggest that the apparent strangeness of that ending results

The Women

The women occur three times in close succession, though the names vary somewhat:

> Mary of Magdala, and Mary the mother of James the younger and Joses, and Salome (15:40).
> Mary of Magdala and Mary the mother of Joses (15:47).
> Mary of Magdala and Mary the mother of James and Salome (16:1).

In 6:3 Jesus' other brothers are mentioned. "Isn't he the son of Mary? And aren't his brothers James, Joses, Judas, and Simon?" Some have suggested that in the three references to Mary, first as the mother of James and Joses and then as the mother only of Joses and finally as the mother only of James, is intended to draw attention to her. Even more, they suggest, she is the same mother mentioned in 6:3. Thus Mark would be putting Mary, Jesus' mother, among the women at the tomb and so continues his bias against Jesus' family.

more from what came afterwards in Matthew, Luke, and John, and from their re-writing of Mark, than from the actual strangeness as a conclusion to this gospel. This ending poses several questions for us:

- Did Mark inherit the empty tomb story?
- Did Mark create the empty tomb story?
- What type of story is it?
- Did Mark know of appearance stories and suppress or omit them?
- What about the women at the tomb?

In order to answer these questions, we first must understand how this conclusion ends Mark's gospel. With some understanding of that in place—what Mark actually says—then we can proceed to a consideration of where the story comes from.

The women approaching the tomb have been mentioned before, as noted, in 15:40–41 at the crucifixion and 15:47 at the burial. Commentators often worry about why the women are coming to anoint the dead body, if that has already taken place at the burial. But a more serious issue poses itself. Even before his death Jesus already had been anointed for his burial. While eating in the house of Simon the leper, "a woman came in carrying an alabaster jar of aromatic ointment made from pure and expensive nard. She broke the jar and poured <the ointment> on his head" (14:3). This startling act provokes a reaction among the bystanders that it would have been better to sell the ointment and give the money to the poor. Then Jesus responds:

> Let her alone! Why are you giving her a hard time?
> She has done a good deed for me.
> Remember, the poor will always be around,
> and whenever you want you can do good for them,
> but I won't always be around.
> She did what she could;
> she has planned ahead by anointing my body for burial.
> Let me tell you:
> wherever the good news is announced in all the world, the
>   story of what she's done will be told in her memory.
>   (Mark 14:6–9)

Jesus' prophecy, "wherever the good news is announced in all the world, the story of what she's done will be told in her memory," has of course remained unfulfilled. She has been quickly forgotten. Nevertheless, this prophecy underlines the significance of what is happening.

The real question is this: Since Jesus has already pronounced his anointment, why are the women coming? In light of 14:6–9, a reader is most likely to conclude that like so many others in Mark's gospel they misunderstand what is happening. Even while approaching the tomb, they wonder who will roll away the stone blocking its entrance. The narrator remarks on its very size in a parenthetical remark, "For in fact the stone was very large" (16:4). This remark only serves to point out their lack of understanding of the task.

Words of seeing are prominently associated with the women.

> Now some women were observing (*theōrousai*) from a
>   distance. (15:40)
> [They] noted (*ethōroun*) where he had been laid to rest. (15:47)
> Then they look up (*anablepsasai*) and discover (*theōrousin*)
>   that the stone has been rolled away. (16:4)

> And when they went into the tomb, they saw (*eidon*) a young
> man sitting on the right. (16:5)

The young man's speech continues this association with words of
seeing.

> Look (*ide*) at the spot where they put him. (16:6)
> He is going ahead of you to Galilee. There you will see
> (*opsesthe*) him. (16:7)

As can easily be observed (pardon the pun), the author uses three
words for seeing. *Theōreō* (to observe, three times), then switches
to *eidon* (to see, twice) and finally *horaō* (to see, once), the same
root that appears in Paul's list (*opsesthe* for *ōphthē*). With all this
accent on verbs of seeing, the reader surely expects to see something.

The young man's speech forecasts the women's failure. He reminds them that Jesus had said he would be in Galilee, "just as he
told you" (16:7). But this foretelling (14:28) had taken place at the
final supper just as Peter swore he would never deny him.

> Peter said to him, "Even if everyone else is shaken and falls
> away, I won't!"
> And Jesus says to him, "Let me tell you: tonight before the
> rooster crows twice you will disown me three times." (Mark
> 14:29–30)

The women are in the wrong place. If they really could see, they
would have recognized that Jesus had already been anointed and
they should go to Galilee. The young man says "There you will
see him" but, because we are looking for the egg of resurrection,
we put the accent on "see" instead of "there." Like Peter, they too
will fail.

Upon seeing the young man, the women "grew apprehensive"
(16:5), a condition the young man recognizes and immediately
picks up on when he says, "Don't be apprehensive (16:6, BBS
Trans). But after hearing the young man's speech, the women do
not recover. Instead his speech apparently provokes a fear they
never overcome and leads directly to the gospel's conclusion:

> And once they got outside, they ran away from the tomb,
> because great fear and excitement got the better of them.
> And they didn't breathe a word of it to anyone:
> talk about terrified. . . . (Mark 16:8)

Literally in the Greek, "they said nothing to no one" (*oudeni ouden eipan*), about as firm a denial as can be.

In Mark 4:12, when explaining the parables, the author quoted Isa 6:9:

> They may look with eyes wide open
> > but never quite see,
> and may listen with ears attuned
> > but never quite understand,
> otherwise they might turn around and find forgiveness.

This gospel is about seeing—not simply physical seeing, but seeing with insight. This the disciples have failed to do and now so do the women. In chapter 8 when confronted by the Pharisees seeking a sign, Jesus responds, "Why does this generation demand a sign? Let me tell you: this generation won't get any sign!" (Mark 8:12). In the very next story, when the disciples are afraid they will starve in the boat because they have no bread, Jesus confronts them, "You still don't get it, do you? You still haven't got the point, have you? Are you just closed-minded? You have eyes, but you still don't see, and you have ears, but you still don't hear" (8:17–18, quoting Jer 5:21).

Mark's empty tomb story ends with the disciples having abandoned Jesus, and the women not seeing, being in the wrong place, and finally out of fear telling no one anything. The author has stripped from the reader every sign from heaven. The ending demands of the reader what all of Jesus' followers have failed to achieve. They have failed to see. Mark's ending challenges the reader to do better.

When 16:1–8 is read as a summation to Mark's gospel and not in light of what Matthew and Luke have rewritten, it makes marvelous sense as a conclusion—so much so that we must see it as Mark's own composition. It is not a story he inherits from the tradition, but one he composes as the dramatic ending to his narrative. Once the thoroughness of Mark's composition becomes apparent, what would be left that he did not add? We are forced to the conclusion that it is Mark's creation.

Interestingly, the story's form is close to that of an assumption story. The young man points out that the body is not there and is not to be found—which, we have seen, is all it takes in the ancient world for an assumption story. In Chariton's novel *Callirhoe* (early first century CE), when Chaereas cannot find the body of his supposedly dead wife, he asks: "Which of the gods has become my rival and carried off Callirhoe and now keeps her with him? . . . But even so she should not have disappeared from the world so quickly or for such a reason (3:3)." She was not actually dead, but the disappearance of the body immediately provokes among the bystanders the supposition that the body has been stolen, and on the part of her husband that she has been taken away by the gods.

The young man's speech has combined both motifs: "He was raised, he is not here. Look at the spot where they put him" (Mark 16:6). "He was raised" comes from the raised up/resurrection tradition, while "he is not here" comes from the taken up/assumption tradition. We have seen both previously. Mark, writing sometime after 70 CE, brings the two traditions together in the composition of his narrative.

Did Mark omit the appearance stories? The very phrasing of that question supposes their existence, and of course once again presupposes the egg. The young man's confession repeats the verb from Paul's gospel: "He has been raised." To this point, we have not found a narrative or account of the event, but only a confession. Mark remains within that tradition.

On the basis of Mark we must conclude that the tradition has not yet produced any appearance stories, that is, stories of visions or appearances of Jesus to his disciples. Mark and the pre-70 tradition testify that God's raising of Jesus from the dead, super-exalting him, taking him up, is a matter of confession and conviction, a metaphor for saying that God has vindicated Jesus.

Further Reading

Collins, Adela Yarbo. *Mark, a Commentary*, Hermeneia. Minneapolis: Fortress, 2007. An important commentary in the traditional historical critical method.

Crossan, John Dominic. "Empty Tomb and Absent Lord." In *The Passion in Mark, Studies on Mark 14–16*, edited by Werner H. Kelber, 135–52. Philadelphia: Fortress, 1976. One of the important articles arguing that Mark created the empty tomb narrative.

Fowler, Robert M. *Let the Reader Understand: Reader-Response Criticism and the Gospel of Mark.* Minneapolis: Fortress Press, 1991. Still one of the best and most convincing analyses of the Mark.

Metzger, Bruce M. *A Textual Commentary on the Greek New Testament.* New York: United Bible Societies, 1971. For the reasons why those editors responsible for the Nestle-Aland and USB Greek text opted against the optional endings of Mark.

Works Cited

Chariton. *Callirhoe.* Loeb Classical Library, 1995.

12 | Matthew and Luke's Take on Mark

uards keep watch at the tomb in Matthew's account, while Luke's gospel contains the journey to Emmaus. Classic paintings of the resurrection have featured these incidents. The guards fainting away as the victorious Christ carrying his victory banner emerges from tomb is a compelling image. Those of Jesus and the two men at table as Jesus breaks bread are even more famous. On the other hand, I cannot find a single image of Mark's empty tomb in the catalogs of classic art. We are now entering a world that has had a magnetic attraction for the western imagination.

In the clear consensus of scholarship Matthew and Luke not only use Mark's gospel as one of their sources but they derive their chronological outline from Mark. So far as we can tell, Mark is the first one to tell a connected story of Jesus and so successful, so powerful is his telling that no one has really been able to tell it in another fashion.

Since Matthew's rewriting of Mark is less ambitious than Luke's and was almost surely done prior to Luke's, we will begin with Matthew.

Matthew

The Guards

Between Jesus' burial and the two women (instead of three) coming to the tomb, Matthew has inserted a story concerning the chief priests and Pharisees request to Pilate that he post guards at the tomb. The narrative stretches the time to three clear days.

"It was dark" (Matt 27:57) when Joseph of Arimathea asks Pilate for permission to bury Jesus. Then "On the next day, which is the day after preparation" (Matt 27:62), the Jerusalem authorities approach Pilate, and finally "After the sabbath, at first light on Sunday" (Matt 28:1), the women come to the tomb. This clearly marks out the movement from day to day.

The story of the guards has a strongly legendary character. The Jerusalem authorities tell Pilate:

> We remember what that deceiver said while he was still alive:
> "After three days I'm going to be raised up."
> So order the tomb sealed for three days so his disciples won't
>   come and steal his body and tell everyone,
> "He has been raised from the dead."
> If that were to happen, the last deception will be worse than
>   the first.
>   (Matt 27:63–64)

In the hearing held at the house of Caiaphas the high priest "two men came forward and said, 'This man said, "I can destroy the temple of God and rebuild it within three days"'" (Matt 26:61). There is never anything public in Matthew about "after three days I'm going to be raised up." That is only addressed to the disciples.

When Pilate refuses their request, they post their own guard. This is part of a theme that establishes Pilate's innocence of Jesus' blood and shifts the blame to the Jews. While Pilate was sitting in judgment, his wife sent him a message: "Don't have anything to do with that innocent man, because I have agonized a great deal today over a dream about him" (Matt 27:19). Despite his wife's warning, Pilate is unable to control the crowd.

> Now when Pilate could see that he was getting nowhere, but
>   that a riot was starting instead,
> he took water and washed his hands in full view of the crowd
>   and said,
> "I'm not responsible for this man's blood. That's your busi-
>   ness!"
>   (Matt 27:24)

Thus Pilate establishes his innocence, but the crowd shouts on: "So, smear his blood on us and on our children" (27:25). Given Philo (*Legation to Gaius*, 299–305) and Josephus' (*Jewish Antiquities*,

18:4:1–2) stories of Pilate's ruthlessness, it is hard to imagine this scene as being historical. Matthew's picture of Pilate as relatively uninvolved in Jesus' death and pronouncing Jesus' innocence implies by extension that Christianity is not a threat to the Roman empire. The outcome of this strategy has been a disaster.

The guards reappear at several dramatic moments in the story of the tomb. The women come "to inspect" the tomb. The problem with the anointing has disappeared. Mark's image of the empty tomb is quite stark, but not so Matthew's. It has a truly epiphanic character.

> And just then there was a strong earthquake.
> You see, a messenger of the Lord had come down from the sky,
> arrived <at the tomb>, rolled away the stone, and was sitting on it.
> The messenger gave off a dazzling light and wore clothes as white as snow.
> (Matt 28:2–3)

While the resurrected Jesus does not appear, the next best thing is there—a dazzling (in Greek, *astrapē*, lightning or star-like) angel. At precisely this moment when the guards could be a decisive witness, they "were quaking with fear and looked like corpses themselves" (Matt 28:4). That is, they faint and so see nothing.

The guards report to the Jerusalem authorities who concoct a plan to bribe the soldiers and "ordered them, 'Tell everybody, "His disciples came at night and stole his body while we were asleep"'" (Matt 28:13). So tame has Pilate become in this retelling that they instruct the soldiers not to worry about him, "we'll deal with him" (28:14). The conclusion tells it all: "And this story has been passed around in the Jewish community until this very day" (28:15). This is a teleological legend, a story invented to prove this point. It indicates that no one knows where the body is.

Not only is the tomb now filled with the dazzling epiphany of an angel of the lord, but the women are no longer embarrassingly silent. "And they hurried away from the tomb, afraid and filled with joy, and ran to tell his disciples" (Matt 28:8).

Jesus himself now appears to the two women to repeat the angel's message (Matt 28:10). Upon seeing Jesus, the women "came up and grabbed his feet and paid him homage" (Matt 28:9). "To pay homage" is a term Matthew frequently employs (13 times, Mark 4, Luke 3) of those who encounter Jesus. The astrologers from the East say that they "have come to pay him homage" (Matt 2:2) and at the gospel's conclusion when the Eleven see Jesus, "they paid him homage" (Matt 28:17).

The language of this appearance story is distinctly Matthean and it corrects the silence of the women in Mark. It does not represent a piece of independent tradition, but a Matthean rewriting of Mark.

Make Disciples

Matthew continues to follow the clues in Mark's narrative, with the disciples following the command to go to Galilee, but there are several interesting notices in the introduction to the so-called "Great Commission" that concludes this gospel. Consider, for example, "The eleven disciples went to the mountain in Galilee where Jesus had told them to go" (Matt 28:16). Unlike Paul who has the Twelve, Matthew has corrected that with "the eleven," taking into account the suicide of Judas narrated in this gospel (see Matt 27:3–10, see also Acts 1:18–19—although the methods of suicide are different). Besides, there is no previous saying about going to the *mountain* in Galilee, although mountain does play a prominent role in this gospel (e.g., the temptation, the Sermon on the Mount, the second feeding, and the transfiguration).

The encounter with Jesus has its own surprises in store. "And when they saw him, they paid him homage; but some were dubious" (28:17). The grammatical structure puts the emphasis on "paid him homage," which is the main verb, while "they saw" appears in a subordinate element (in Greek a participle). It is surprising that, in an appearance story, "seeing" is not rhetorically stressed. Even more, the sentence ends with the disturbing note, "but some were dubious." Matthew does not understand faith as an absolute quality, but sees it as ambiguous; he acknowledges that "little faith" or "meager trust" is sufficient.

> If God dresses up the grass in the field,
>> which is here today and is thrown into an oven tomorrow,

won't <God care for> you even more, you with your meager
   trust?
So don't fret.
Don't say, "What are we going to eat?"
      or "What are we going to drink?"
      or "What are we going to wear?"
These are all things pagans seek.
After all, your heavenly Father is aware that you need them all.
Seek God's empire and his justice first, and all these things will
      come to you as a bonus.
      (Matt 6:30–33)

This passage establishes the theme—even meager trust is enough.
It is enough to move mountains (Matt 17:20). Being dubious is
not a problem.

The appearance story concludes with a saying of Jesus in
which he tells his disciples to "make disciples of all peoples" (Matt
28:19). The Greek word translated here as "all peoples" is the same
word used in Matt 6:32 for "the pagans." Now the risen Jesus is
telling the disciples to make disciples of those same pagans.

The baptismal formula is attested in the Didache, which like
Matthew probably comes from Syria. He is repeating this community's baptismal formula.

These last words of Jesus form a conclusion to Matthew's gospel, picking up the essential themes of that gospel in Matthew's
own language. Jesus' final words are, "I'll be with you day in and
day out, as you'll see, until the culmination of the age" (Matt
28:20). "The culmination of the age" is a term that in the gospels

---

Didache on Baptism

Concerning Baptism, baptize thus: Having first rehearsed
all these things, "baptize in the Name of the Father and of
the Son and of the Holy Spirit," in running water
      (Didache 7:1).

The Didache was probably written in Syria towards the end of
the first century.

occurs only in Matthew. In Matt 18:20 Jesus had promised, "In fact, wherever two or three are gathered together in my name, I will be there among them." The name Emmanuel announced by the angel before his birth means "God with us."

Just as Mark composed the empty tomb story as an appropriate and powerful ending of his gospel, so Matthew has re-written Mark and followed up on the clues in Mark' story to construct his own ending, an ending which, with its images of the guards and the commissioning, has had a powerful influence.

In this gospel Peter plays a prominent role: in Matt 16:18 Jesus promises, "Let me tell you: you are Peter, <'the Rock'>, and on this very rock I will build my congregation." Yet Peter plays no role in Matthew's resurrection account, which is not used to establish Peter's authority, but rather employs the resurrected Jesus to establish his community's mission to make disciples of the pagans.

Matthew's gospel was written probably between 85 and 95 CE, and does not appear to know any traditions about the resurrected Jesus' appearance other than Mark's. Like Mark he is left to compose his own accounts. Ironically, the appearance of the angel at the tomb is more epiphanic than Jesus' appearance either to the women or to the disciples on the mountain.

In this narrative of Jesus' appearance we should carefully observe Matthew's language. The angel uses Mark's language to speak of Jesus' rising from the dead and Jesus repeats the angel's language. The women do not "see" Jesus, but "meet" him. In the story of Jesus' "appearance" on the mountain, the Eleven "see" Jesus, but as we noted, the verb of seeing is in a subordinate element. The actual construction of this concluding scene is in the standard form of an apothegm. Except for what he inherits from Mark, the technical language of raising up and taking up is missing from Matthew's narrative.

Luke

Empty Tomb, Take 3

Like Matthew, Luke follows and rewrites the Mark's story of the empty tomb, but he rewrites with a heavier hand. The women, for example, remain nameless, as they did at the crucifixion and burial, until after they have reported to the Eleven "and to everybody else" (Luke 24:9). And their names are somewhat different: "The group included Mary of Magdala and Joanna and Mary the mother of James, and the rest of the women companions." Salome has disappeared, Joanna takes her place, and the group has been enlarged with even more unnamed companions. Further, their report is doubted: "but their story seemed nonsense to them, so they refused to believe the women" (Luke 24:11).

Matthew had ignored the issue of the anointing, but Luke prepares for it by noting that at the time of burial "the Sabbath was about to begin" (Luke 23:54), and thus implying that there was no time for a proper burial. The women "went home to prepare spices and ointments. On the Sabbath they rested in observance of the commandment" (Luke 23:56). The notice about observing the Sabbath helps establish the time sequence of three days and points out that they are observant Jews.

By careful rewriting, Luke elongates Mark's empty narrative. The women's discovery that the stone had already been rolled away replaces the awkward wondering about who will roll it away. Once again, the moment of resurrection is missed and remains unnarrated: "But when they went inside they did not find the body of the Master Jesus" (Luke 24:3). They discover the tomb empty, and its emptiness does not have to be pointed out to them. It simply perplexes them.

Then "two men in dazzling clothes suddenly appeared and stood beside them" (Luke 24:4). Two men replace one young man and their clothing is "dazzling." The Greek, *astraptō*, derives from the root *astr-* meaning "star." In the verb form it often means "lightning" and when used of a person means "brilliant." The astral notion is important here because it identifies the two men as angels. By employing the *astr-* root, both Matthew and Luke remove the ambiguity of Mark's young man and turn the empty tomb, a story that would normally lead to a narrative of assumption, into an angelic epiphany.

If the vacated tomb only perplexed the women, the two angels terrify them. Matthew and Luke have each dealt differently with Mark's final picture of the women in fear and saying nothing. In Matthew, they leave the tomb "afraid and filled with joy" (Matt

28:8): in Luke, upon seeing the angels, "They were terrified and knelt with their faces to the ground" (Luke 24:5). So much for the theme of fear.

The angels propose a simple riddle: "Why are you looking for the living among the dead?" (Luke 24:5). Then, in a clever maneuver, Luke has the angels report, "Remember what he told you while he was still in Galilee" (24:6). Since Luke's gospel is pointed towards Jerusalem, not Galilee, the young man's promise in Mark, "He is going ahead of you to Galilee" (Mark 16:7), is rewritten to "while he was still in Galilee." Then the angels in a somewhat pedantic fashion quote a specific saying, as though they were engaged in a scribal argument.

Unlike Mark, this gospel does not report the women's response to this message. Instead they go directly to the Eleven and make their report to the apostles, "but their story seemed nonsense to them, so they refused to believe the women" (Luke 24:11). The women are clearly subordinated to the apostles.

Just as Matthew had followed and rewritten Mark up to 16:8, so also does Luke. From this point on, the narrative is of the author's construction. Everything takes place on one day, in and around Jerusalem. The day ends with the assumption of Jesus at Bethany, even though the Acts of the Apostles has the assumption forty days later. It is difficult to explain this inconsistency by a supposedly common author.

This one day of activity is arranged around three scenes:

- The empty tomb rewritten from Mark
- The disciples on the road to Emmaus
- Jesus' appearance to the Eleven

Between the Emmaus story and Jesus' appearance to the Eleven is a report of an appearance to Peter and the day is brought to a conclusion with Jesus' assumption.

Road to Emmaus

The centerpiece of this day's activity is the journey of two disciples to Emmaus, a scenario of Luke's own construction. The vocabulary is replete with words frequently found in Luke. The scene is carefully set. Two people are on the road to Emmaus and

Textual Issue

Two verses in Luke's resurrection account have long been debated as to whether they were in the original. After the women make their report, some manuscripts read: "But Peter got up and ran to the tomb. He peeked in and saw only the linen wrappings, and returned home, marveling at what had happened" (24:12). When Jesus appears to the Eleven it reads, "Touch me and see—a ghost doesn't have flesh and bones as you can see that I have" (24:39). But then a number of manuscripts add, "And when he had said this, he showed them his hands and his feet" (24:40).

Because these two verses have a strong resemblance to the gospel of John, many scholars argue that they were added to the text from that gospel. But the additions appear in many very early manuscripts, so such an addition would have to have taken place very early. Other scholars think that the authors of Luke and John knew a common source. I find this highly unlikely, and therefore consider these two verses a later addition.

one of them is even named Kleopas. While the artistic tradition has imagined these two travelers as males, it may be otherwise. When a male is named and the other character remains unnamed, ancient convention normally dictates that the unnamed character is female. Such are the assumptions of patriarchy. Perhaps Luke wants the reader to imagine a husband and wife.

The couple are discussing the just narrated events—Jesus' crucifixion and the report of the women who had gone to the tomb. Their identification of Jesus as "a prophet powerful in word and deed in the eyes of God and all the people" (Luke 24:19) is a regularly recurring theme for this author (Luke 4:24; 13:33; Acts 2:22; 3:22; 7:37). Further, they had thought that Jesus was the one to ransom or redeem Israel, a description of Jesus' mission (Luke 1:68; 2:38; Acts 2:30–36; 13:32–34). They are sad, what we call "down," "blue," or depressed. The women's story does not suggest to them that Jesus has been raised up, for they seem to agree with the Eleven that the women's story is an "idle tale" (Luke 24:11), i.e., gossip.

The Emmaus story underlines three themes important for Luke: the necessity of Jesus' death, resurrection is not proof, and the meal as recognition.

Divine Necessity

After Kleopas' summary of the events they had been discussing, the unrecognized Jesus turns on them and accuses them (and by implication all the disciples and probably the readers as well) of being foolish: "You people are so dim, so reluctant to trust everything the prophets have said!" (Luke 24:25). After castigating them, Jesus makes a remarkable statement, "Wasn't the Anointed One destined to endure these things and enter into his glory?" (24:26). This states precisely the problem: Why was his death necessary? Surely the Anointed was to defeat his enemies, not be defeated by them. Making the scandalous paradox obvious obviates Paul's understanding of the cross as scandal. Solving this enigma is a key issue in Luke-Acts, in which the death and raising into glory of Jesus is part of God's plan, the fulfillment of scripture. Jesus' predictions of his passion (Luke 9:22; 17:25) foretell its necessity and Peter's speech in Acts makes the same point.

> Fellow Israelites,
> I may say to you confidently of our ancestor David that he
>   both died
> and was buried,
> and his tomb is with us to this day.
> Since he was a prophet,
> he knew that God had sworn with an oath to him that he
>   would put one of his descendants on his throne.
> Foreseeing this, David spoke of the resurrection of the
>   Messiah, saying,
> "He was not abandoned to Hades,
> nor did his flesh experience corruption."
> This Jesus God raised up, and of that all of us are witnesses.
>   (Acts 2:29–32)

The angels in the tomb (Luke 24:7), Jesus in the Emmaus story, and likewise his immediately following appearance to the disciples all stress this necessity (24:26, 44–45). Why was it necessary?

While Jesus explained the scriptures to them, no explicit references are quoted. The same pattern holds true later in Luke 24:45 when Jesus "prepared their [the Eleven's] minds to understand the scriptures. He said to them, 'This is what is written: the Anointed One will suffer and rise from the dead on the third day. And all peoples will be called on to change their hearts for the forgiveness of sins, beginning from Jerusalem. You are witnesses to this'" (24:45–48).

Is Luke thinking of proof texts, the use of specific texts to prove the point? That seems unlikely, since in general the author of Luke-Acts does not employ scripture in that fashion. In both 24:27 and 44 the reference is made to "Moses and all the prophets," not to individual texts. Luke has in mind a grand, sweeping view of the biblical story. Stephen's speech in Acts 7 makes exactly this type of move:

> You stiff-necked people, uncircumcised in heart and ears,
> you are forever opposing the Holy Spirit, just as your ancestors
>   used to do.
> Which of the prophets did your ancestors not persecute?
> They killed those who foretold the coming of the Righteous
>   One,
> and now you have become his betrayers and murderers.
>   (Acts 7:51–52)

Likewise Jesus has made a similar claim in the gospel:

> Still, today and tomorrow and the day after, I have to move on,
> because it's impossible for a prophet to die outside of
>   Jerusalem.
> Jerusalem, Jerusalem, you murder the prophets and stone
>   those sent to you!
> How often I wanted to gather your children as a hen
>   <gathers> her own chicks under her wings,
> but you wouldn't let me.
>   (Luke 13:33–34)

For Luke, the fate of the Anointed is the same as that of the prophets, and Jesus is the prophet *par excellence*. This is the Deuteronomic pattern we saw in the Q-gospel. The prophet/

Anointed proclaims God's word and is always rejected, persecuted, and killed, and yet God affirms the prophet. Such is the
pattern of divine necessity. The same fate lies in store for the
disciples. In the gospel, when Jesus for the first time prophesies
his own death, he immediately makes his fate the disciples' fate:
"If any of you wants to come after me, you should deny yourself,
pick up your cross every day, and follow me!" (Luke 9:23). Only in
Luke is this made a *daily* part of being Jesus' disciple. In Acts 9:16
the risen Lord charges Ananias that Paul is to go to the gentiles
and "I myself will show him how much he must suffer for the sake
of my name." Suffering marks Paul's mission at every turn in Acts.

For Luke, the divine plan made known in scripture is not in
accord with human standards. The proclamation of God's word,
rejection, suffering, and finally resurrection are how God operates. In Luke's view, the resurrection does not banish the suffering
of Jesus' death, but acknowledges that this is how God operates.

Recognition

The illusion persists that seeing the risen Jesus would prove everything. Luke's resurrection accounts argue against this. The
apostles (Luke 24:11) and the couple on the road to Emmaus
reject the women's account, actually demean it. When Jesus walks
alongside the couple, they do not recognize him and his strangeness is emphasized in the story when Kleopas addresses him as
"visitor" or "stranger" (Luke 24:18). Likewise in the immediately
following story of the disciples, when Jesus first appears they are
frightened and think they have seen a ghost or spirit (*pneuma*)
(Luke 24:37). Luke argues strongly against the notion that an appearance of the resurrected Lord would answer all questions and
provide definitive proof of the resurrection.

Jesus "took a loaf, and gave a blessing, broke it, and started
passing it out to them" (Luke 24:30). This fourfold pattern recalls
a ritual gesture by closely paralleling two prior references to the
ritual. One is the feeding story: "Then he took the five loaves and
two fish, looked up to the sky, gave a blessing, and broke them,
and started handing them out to the disciples to pass around
to the crowd" (Luke 9:16). The other is the last supper: "And he
took a loaf, gave thanks, broke it into pieces, offered it to them"

(Luke 22:19). It also looks forward to the meals in Acts (2:42, 46; 20:7, 11). As the references to Acts make clear, "breaking bread" becomes a summary of this ritual formula. The Emmaus story concludes with the couple reporting, "how they came to recognize him in the breaking of bread" (Luke 24:35).

Besides looking back to the meals of the gospel narrative and forward to those in Acts, the formula of the breaking of the bread also points outside the narrative to the community's actual practice. The breaking of the bread is the community's recognition of the resurrected Jesus. Where is the resurrected Jesus? Luke answers, "Where he has always been, in the breaking of the bread." What was true for the original followers—in the feeding, at the last supper, at Emmaus—was true in the gospel reader's day late in the first century. For Luke, the breaking of the bread is where God's plan as foretold in scripture becomes evident.

He Has Appeared to Simon

In between the story of the couple on the road to Emmaus and Jesus' appearance to the Eleven is a report of an appearance to Simon. Because the referent of "they" shifts around in the passage, most English translations are confusing, and the Greek only a little less so. The attention falls on the nouns "the Eleven" and "Simon." In the first line, "they" refers to the Emmaus couple, in line 2 it is the Eleven who report the appearance to Simon, and in line 3 and 4 the Emmaus couple summarize their experience, and finally in line 5 "they" is the whole group.

> And when they found the Eleven and those with them gathered together,
> who were saying, "The Master really has been raised, and has appeared to Simon!"
> Then those ones described what had happened on the road,
> and how they came to recognize him in the breaking of bread.
> While they were talking about this, he himself appeared among them.
> (Luke 24:33–36, SV revised)

While this passage is short, it is central in Luke's overall construction of the resurrection appearances and in his overall project.

The gospel of Luke makes Peter the central character among Jesus' followers and protects his status. We can observe this in three key passages where the author modifies Mark, a primary source for the gospel.

The calling of the first disciples is quite different in Luke than in Mark (or Matthew). Only the punch line remains somewhat the same. Luke employs the story of the miraculous catch of fish, a story similar to the appearance story in John 21, an appendix to the fourth gospel. The set up is the following: Jesus borrows Simon's boat to teach from it, and when finished he tells them to put out into deep water. Simon tells him, "Master, we've been hard at it all night and haven't caught a thing" (Luke 5:5). But they put out anyway and the catch was so huge "their nets began to tear apart" (5:6). At this, "Simon Peter fell to his knees in front of Jesus and said, "Get away from me, Master; I'm a sinful man" (5:8). Jesus tells him "Don't be afraid; from now on you'll be catching people" (5:10). At which point they "abandoned everything, and followed him" (5:11).

The changes from Mark (1:16–20) are significant. It is now a miracle story, not just a calling story. The focus is on Peter; Andrew has disappeared and James and John have faded into the background. At the punch line, "you'll be catching people," the "you" is tellingly singular, referring only to Peter, not plural as in Mark.

Even more telling is the parallel to the confession at Ceasarea Philippi (Mark 8:27–33; Luke 9:18–22). Whereas Luke expanded the calling story, now Mark's objectionable cursing of Peter ("Get out of my sight, you Satan, you, because you're not thinking in God's terms, but in human terms," Mark 8:33) is totally omitted. All that remains is Peter's confession, "God's Anointed One!" (Luke 9:20).

In the prediction of Peter's denial we once again observe the same protection of Peter. Even before the prediction of the denial, Jesus tells Peter,

> Simon, Simon, look out: Satan is after all of you, to sift you like wheat.
> But I have prayed for you that your trust won't give out.
> And once you've recovered,

you are to shore up these brothers of yours.
(Luke 22:31–34)

Following this promise of recovery, and only then, comes the prophecy of denial. In Mark, we never discover Peter's fate, but in Luke's gospel, Jesus makes him the foundation "to shore up these brothers of yours."

While the story of the couple on the road to Emmaus is elaborated in Luke, the report of the appearance to Simon is central, the pivot around which the whole chapter rotates. The construction subordinates the couple's report of their experience to a report about Simon. This has the effect of making the appearance to Peter prior, even though that to the couple is narrated first. Only after the Eleven report to the couple that the Master (lord) has appeared to Peter are the couple allowed to give their account.

The phrasing of the report is important. "The Master really has been raised (*ēgerthē*), and has appeared (has been seen, *ōphthē*) to Simon!" (Luke 24:24). The Greek is very close to the language employed in Paul's gospel-statement and list, so much so that one almost thinks that it has to be the source.

If the author does not know Paul's list from 1 Corinthians 15, he surely knows the language of the list. What is even more amazing is that his "appearance" is reported in a kerygmatic form. There is no actual account of the appearance. The author certainly does not know a story about an appearance to Peter; what he knows is the confession of the kerygma, the preaching. This reinforces the argument that in Paul "he has been seen for" (*ōphthē*) represents a revelatory formula, not language about visions. The narration of apparitions and visions is clearly a product of the mid-80s CE and later.

When seen in context, it is clear that Luke's depiction of Simon Peter is what makes Peter the "foundation" of the resurrection belief.

The Eleven

When Jesus suddenly stands among the Eleven, they "were terrified and frightened, and figured that they were seeing a ghost" (Luke 24:37). Strangely enough, the appearance to Simon mentioned in verse 34 has not resolved the issue, but fear picks up a theme from the Emmaus story. Appearances of the risen Jesus do not in themselves provoke belief in the resurrection. More is needed.

Flesh and Bone

Jesus then shows them his hands and feet (not his side as in John) to prove that indeed it is he. The resurrected Jesus is the crucified Jesus. The resurrection does not eliminate or overcome the crucifixion, but indicates that the crucifixion is God's way.

Then Jesus concludes, "Touch me and see—a ghost doesn't have flesh and bones as you can see that I have" (Luke 24:39). This reference to the physical character of the risen Jesus is the strongest such reference in the New Testament. John, like Luke written around the end of the first century, does not go quite this far in portraying the physical character of the risen Jesus. Matthew, probably written in the mid-80s, has a very brief appearance story and avoids the issue of what kind of body the risen Jesus has. In Mark, written shortly after the destruction of the Temple, the empty tomb ends the story and so the risen Jesus makes no appearance. A clear trajectory emerges: in the earliest gospel, Mark, there is no mention of the body of the risen Jesus, but by the end of the first century the physical character of the risen Jesus is being emphasized. Clearly, at the end of the first century this has become an issue, perhaps as a result of the debate with emerging Gnosticism or docetism.

When we turn to Paul, who wrote even earlier than any of the gospels, the contrast could not be stronger. In 1 Corinthians 15 Paul draws a clear distinction between the physical body and the spiritual body. It is sown a soul-body; it is raised up a body whose breath is God's (see chapter 9). The body will rise; however, it will not be a physical body, but a spiritual body. Paul drives his argument home with the conclusion, "flesh and blood is not capable of inheriting the coming Empire of God, no more than the corruptible can inherit the incorruptible" (1 Cor 15:50).

Paul and Luke are at opposite ends of the pole. Nor is there any easy way to reconcile them. When we add in the evidence discussed above a clear trajectory emerges. Paul in the 50s, the earliest discussion of the resurrection, argues for a spiritual body.

Luke at the end of the first century argues for a physical understanding of the resurrection. Yet even for Luke the physical body
of the risen Jesus is not like an ordinary physical body since the
couple on the road to Emmaus do not recognize Jesus, and he
suddenly appears among the Eleven. His cannot be a normal
physical body. Perhaps this is an effort to compromise with Paul's
spiritual body. Given the aversion of Greeks to resurrection of the
body, this insistence on a semi-physical body, a body that bears
the marks of crucifixion, can be seen as an effort to maintain a
"body" resurrection.

There is no biblical position on the resurrected body—there
are differing positions. What the two extremes have in common is
their attempts to affirm the reality of the resurrection. Both Paul
and Luke would agree that it is not a ghost or a phantom. What
both lack is an anthropology to explain resurrection, so they operate within the anthropological models they have.

Divine Necessity Once Again

After establishing the reality of his resurrection, "he prepared
their minds to understand the scriptures " (Luke 24:45). This returns to a major theme of the angels in the tomb and the Emmaus
story, pointing to its importance and centrality in Luke's resurrection narratives. The Human One prophesying his death and
resurrection now becomes an Anointed One saying, "This is what
is written: the Anointed One will suffer and rise from the dead
on the third day" (Luke 24:46, see 9:21; 17:25; 18:32). Jesus does
not appeal to specific scriptures to prove that he is the Anointed,
but to the pattern of scripture as indicated in the stories of Moses
and the prophets. The prophets and the Anointed proclaim God's
word and are always rejected, persecuted, and killed, yet God still
affirms them. That is the pattern of divine necessity.

What is now added is "all peoples will be called on to change
their hearts for the forgiveness of sins, beginning from Jerusalem"
(Luke 24:47). This moves beyond the announcement of the angels
and the Emmaus story. The theme of repentance and forgiveness
of sins extends back into the gospel and looks forward to Acts.

John the Baptist had proclaimed repentance. "And he went
into the whole region around the Jordan, calling for baptism and

a change of heart that lead to forgiveness of sins" (Luke 3:3). In Jesus' inaugural speech in the synagogue in Nazareth, a critical passage in Luke's gospel, the Isaiah 61 passage summarizes Jesus' ministry. That quote begins, "The spirit of the Lord is upon me" and includes the phrase, "He has sent me to announce pardon for prisoners" (Luke 4:18; Isa 61:1 LXX). The Greek word translated by "pardon" is the same one used for forgiveness in Luke 3:3 and 24:47. Furthermore, in Nazareth Jesus announces that the spirit of the Lord is upon him, while in this appearance story he tells the disciples to remain in Jerusalem until clothed in power (Luke 24:49).

Making the tie to Acts, Peter tells those in Jerusalem, "Repent, and be baptized every one of you in the name of Jesus Christ so that your sins may be forgiven; and you will receive the gift of the Holy Spirit" (Acts 2:38). And in defending himself before Agrippa, Paul summarizes his ministry thus: "but [I] declared first to those in Damascus, then in Jerusalem and throughout the countryside of Judea, and also to the gentiles, that they should repent and turn to God and do deeds consistent with repentance" (Acts 26:20).

Luke pulls together a number of major themes in both the gospel and Acts. He is frequently credited with creating the Christian periodization of history, the period of Israel, Jesus as the Middle of Time, and the period of the Church. Yet here at the gospel's end he makes another move. He paints with a broad brush outlining and hinting at a grand sweep of divine history. The fate of the prophets is still the fate of Jesus and the disciples. Jesus fulfills the divine plan. But that plan looks forward to reaching the whole world and its pattern is always the same. God's word meets rejection because it opposes the powers of the world and brings release to the captives. Just as the gospel ends with Jesus confronting Rome, so Acts will end with Paul awaiting his confrontation with Rome. There is no doubt how the empire will act. Empires always act in the same way. Yet the resurrection announces that this is still the way God counter-acts.

To conclude this one-day resurrection account, Luke employs a motif from the assumption tradition, and he "was carried up into the sky" (Luke 25:41). The assumption tradition offers a better explanation of where Jesus is than the resurrection tradition. Luke has explicitly combined the two models.

Unlike the gospels of Mark and Matthew, the author of the gospel of Luke has created a full theology of the resurrection. The former employ their resurrection accounts to conclude their respective gospels. Luke does that and more. These stories provide a bridge to the Acts of the Apostles and summarize the main themes of the gospel.

Further Reading

Conzelmann, Hans. *The Theology of St. Luke.* Reprint 1982 ed. Philadelphia: Fortress Press, 1960.

Brock, Ann Graham. *Mary Magdalene, the First Apostle: The Struggle for Authority.* Vol. 51, Harvard Theological Studies. Cambridge: Harvard University Press, 2003.

Fitzmyer, Joseph. *The Gospel According to Luke.* 2 vols. 28A, Anchor Bible Series. Garden City, NY: Doubleday & Co., 1985.

Tannehill, Robert C. *Narrative Unity of Luke-Acts, a Literary Interpretation: The Gospel According to Luke.* Vol. 1, Foundations and Facets. Philadelphia: Fortress Press, 1986.

Tannehill, Robert C. *Luke*, Abingdon New Testament Commentaries. Nashville: Abingdon, 1996.

Works Cited

The Apostolic Fathers. *The Didache.* Loeb Classical Library, 1912.

13 The Empty Tomb Again

Chapter 20 in the fourth gospel is a long and complete unit divided into four parts.

- Empty tomb
- Mary Magdalene
- The disciples
- Thomas

It originally served as the gospel's ending. Chapter 21 was later added on, probably in the early second century (see chapter 14). Its themes and setting are different.

No consensus exists as to whether the fourth gospel knows the synoptic gospels, although there is a growing position that its author knows Mark. Since he follows the traditions of the empty tomb, the women, Peter, and the disciples, he is certainly working within the same stream of tradition that flows into the synoptic gospels. John has elaborated the tradition by focusing on one individual in each scene to bring out each story's significance.

The Empty Tomb

The two male characters in this scene have played central roles in the gospel: Peter since the very beginning, and the mysterious and anonymous beloved disciple who first appears in John 13:23, and whose identity remains a mystery despite efforts to solve it. Mary Magdalene, on the other hand, was mentioned only once before, when she appeared with Mary, the mother of Jesus, and Mary, the wife of Klopas, at the foot of the cross (John 19:25). This double presence is no accident. For John, Jesus' death is essential to his exaltation. "'And if I'm elevated from the earth, I'll take everyone with me.' (He said this to show what kind of death he was going to die)" (John 12:32–3). Mary Magdalene, a witness to Jesus' death/exaltation, will also be the first witness to hear the risen Jesus' voice. Like Nicodemus (John 3:1–2), Mary comes while it is still dark and darkness is tied to negative themes in John (8:12; 12:35, 46). Mary's report to Peter and "the other disciple" reveals that she believes that "they" have taken the body of Jesus. Hers becomes the first response to the evidence of the missing body.

While Mary's report initially seems to confirm the rumor in Matthew's gospel (27:64) that the body of Jesus was stolen, John's gospel decidedly rejects this rumor by the recurring phrase "the strips of burial cloth lying there" (John 20:5). The accent on the neatness and tidiness of the burial clothes implies that the body is missing but not stolen, for otherwise the burial garments would also be missing. His body does not require clothes. Unlike Lazarus who has to be freed from the bondage of his burial clothes, Jesus is free. As we have noticed before, the empty tomb has overtones that fit well with the assumption tradition.

Mary does not see this evidence, but only Peter and the other disciple. The phrasing "the other disciple ran faster (in Greek *pro-* 'in front of') than Peter" and "was the first" (*protos*) accents this disciple's priority. The one whom Jesus loved is the first to the tomb and the first to believe, thus setting up a decided contrast with Peter.

He came, he saw, he believed—this describes the activity of the beloved disciple. This is the way he is: he believes. Coming, seeing, believing define his character. He needs no more. In contrast to Peter, his portrait is strongly focused. There is no indication what the disciple believes or why, but he presents an image of belief. Somewhat like the case of the empty tomb in Mark, the beloved disciple believes on the basis of what he does not see. The ambiguity of what he believes is compounded by the concluding statement: "But since neither of them yet understood the prophecy that he was destined to rise from the dead, these disciples went back home" (John 20:9–10). Yet the beloved disciple becomes the first example in the fourth gospel of faith in the resurrection. As the model for the community that claims his heritage, his faith is the archetype or the standard by which to judge the others. That faith is not based on hearing, seeing, or touching the resurrected Jesus.

This first section presents three points of view on the empty tomb. Peter draws no conclusion; Mary Magdalene assumes that someone has stolen the body; only the beloved disciple comes, sees, and and believes. But what does he believe?

A Voice in the Garden

The introduction of Mary Magdalene follows the pattern of the other disciple and Peter. Like the other disciple she was first to reach the tomb and both of them bend down to look into the tomb. But whereas Peter observes linens, she observes two heavenly messengers. She contacts heavenly realities; he contacts left over artifacts. Yet the messengers have no portentous message and there is no dazzling epiphany. While an audience could draw from their appearance a sign that Jesus has risen, Mary draws the same conclusion as when she had seen the stone rolled away. Mary's response to the angels is to repeat her report to the disciples, reinforcing the point that not even the sight of heavenly messengers produces faith.

Mary is described four times as weeping—twice in rapid succession at the section's opening, and then when both the messengers and Jesus ask why she is weeping. Mary sees but does not know that it is Jesus. Physical seeing does not produce recognition or belief.

Jesus repeats the messenger's question with a significant addition, "Who is it you're looking for?" (John 20:15) and thus echoes the question he asked the two unnamed disciples of John the Baptist (John 1:38). Notably, their address of Jesus as Rabbi parallels Mary's.

A single exchange of words between Jesus and Mary constitutes the heart of the section and subtly draws the audience into the story's creative performance. Two words are exchanged, "Mary" and "Rabboni," and the audience must fill in a great gap. There is strong dramatic irony in the passage, since the audience knows more than Mary and keeps waiting for her to find out what is happening. Yet the audience must deal with such traps as the heavenly messengers. An audience can over anticipate. When Jesus says Mary's name and she responds, the audience must supply her joy or emotion. While weeping is expressed, its opposite is implied in her voice. The recognition of Jesus when he says her name recalls Jesus' saying, "The sheep recognize his voice; he calls his own sheep by name and leads them out" (John 10:3, 14). The voice that she recognizes draws attention to the risen Jesus as the earthly Jesus. She may mistake the embodiment for a gardener, but she does recognize the voice. Here the narrator drops a clue for the audience. This is Jesus but not the physical Jesus. Voice, like breath, is a perfect model for the spirit. It has body, but it is not physical (John 3:8).

At Jesus' pronouncing of Mary's name, she responds, "Rabboni." Its foreignness draws attention to her response; the Hebrew produces verisimilitude. She "turns around" and this focuses attention on her action and may perhaps have a double meaning. She turns around physically, but "turning around" is a Hebrew metaphor for conversion, a change of perspective or commitment.

Jesus' response to Mary has often been mistranslated. The Vulgate phrase, *noli tangere* ("do not touch"), has been fixed in art and the Western imagination. But such a translation is hardly likely, given the Thomas story that follows. Such a rendering would involve either a serious contradiction (over which exegetes have strained) or a terrible sexism. A more proper translation is "Let go of me" or "Don't keep clinging to me."

Jesus gives as his reason for demanding that Mary let go of him that he has not yet ascended to his Father. In John the ascent to the Father refers to Jesus' death, something to which Mary Magdalene was a witness. The classic references are John 3:13 and 6:62. "No one has gone up to heaven except the one who came down from there: the Human One" (John 3:13) and "What if you were to see the Human One going back up to where he was to begin with?" (John 6:62). The fourth gospel is combining two different views—the assumption/exaltation model and the raising up from the dead model.

Jesus does not explicitly send Mary Magdalene to the disciples, but she does go to them proclaiming, "I have seen the Master" (John 20:18). In the fourth gospel she becomes the first one both to see the resurrected Jesus and to proclaim the resurrection faith. The beloved disciple believes, but has no voice; Peter sees the tomb, but is otherwise silent.

Behind Closed Doors

Verse 19 exhibits multiple signs of a major shift; clearly, the stories of the beloved disciple and Mary Magdalene form one unit and those of the disciples a second unit. The reference to the "first day of the week" repeats the similar time notice from verse 1. But a time shift has occurred. And although it is now evening rather than morning, both episodes begin in the dark. The locked doors and the disciples' fear reinforce the darkness theme.

Jesus' "Peace" (*shalom*, 20:19) is a normal Jewish greeting. While obviously contrasting with the disciples' fear, it is still a normal greeting.

Jesus came and stood. Coming and standing is the way of describing Jesus' resurrection experience to the disciples. John does not use the appearance language "he has been seen" (*ōphthē*) that Paul does in 1 Corinthians 15. Rather he uses very physical terms: he came and stood.

Furthermore he shows them his hands and his side. The reference to the hands and side involves the audience's formation of a complex gestalt. First, the hands and the side show that the risen Jesus is the crucified Jesus, a theme before implied, now forcibly proclaimed. "Side" also harks back to the passion's conclusion (John 19:31–37). The truth of what was reported was guaranteed by the witness of the beloved disciple "so you too will believe" (19:35). Then a clause from the second part of Zech 12:10 is quoted: "They shall look at the one they have pierced" (19:37). Finally in this section the first part of the verse from Zechariah will be fulfilled in the disciples commission. "And I will pour out on the house of David and the inhabitants of Jerusalem a spirit of compassion and supplication, so that, when they look on him whom they have pierced, they shall mourn for him, as one mourns for an only child, and weep bitterly over him, as one weeps over a first-born."

The disciples are strongly contrasted with Mary Magdalene. Their fear while hiding behind locked doors contrasts with her boldness of action; their joy contrasts with her weeping. They see and are filled with joy, whereas she sees and does not recognize, but believes at the sound of his voice. An audience begins to notice a progression in the points of view. The beloved disciple saw only an empty tomb and believed; Mary heard Jesus' voice and believed. Now the disciples see the hands and side of Jesus and they believe. The images are becoming progressively more physical.

Jesus commissions the disciples with, "Just as the Father sent me, so now I'm sending you." His own sending by the Father is in Greek in the perfect tense, indicating its past point of origin but its continuing validity, while Jesus' sending of the disciples is in the present. Jesus' sending is not over as the English past tense would imply, but continues on and is the basis for the disciples' sending.

The commission refers back to Jesus' promise in the farewell discourse. "I sent them into the world just as you [the Father] sent me into the world" (John 17:18). The attentive listener would pick up many strong echoes to the farewell discourse in John 17— peace, joy, mission and Spirit.

"He breathed over them" (John 20:22) alludes to Gen 2:7, where God "formed man of dust from the ground, and breathed into his nostrils the breath of life." The LXX uses the same Greek word as in John. Thus the commissioning is a type of creation story.

"Holy spirit" is rare in John (normally John uses "Spirit"). This is not a Trinitarian reference, but in connection with the allusion to Genesis refers to God's creating, life giving spirit or breath. The saying about forgiveness has to do with preaching and being sent, as the context makes clear. The community preaches to the world and offers forgiveness. In John 1:29 John the Baptist introduced Jesus as "the lamb of God, who takes away the sin of the world." In this commission, that announcement finds its fulfillment. This section began with a reference to the disciples' fear of the Judeans and Jesus showing them his side. The audience now begins to put the pieces together. The Zechariah quote, the creation story in Genesis, and the announcement of John the Baptist form the context in which this commission is understood.

Touching and Feeling

Thomas the Twin, one of the Twelve, is the next character to be identified. The foreign name, Thomas, is translated for the benefit of a Greek speaking audience. "Thomas" in Aramaic means "twin." In his first appearance in the gospel narrative (John 11:16), the translation "Twin" was also given. The phrase "Thomas, the one called the Twin" may well function as a way to recall to the audience's mind a whole series of extra-textual references. With the discovery of the gospel of Thomas, we may well be in a position to speculate about those extra-textual references triggered by "Thomas the Twin." In that gospel, Thomas is referred to as "Didymos Judas Thomas." In Greek "Didymos" means "twin." Therefore his name is Judas. Thomas and Didymos are nicknames meaning "twin."

In the gospel that bears his name Thomas is the great mystic seer, in contrast to his function in the fourth gospel. His commissioning scene in the gospel of Thomas brings out the difference.

> Jesus said to his disciples, "Compare me to something and tell me what I am like."
> Simon Peter said to him, "You are like a just angel."
> Matthew said to him, "You are like a wise philosopher."
> Thomas said to him, "Teacher, my mouth is utterly unable to say what you are like."
> Jesus said, "I am not your teacher. Because you have drunk, you have become intoxicated from the bubbling spring that I have tended."
> And he took him and withdrew, and spoke three sayings to him.
> When Thomas came back to his friends, they asked him, "What did Jesus say to you?"
> Thomas said to them, "If I tell you one of the sayings he spoke to me, you will pick up rocks and stone me, and fire will come from the rocks and devour you."
> (Thomas 13)

In the gospel of Thomas, Thomas is the hero, while the other disciples play the role of buffoons. But in the gospel of John, Thomas does not understand. He takes a very literal position. In John 11:16 when Jesus goes to Bethany to raise Lazarus, Thomas tells the other disciples he will go with Jesus to Jerusalem to die, while in the farewell discourse Thomas complains "Master, we don't know where you're going. How can we possibly know the way?" (John 14:5). It is not hard to imagine that among the community of the beloved disciple the claims of Thomas' followers as represented in the tradition of the gospel of Thomas are viewed with a certain skepticism and scorn.

Thomas' response to the disciples' declaration, "We have seen the Master," is harsh and negative. The repetition of "mark of the nails" and the escalation from sticking in his finger to inserting his whole hand create an exaggerated physical definition for the need of proof. The Greek original of "I'll never believe" (John 20:25) involves an emphatic negative in the future, more like "Never ever will I." Jesus' command to Thomas on the other hand is constructed very differently. Where Thomas is harsh and negative, Jesus is elegant and pleading. "Put your finger here, and look at my hands." So magnificently composed is this scene, so strong is the contrast, that it has inspired magnificent art (e.g., Caravaggio).

Jesus' command ends in Greek with an aphoristic wordplay: *apistos alla pistos*, "Stop doubting and start believing." But "doubting" panders to a much later tradition. John's sense is more "Be not faithless, but faithful."

Commentators often take Thomas' response to Jesus' command as the climax to the gospel. Rarely in the New Testament is Jesus called God. The closest parallel to Thomas' confession is the title of the Emperor Domitian who ruled during the gospel's time frame (81–96 CE). He required that he should be addressed as "our Lord and God" (*dominus et deus noster*, Suetonius, *Domitian*, 13). John has used imperial titles before. At the end of the Samaritan woman's narrative, Jesus is proclaimed as savior of the world (John 4:42), clearly an ironic usage. Here too Thomas' confession exposes the pretensions of the Roman emperor. Thomas' confession acknowledges what Jesus has already told Mary: Jesus is God's agent, the bridge between my God and your God, creating the new family of God. "Anyone who has seen me has seen the Father" (John 14:9).

Jesus responds to Thomas' confession with a question and a beatitude. The question, "Do you believe because you've seen me?" (John 20:29) is slightly ironic, challenging Thomas to examine his belief. The beatitude contrasts seeing and believing: "Congratulations to those who believe without seeing"—as do the beloved disciple and Mary Magdalene. In the end, the narrative comes back to its first examples of faith, the beloved disciple and Mary Magdalene. Thomas is in the same position as a gospel reader who has not seen the risen Jesus. Thomas should have no need to see, touch, and feel.

The Ending

Verses 30–31 conclude the chapter and originally the whole gospel. The book is center stage. Writing in the ancient world was strongly connected with auditory activity. One writes so that others may hear. Silent reading was almost unknown. The purpose of the writing/hearing is to bring one to faith in Jesus the Anointed, the son of God. "[T]hese are written down so you will come to believe that Jesus is the Anointed One, the son of God—and by believing this have life in his name" (John 20:31). The very writing/hearing of the book is the voice of the risen Jesus. There is no need to see or touch and feel—only to hear.

This concludes the argument of the chapter. Faith now comes through hearing, not seeing. The audience who hears the book confronts in its reading/hearing the conditions for believing. They have experienced the risen Lord. They fulfill the beatitude: "Blessed are those who have not seen and yet have come to believe."

Just as each of the synoptic gospel writers constructed a resurrection narrative as an ending for his gospel, so the author of the fourth gospel has done. The author knows the tradition of the empty tomb, Mary Magdalene and the disciples. But he feels free to assemble these elements in his own way to create a fitting conclusion to his unique gospel.

Further Reading

Ashton, John. *Understanding the Fourth Gospel*. Oxford: Clarendon Press, revised 2009.

Lindars, Barnabas. *The Gospel of John, New Century Bible*. London: Oliphants, 1972,

Schnackenburg, Rudolf. *The Gospel According to St. John.* Translated by David Smith and G. A. Kon. 3 vols. Vol. 3. New York: Crossroad, 1982.

14 Mary Magdalene First?

A number of scholars have charged that Paul deliberately omitted Mary Magdalene's name from his list of those to whom Jesus had been seen in 1 Cor 15: 5–8. They have argued that Mary Magdalene was the first to see the resurrected Jesus, that she was the first apostle. They have made a strong case and marshaled impressive arguments to which we must give serious attention.

In this chapter and the next we are nudging towards a question that we set aside at the beginning, what really happened? We have been following the textual evidence in chronological order and asking what these writings meant. Now we will be probing into the mists behind and beyond our textual evidence.

The Case for Mary Magdalene

How does one make a case for Mary Magdalene? We have already seen much of the evidence, but as in all historical argument, arrangement is everything. The elements of the case are as follows.

A Female List

Mary Magdalene is mentioned prominently among those who witness the crucifixion and burial of Jesus in Mark, Matthew, and John. While acknowledging the arguments against the historicity of these stories, these scholars argue that the three gospels represent impressive support for the historicity of the women being

Mary Magdalene as Prostitute

The gospel of Mark mentions Mary Magdalene three times: at Jesus' death, at the burial, and upon coming to the tomb. She is among the women who followed and provided for Jesus in Galilee. She is viewed positively. In Matthew's gospel, for which Mark is a source, the situation is much the same, with one exception. After leaving the tomb, she and "the other Mary" are the first to see the Master. Likewise, in the gospel of John she is the first to recognize Jesus by voice and then announces to the disciples, "I have seen the Master" (John 20:18).

Mary enters the stage much earlier in Luke chapter 8. Jesus is preaching the good news with the Twelve, and travelling with them are "some women whom he had cured of evil spirits and diseases: "Mary, the one from Magdala, from whom seven demons had departed . . ." (Luke 8:2). This note about the seven demons also occurs in the longer and later ending of Mark's gospel (16:9). Immediately preceding the mention of Mary Magdalene in Luke is a story of the unnamed sinful woman who "suddenly showed up with an alabaster jar of aromatic ointment, and stood there behind him weeping at his feet. Her tears wet his feet, and she wiped them dry with her hair; she kissed his feet, and anointed them with the ointment" (Luke 7:37–38). Clearly, Luke's gospel starts Mary Magdalene on the road to prostitution.

The final step was in the fifth century when Pope Gregory the Great proclaimed:

> She whom Luke calls the sinful woman, whom John calls Mary, we believe to be the Mary from whom seven devils were ejected according to Mark. . . . It is clear, brothers, that the woman previously used the unguent to perfume her flesh in forbidden acts. What she therefore displayed more scandalously, she was now offering to God in a more praiseworthy manner (Quoted in Schaberg, *Resurrection*, 82).

The pope conflates three passages that are unrelated to create the picture that has dominated the imagination ever since.

Women at the Death of Jesus	
Mark 15:40	**John 19:25**
Mary Magdalene	[Mary] His mother
Mary the mother of James the younger and of Joses	his mother's sister, Mary the wife of Clopas
Salome	Mary Magdalene

present at the death and burial of Jesus. This is especially impressive if John's account is independent of Mark's. Since John's listing of the women at the death is different from Mark's, this would point to John's list being independent.

Empty Tomb

All four canonical gospels testify to the empty tomb. While many scholars deny its historicity and I argued above it was a creation of Mark, the women's care for the dead is well established, so it is plausible that a group of women went to the tomb and found it empty. Jane Schaberg powerfully summarizes the argument:

> This means that the emptiness of the tomb rather than the resurrection appearances was the trigger of the resurrection faith, the inspiration of that faith. This does not reduce the resurrection to the women's spiritual experience, rather, it is their physical and intellectual experience that leads them to the spiritual insight that something has happened to Jesus. They were ready to believe it. In the context of the basileia movement, scriptures like Daniel 7 and 12 and stories about the ascension of Elijah to heaven were valuable for thinking about the current struggles against injustice. The people of the basileia movement—like many movements for change— longed for an end to unjust suffering. The emptiness of the tomb profoundly evokes hope and even faith that God has finally begun to vindicate the suffering righteous.
> (*Mary Magdalene Understood*, pp. 117–18)

The historicity of the discovery of the empty tomb is pivotal to this line of argumentation. A strength of this position is its tying

Jesus' *basileia* (empire/kingdom) movement to the proclamation of his being raised from the dead.

Appearance to Mary Magdalene

Once the empty tomb story is accepted as historical, then the next step is to inquire into the appearance to Mary Magdalene. Schaberg, for example, sees strong parallels between the longer ending of Mark, Matthew, and John. She has a list of 15 common items in these three accounts. For her, this commonality points to a source that predates the current abrupt ending of Mark at 16:8 and tells of the first vision of Jesus to Mary Magdalene.

Paul's List

In this reconstruction, the empty tomb discovered by a group of women provokes resurrection faith, and the first appearance of the resurrected Jesus is attributed to Mary Magdalene. The question therefore arises as to why Mary Magdalene does not appear on Paul's list in 1 Cor 15:5–8?

There are several possible answers. Paul shows no evidence of knowing an empty tomb tradition. Perhaps such a tradition was suppressed by the Jerusalem group because of their fear of women or the association of grave visitations with necromancy or other troubling traditions. Paul also has trouble in Corinth with female prophets and he does not support their position. Perhaps they are appealing to the Mary Magdalene or some other female tradition for backing, and so Paul suppresses any mention of women from the list.

Luke's Erasure of Mary Magdalene

The gospel of Luke is often seen as favorable to women because of its frequent mention of women, more often than any other gospel. But on closer analysis this is difficult to sustain. A good example of Luke's treatment of women is his extensive reworking of Mark's story of the anointing in Bethany. So extensive is this reworking that some have doubted whether it is the same story, but recent analysis has clearly shown that Luke has reworked it. In Mark this story occurs at a pivotal point toward the narrative's end in Jerusalem. The conflict in the temple has concluded and next comes Jesus' final meal. While eating at the house of Simon the leper, "a woman came in carrying an alabaster jar of aromatic ointment made from pure and expensive nard. She broke the jar and poured <the ointment> on his head" (Mark 14:3). Following a discussion about whether the monetary equivalent might better have been given to the poor, Jesus comes to the woman's aid, remarking that she has anointed him (i.e., marked him as the Anointed) for his burial and prophesying, "Let me tell you: wherever the good news is announced in all the world, the story of what she's done will be told in her memory" (Mark 14:9). Needless to say, this is one prophecy of his that has not come true.

In Luke's version of this story, the details are significantly different. The narrative now appears earlier in the gospel story, thereby losing its possible significance as an anointing story. Furthermore the woman is a sinner and the anointing is much more elaborate. "She suddenly showed up with an alabaster jar of aromatic ointment, and stood there behind him weeping at his feet. Her tears wet his feet, and she wiped them dry with her hair; she kissed his feet, and anointed them with the ointment" (Luke 7:37–38). No longer is Jesus' head anointed, as was the case with Israel's kings, but now it is his feet. The woman becomes an example of how Simon should have welcomed Jesus, and at the story's conclusion Jesus forgives her many sins. The whole character of the story is radically different in Luke than in Mark. The sinful woman becomes an example for the Pharisee Simon.

As we saw in dealing with Luke's resurrection narrative, the role of the women has been subtly but significantly shifted. Mark lists the names of the women on three separate occasions—at the crucifixion, at the burial, and early on Sunday morning. On the other hand, Luke does not name the women at the crucifixion or the burial. At the beginning of the empty tomb narrative, the women are introduced with the simple "they came," in Greek *ēlthon*, with the "they" implied by the verb. "On Sunday, at daybreak, they made their way to the tomb, bringing the spices they had prepared" (Luke 24:1). Only after returning from the tomb, and reporting everything to the Eleven, are they finally named.

> And returning from the tomb, they related everything to the
> Eleven and to everybody else.
> The group included Mary of Magdala and Joanna and
> Mary the mother of James, and the rest of the women
> companions.
> They related their story to the apostles;
> but their story seemed nonsense to them, so they refused to
> believe the women.
>   (Luke 24:9–11)

In editing and rewriting Mark, Luke has bracketed the naming of
the women with a mention of the Eleven and the apostles, subor-
dinating the women to the men. Furthermore the three women
are now part of a larger group, "the rest of the women companions."

This editing diminishes the prominence of the women in favor
of Peter who in the gospel of Luke receives the first resurrection
appearance. And in this gospel, as we have seen, the appearance
to Peter is the foundation of the resurrection faith. In the gospel
of Luke, Peter comes to prominence at the expense of the women.

Later Conflict

Gospel of Thomas

In the gospel of Thomas, the disciple with correct insight is
Thomas. In logion 13, he gives the correct response as to who
Jesus is: "Teacher, my mouth is utterly unable to say what you are
like." Jesus responds,

> "I am not your teacher. Because you have drunk, you have
> become intoxicated from the bubbling spring that I have
> tended."
> And he took him, and withdrew, and spoke three sayings
> to him.

But in Thomas we also see conflict between Peter and Mary
(Magdalene). This is especially evident in the gospel's notorious
final saying.

> Simon Peter said to them, "Make Mary leave us, for females
> don't deserve life."
> Jesus said, "Look, I will guide her to make her male,
> so that she too may become a living spirit resembling you

males. For every female who makes herself male will enter
the kingdom of Heaven."
(Thomas 114)

The interpretation of this saying is complicated and may well play
into themes of androgyny in the ancient world. But with regard
to our present concern, it indicates conflict between Peter and
Mary. Peter wants Mary expelled from among the disciples, and
this Jesus refuses.

The gospel of Thomas represents a community in which Mary
is held in high esteem, Peter less so. This final saying may well
represent a debate between those who value the leadership role of
women and so appeal to Mary Magdalene against those who appeal to Peter. The gospel of Thomas sides with Mary Magdalene.

Gospel of Mary

In the gospel of Mary, a late first or early second-century gospel,
Mary is the clear hero. She reports a vision of the lord:

> She said, "I saw the Lord in a vision and I said to him, Lord,
> I saw you today in a vision. He answered me, 'how wonderful
> you are for not wavering at seeing me! For where the mind
> is, there is the treasure.'"
> (Mary 7:1–4, translation from King, *The Gospel of Mary of
> Magdala*)

Mary "turned their [the disciples] heart [to]ward Good, and
they began to deba[t]e the wor[d]s of [the Savior]" (Mary 5:9–10).
But Andrew and then Peter reject Mary's teaching, and Peter specifically because she is a woman.

> He [Peter] questioned them about the Savior: "Did he, then,
> speak with a woman in private without our knowing about
> it? Are we to turn around and listen to her? Did he choose
> her over us?"
> (Mary 10:3–4)

Mary responds by asking why he thinks she is telling lies about the
Savior, and Levi comes to her defense:

> Peter, you have always been a wrathful person. Now I see
> you contending against the woman like the Adversaries. For
> if the Savior made her worthy, who are you then for your
> part to reject her. Assuredly the Savior's knowledge of her is

completely reliable. That is why he loved her more than us.
(Mary 10:7–10)

This anti-Petrine gospel values Mary Magdalene above her male counterparts.

John 21

Chapter 21 of the gospel of John is usually considered an appendix added to the fourth gospel at a later date, probably in the early second century. Moving from John 20 to this later appendix, we observe development. In John 20, Peter plays a minor role. He arrives at the tomb after the "other disciple" who sees and believes. Peter just leaves. Mary Magdalene is the first to see the risen Jesus, and she is commissioned to announce the resurrection to the disciples: "I have seen the Master" (John 20:18). Jesus appears to the disciples who are locked away in a room out of fear of Jewish authorities. Only Thomas is singled out from this group, and even his beatitude is a put-down. John 20, like the whole of the gospel, is anti-apostolic, pro the beloved disciple. Mary Magdalene is a foil in this project.

John 21 reverses this. While the disciples are fishing in Galilee, Jesus appears to them. Peter is the first to recognize him, "It's the Master!" (21:7). This is the first or earliest narration of an appearance to Peter! In Luke it only is reported that Jesus has appeared to Peter. "They said, 'The Master really has been raised, and has appeared to Simon!'" (Luke 24:34). There is no actual report of an appearance. John 21, an appendix to the original gospel of John, is the first actual account of an appearance to Peter. Its form is that of a miracle story similar to Luke 5:1–11 and it concludes with a Eucharist: "Jesus comes, takes the bread, and gives it to them, and passes the fish around as well" (John 21:13). The similarity of the ending of this miracle/appearance story to the ending of the Emmaus story in the gospel of Luke is striking. Both are attempting to argue that the Eucharist represents the presence of the resurrected Jesus in their communities.

The author of John 21 has reworked a miracle story into an appearance story. Just as Luke had no story of an appearance to Peter, neither did the author of John 21. He created the account out of a miracle story.

Jesus now confronts Peter three times:

> Jesus says to him a third time, "Simon, son of John, do you
>   love me?"
> Peter was hurt that he had asked him for the third time, "Do
>   you love me?" and he says to him, "Master, you know ev-
>   erything; you know I love you."
> Jesus says to him, "Feed my sheep."
>   (John 21:17)

The three-time repetition most likely refers to Peter's triple denial of Jesus. In the tradition of those who preserved the fourth gospel, this miracle/appearance story and threefold confrontation represent Peter's restoration, but they do not represent a diminution of the status of the anonymous beloved disciple. When Peter asks Jesus about this one, Jesus replies, "What's it to you if I want him to stay around till I come? You keep on following me" (John 21:22). The gospel concludes with the assurance that this disciple is the one in whose tradition the gospel stands.

John 20 and 21 show that during the end of the first century and the beginning of the second, some Christian communities were symbolizing their issues with authority and leadership by appealing to various apostolic figures. The gospel of Thomas appealed to Thomas against Peter. The fourth gospel (John 20) appealed to the Beloved Disciple, likewise against Peter. Both of these employed Mary Magdalene in a supporting role against Peter. The gospel of Mary directly appeals to Mary Magdalene against Peter. The gospel of Luke, which privileges Peter above all the others and makes him the foundation of resurrection faith, severely diminishes the role of Mary Magdalene. The gospel of Peter does likewise.

Thus at the end of the first century there is clearly a conflict between the followers of Peter and Mary over the status of women in the church. Those supporting women's role appeal to Mary Magdalene; those supporting male roles appeal to Peter. Each character is a stand-in for a different view of Christianity.

But this raises yet another question. Does this conflict extend back to the beginning? Where there is smoke there is fire. Those who would argue that Paul omitted Mary Magdalene from the list in 1 Cor 15:5–8 maintain that these debates at the end of the first century extend back to the very beginning of the Jesus movement. Paul took his version of tradition from Peter and Jerusalem, and either omitted or did not know of the Mary Magdalene tradition.

Evaluation

How do we reevaluate this claim, a project that actually calls for a reconstruction of the origins of Christianity? Did belief in the resurrection actually originate with Mary Magdalene and the women?

Denying that Mary Magdalene was first or claiming she was omitted from the list by Paul does not mean that Peter is first in the sense of being the foundation of resurrection belief. Nothing in Paul's list indicates that Cephas is the foundation; he is only first on the list. Nor does being on the list make one an apostle. The gospel of Luke created the notion of Peter's primacy. Although the argument is often framed as an either/or between Mary Magdalene and Peter, that in my judgment is a false option.

There are several linchpins in this argument. Does the obvious conflict between the followers of Mary Magdalene and those of Peter in the late first century translate into that debate also being present from the beginning? Scholars often argue that later writings can and do preserve evidence of earlier events, but while that is a standard argument, the burden of proof lies on the one claiming that a later composition preserves earlier memories.

The following issues call this reconstruction into question.

The author of Mark's gospel created the empty tomb story. We saw that clearly in our discussion. There are no appearance stories in this, the first gospel. This is a major linchpin in the argument of those asserting the priority of Mary Magdalene. Yet their argument fails. Not only is the stronger argument that Mark composed the empty tomb narrative, but the early Christian movement shows no interest in the location of Jesus' tomb nor is any cult associated with Jesus' tomb, even though there is ample evidence in early Christianity for cults of the dead associated with the tombs of martyrs. The cult of the tomb of Jesus begins during the reign of Constantine, when his mother Helena thought she had discovered the tomb (325 CE). This leads to the conclusion that the earlier tradition did not know where Jesus was buried.

In our examination of Matthew we saw that he was following and rewriting Mark. Jesus' appearance to the women in Matthew corrects what Matthew deemed an unacceptable ending to Mark's gospel. The author of Matthew has no tradition about the resurrection independent of Mark. This gospel is not a source for an appearance to Mary Magdalene.

This reinforces the notion that, like Mark, the author of Matthew does not view Peter as the foundation of the resurrection experience.

Again the gospel of John in chapter 20 is following Mark. There is no indication that the author has an independent tradition, but constructs his own elaborate appearance stories as a conclusion to the fourth gospel. John 20 may well represent a rejection of the apostolic tradition in favor of that of the beloved disciple, in which the appearance of Jesus to Mary Magdalene serves as a foil.

Luke is likewise following and rewriting Mark. He does not omit an appearance to the women or Mary Magdalene. He would have to know Matthew or John. What is apparent is that Luke is responsible for putting Peter at the center, and he does severely downgrade the role of women and Mary Magdalene in particular.

The appendix to the fourth gospel, chapter 21, gives Peter a primary role, while not diminishing that of the Beloved disciple.

As is so often the case, when one follows the evidence chronologically, it begins to clarify itself. Matthew and John have independently created their own stories of an appearance to Mary Magdalene, while Luke reports an appearance to Peter and the author of John 21 constructs an elaborate miracle/appearance story and story of Jesus testing Peter. In none of these cases is there independent attestation for appearance stories. They appear to be created by the authors in the period after 85 CE. While Paul's list in 1 Cor 15:5–8 reports in a formulaic pattern a list of those to whom "he has been seen for," no evidence indicates that this list was supported by actual narratives until the last quarter of the first century, and then only selected elements of the list were recorded.

While there was no original appearance to Mary Magdalene, that does not mean that her name cannot or should not be on Paul's list in 1 Cor 15:5–8. In fact, I would argue that she already is on the list. Paul's list is both complete and incomplete. Complete in the sense that Paul most likely means it to be inclusive— everyone to whom the Anointed has been seen is on the list. But incomplete in the sense that we know a great deal less about those on the list than we think we do. Consider the following.

- Is Cephas Peter?
- Who are the Twelve?
- Who are included in the 500?
- Who are included in the apostles?

As we saw in chapter 7 it is not absolutely clear that Cephas is Peter, yet most scholars assume that Cephas is Simon Peter. Furthermore, few have recognized the influence of Luke and John 21 on the interpretation of "he has been seen for Cephas." That gets understood as "he has appeared to Peter" (it's even trans- lated that way in the NIV), and those later stories and traditions about Peter are then read into and understood as implied in that statement. But that is unwarranted. Paul's list does not imply any priority to Peter nor does Paul ever in his letters imply such, even if Cephas is Peter. At best, Paul recognizes Cephas as *one* of the pillars, not *the* pillar.

As we saw when we examined the list in chapter 7, Paul knows at least one female apostle, Junia, mentioned in Rom 16:7. She is certainly included in the "apostles." Actually, were it not for the rhetorical use Paul is making of the list, his own name would not occur on the list, but would be subsumed like Andronicus and Junia in "apostles." There is every reason to think that Mary Magdalene's name also is subsumed in that word "apostles." We have no idea how large a number is included in "apostles." The 500, many of whom were women, warns us that "apostles" surely includes many more than 12, as Luke's conflation of the Twelve and apostles would lead us to believe.

Finally, there remains the issue of where Mark got the names of the women. Kathleen Corley in a recent book, *Maranatha,* has argued that women's funerary rituals are the tradition out of which grew the oral tradition that underlies the passion account. Her argument is elaborate and largely convincing. If the passion account emerged from women's funerary rituals, "he was buried" in Paul's gospel-statement may well represent that effort. In the ritual retelling of this story in the tradition of the noble death, the names of the women could have become attached to a tradition that supplied Mark with the women's names. There is no more reason to doubt that the names Mary Magdalene et al. were as prominent in the emergence of the post-mortem Jesus traditions, than there is to doubt Cephas, James, Peter, and Paul.

Further Reading

Brock, Ann Graham. *Mary Magdalene, the First Apostle: The Struggle for Authority.* Harvard Theological Studies, Vol. 51. Cambridge: Harvard University Press, 2003.

Brown, Raymond. *The Community of the Beloved Disciple: The Life, Loves, and Hates of an Individual Church in New Testament Times.* New York: Paulist Press, 1979.

Corley, Kathleen E. *Maranatha, Women's Funerary Rituals and Christian Origins.* Minneapolis: Fortress, 2010.

Schaberg, Jane with Melanie Johnson-DeBaufre. *Mary Magdalene Understood.* New York: Continuum, 2006.

Schaberg, Jane. *The Resurrection of Mary Magdalene.* New York: Continuum, 2003.

Schnackenburg, Rudolf. *The Gospel According to St. John.* Translated by David Smith and G.A. Kon. 3 vols. Vol. 3. New York: Crossroad, 1982.

Schussler-Fiorenza, Elizabeth. *In Memory of Her: A Feminist Theological Reconstruction of Christian Origins.* New York: Crossroad, 1992.

Smith, Jonathan Z. *Drudgery Divine, on the Comparison of Early Christianities and the Religions of Late Antiquity.* Chicago: University of Chicago Press, 1990.

Works Cited

King, Karen. *The Gospel of Mary of Magdala, Jesus and the Woman Apostle.* Santa Rosa: Polebridge, 2003.

Schaberg, Jane. *The Resurrection of Mary Magdalene.* New York: Continuum, 2003.

Schaberg, Jane with Melanie Johnson-DeBaufre. *Mary Magdalene Understood.* New York: Continuum, 2006.

15 What Happened?

Four Models

Well before 70 CE the early believers in the Anointed employed four metaphorical models:

- raised up
- he has been seen for
- taken up
- exalted

Each of these metaphorical models has its own coherence, and at times they are combined in various ways, but it remains difficult to sketch out an evolutionary development. To make a rhetorical point or fit a particular circumstance, an author employs the fitting model. "Raised up" is the dominant metaphor and may be the first one, although that is not evident. "Taken up" also has a high claim for being first. By the time of our earliest glimpse at the evidence all four models are already in play.

Raised Up

"Raised up" is based on the analogy of getting up from sleep. The dead are asleep and they awake or are raised up, just as one gets up out of bed. In the noun form it means "standing up" and eventually is translated into Latin as *resurrectio*, from the verb *resugo*, to rise or raise one's self. "Resurrection" is an English transliteration of the Latin, not a translation. When in a later period (probably in the second century) the Greek becomes a technical theological term, it still retains its everyday meaning, though this is not the case in English.

The "raising up" metaphor was applied to the people of Israel, and Daniel is among the first to apply it to those Jews who were martyred by Antiochus Epiphanes. Daniel creates around this metaphor an apocalyptic scenario in which God will vindicate the martyrs by raising them up from the dead. This metaphorical system also has overtones of God as creator who will restore creation. The God who created out of nothing can also raise up the dead from the dust of the grave.

In order to apply this scenario to Jesus, the earliest believers had to shift the model by claiming that a single individual, Jesus, was raised up so as to inaugurate the eventual resurrection of his faithful followers. In Jewish thought raising up is always corporate; thus the basic model needed adaptation. This raising up of an individual is not something Daniel 12 or its successors had anticipated. The corporate nature of resurrection is why in the earliest mention of Jesus' resurrection in 1 Thessalonians, Paul moves from Jesus' being raised to his return and in 1 Corinthians 15 he insists upon the resurrection of the body. Yet because Daniel's model left much unanswered, Paul, especially as he confronts the Greco-Roman culture of his converts, has to make further innovations to the model. Will those already dead be disadvantaged as regards those who are alive at the coming of the Anointed? With what kind of body will they be raised up? As we have seen, he answered these questions from within his Jewish heritage.

He Has Been Seen For

The "he has been seen for"(ōphthē) is a model borrowed from the Septuagint (LXX). While based on the metaphor of seeing, it is not physical seeing, but seeing as insight or revelation. In the LXX ōphthē is used to note a revelatory event by God. This metaphor is prominent in Paul's list, and along with "raised up" is surely part of the early preaching and confession. Paul invokes this metaphor explicitly in describing his own call and experience of Jesus raised up as "revelation" (apocalyps-revelation).

This metaphorical model evinces a long afterlife, especially after 85 CE, when it is taken literally and gospel writers begin to construct appearance stories, i.e., accounts in which Jesus actually appears, as conclusions to their gospels. While from the beginning Anointed-believers used "seeing" as a metaphor for their experience, there is no evidence of appearance stories before 85 CE. As astonishing as that may seem, that is the evidence we have uncovered. Early Christianity's avoidance of narrating the actual raising up of Jesus from the grave is evidence of the late character of appearance stories. Only the gospel of Peter actually narrates the resurrection itself.

> Early, at first light on the Sabbath, a crowd came from Jerusalem and the surrounding countryside to see the sealed tomb. But during the night before the Lord's day dawned, a loud noise came from the sky, and they saw the skies open up and two men come down from there in a burst of light and approach the tomb. The stone that had been pushed against the entrance began to roll by itself and moved away to one side; then the tomb opened up and both young men went inside.
>
> Now when these soldiers saw this, they roused the centurion from his sleep, along with the elders. (Remember, they were also there keeping watch). While they were explaining what they had seen, again they see three men leaving the tomb, two supporting the third, and a cross was following them. The heads of the two reached up to the sky, while the head of the third, whom they led by the hand, reached beyond the skies. And they heard a voice from the skies that said, "Have you preached to those who sleep?" And an answer was heard from the cross, "Yes!"
>
> (Peter 9–10)

Taken Up

The "taken up" or assumption metaphor is also present prior to 70 CE. This model is widely used in second temple Judaism in connection with Elijah and Enoch, and also in Greco-Roman culture. The Q-community is convinced that God has restored and will vindicate Jesus against his enemies (personified as Jerusalem), and that God has taken him up into heaven like Elijah or one of the murdered prophets of old, and that he will come again as the apocalyptic judge, the son of man (the Human One in the SV translation).

Because the Q-gospel is a hypothetical, reconstructed text, some tend to marginalize it and prefer the canonical Paul as the representative of what the early movement looked like. This is clearly indefensible. The very controversy with which Paul was met indicates that the early Jesus movement was quite diverse. Maybe we should speak of movements. Nor should we imagine these movements as unified or even in constant contact. Neither James nor Cephas is acting in Jerusalem as some latter day pope sending out orders and missionaries.

The Q-gospel has a high claim on our attention. It originates in Galilee in the 50s and 60s, and surely comes from those groups that were originally with Jesus. It represents their response to Jesus' death. Instead of the martyr view and subsequent raising up as in Daniel 12, they understand Jesus from within the Deuteronomic viewpoint: as a righteous prophet whom the people have murdered, whom God has taken up or assumed into heaven, and who will come as judge. This response to Jesus' death has a claim to be at least as old as the "raised up from the dead" model. Both are Jewish models employed to understand what happened.

The assumption model likewise explains where Jesus is and indicates that he will come again as judge. The righteous one in the Wisdom of Solomon offers a compelling vision of what has happened to Jesus.

Interestingly, the resurrection model leads to accounts of Jesus actually being seen (ōphthē), while the assumption model is based on his not being seen. Fundamental to that latter model is the missing body, which provokes the postulation of assumption.

Exaltation

"Raised up" or "standing up" were not the only models available. In 1 Thess 1:10, along with the first instance we saw of "raised up," Paul himself also used exaltation: "to wait for God's 'son' from heaven, whom God raised from among the dead." "From heaven" implies an exaltation *to* heaven.

The gentile Anointed-believers in the colony of Philippi apparently responded with their own praise speech, which Paul incorporated into one of his letters to them. The Philippians praise speech indicates how a group of gentile Anointed-believers responded to Paul's preaching. They interpreted it by employing the Adam model and an exaltation model derived both from the LXX and Roman imperial theology. As a product of gentiles converted by Paul, this praise speech is, as one might expect, a mixing of a Hellenistic Jewish model with an imperial model. Its themes differ from those of Paul, yet are reminiscent of him. The Adam motif is Pauline, but used in a strikingly dissimilar fashion. The exaltation has overtones of the Roman ritual of triumph, which from Augustus onward was reserved to the imperial family. Both the martyr motif (although reinserted by Paul, "even death on a cross") and the apocalyptic motif are missing. In its place is a notion, again borrowed from Paul but used differently, of God's triumph in the Anointed over all of reality. The Philippians share the conviction that God has acted in Jesus, vindicated him, super-exalted him, and will ultimately claim all the world.

Seeing the Philippians praise piece as a product of Paul's gentile converts allows its distinctiveness to stand out. But Paul's use of it in his letter to Philippians indicates that he can accept this model as well as the raised up from the dead model. It is not his preferred model, but he does not reject it. Paul himself can combine "has been raised" (resurrection) with "who is at the right hand of God" (exaltation) in Rom 8:34 (also 1 Thess 1:10).

Even if one rejects the argument that the praise piece was composed by Paul's gentile converts and instead argues that Paul himself was the author, that does not change the situation. It still represents a different model, although in my judgment it is more difficult to explain why Paul would have composed it. But on any theory of composition, the Philippians praise piece indicates that Paul and his community know and can use more than one model.

Finally, the exaltation model, like the assumption model, can better explain where Jesus is (in heaven, at the right hand of God) and his future role (to subject all the world to God). A combination of the two models expands the metaphors available for understanding the situation.

Like the raising up model, the exaltation model also sees that creation, the world, is at stake; and therefore the ultimate outcome of the exaltation is the subjection of the world, including Rome, to God the Father. The emperor claims to be father of the country (*pater patriae*), but God is the true father of the world.

This image finds intermittent use. It appears in Peter's speech in Acts to the high priest's council:

> God exalted him at his right hand as Leader and Savior that he might give repentance to Israel and forgiveness of sins. And we are witnesses to these things, and so is the Holy Spirit whom God has given to those who obey him.
> (Acts 5:31–32)

The author of Hebrews, who does not employ the "raised from the dead" model, nonetheless sounds at the letter's very beginning a theme that is similar to the praise piece from Philippians:

> When he had made purification for sins,
> he sat down at the right hand of the Majesty on high,
> having become as much superior to angels as the name he has
>   inherited is more excellent than theirs.
> (Heb 1:1–4)

This is almost a commentary on Ps 110:1:

> The Lord says to my lord,
> "Sit at my right hand
> until I make your enemies your footstool."

What Happened?

Our written evidence takes us back to the late forties and early fifties. By that time all four models we have studied are in play. Can we go back further? Can we peer into the mists before Paul and the Q-gospel? As we have seen, the gospels, all written after 70 CE and the Acts of the Apostles written between 90–120 CE, are of no help in this regard. Our evidence is not direct, but inferential. We have to construct hypotheses to answer this question. We are guessing in the twilight, but not in total darkness. We must be clear about what we know and what is hypothesis. No datum can surrender its meaning if we lack a hypothesis with which to understand it. We should also be clear that the early Anointed-believers were doing the same thing—making inferences from the facts and their past experience.

Data

Where to start seems obvious to me.

- Jesus was crucified by Rome.

This is the strongest historical datum with which to begin. We do not have to solve the many questions connected with the crucifixion. Were the Judean authorities involved? What was the charge? Was there a formal trial? While important questions, they are irrelevant for our concern. The important issue is that Rome crucified Jesus and thereby signaled that Rome won.

The second point is more contentious and involves an inference.

- They did not know where the body was.

Pre-Constantinian Christianity has no cult of the tomb of Jesus, even though they have rituals associated with the tombs of martyrs and the dead. Mark's empty tomb story and the use of his story by the other gospels assume they do not know where the body is. Further, the report in Matthew of the rumor among the Jews that the disciples stole the body makes the same assumption. Since they did not know where the body was, each side is free to tell its own story. At least that hypothesis best explains the evidence. It also seems likely that they did not know where the grave was.

An Hypothesis

Before Jesus' crucifixion the group with him had experienced healings, exorcisms, common meals, parables and aphorisms, and the empire (kingdom) of God. Following Jesus' crucifixion they

---

Q-Gospel on the Death of Jesus

The Q-folks do not explicitly address Jesus' crucifixion. Their model of "taken up" does not demand it. Since they employ the Deuteronomic viewpoint, they apparently blame Jerusalem for Jesus' death; she is the city who kills the prophets.

continued to experience healings, exorcisms, common meals, parables and aphorisms. But most important,

* They continued to experience the empire of God.

Rome crucified the prophet of God's empire. She crushed him. Yet God's empire was still present; therefore, God must have acted.

The parables and aphorisms of Jesus do provide a ground for a conviction that God will act. The parables prepare their listeners for the empire of God as a re-imagined world. The imagined world of God's empire stands over and against the real world of Rome. It is a world in which a Samaritan will come to the aid of a Jew in the ditch, in which a rich man will throw a banquet for the destitute, in which the empire of God resembles not the empire of Rome, but something more like leaven (a symbol of corruption) or a mustard plant (a weed). None of these can be appropriate metaphors for Rome, but for Jesus they are subversive but true portraits of God's empire.

There is a double pivot. Rome crucified Jesus and the experience of the empire of God continues. Jesus must then be a prophet or a martyr whom Rome had killed, just as Antiochus Epiphanes had killed those Jews faithful to God's Torah. Despite Rome's apparent victory, whenever the group came together again—the group that had gathered around the parables and aphorisms, the healings and exorcisms, and the common meals—they discovered that the re-imagined world of God's empire continued to exist, it was still present. To explain this, they turned to their tradition—to the stories of their ancestors. We have followed this effort in some detail in this book.

We need not imagine this happening all at once, on the third day, so to speak. Nor need we imagine it as a unified process. At different times and in different places it took place along different paths. It is but a pious myth that all early followers of Jesus believed in the resurrection, that Jesus had been raised up. That is simply not the case. The Q-gospel irrefutably makes that point. Very likely there is no oldest resurrection tradition, but rather a variety of traditions. They employed a variety of metaphors to explain their conviction that Rome had not triumphed, for God had acted.

Objections

For some this may seem too ephemeral. Surely there was a more dramatic, single moment, a big-bang so to speak.

Paul

Paul presents an interesting test case for this objection. He describes his own experience as revelation (*apocalyps*-revelation) and uses metaphors of seeing: "I have seen the Lord" and "he has been seen for" (*ōphthē*). He says that God revealed his son to/in him and he "would proclaim God's world-transforming news to 'the nations'" (Gal 1:16). But in this regard he never details a vision or narrates an appearance. He remains silent about his subjective experience.

The situation in Acts is very different (see Acts 9:1–19; 22:6–16; 26:12–18). Paul is traveling from Jerusalem to Damascus, armed with letters from the high priest, when a blinding light surrounds him. He hears a voice saying the famous words, "Saul, Saul, why do you persecute me?" (Acts 9:4). Those traveling with him hear the voice, but see nothing. He enters Damascus and "For three days he was without sight, and neither ate nor drank" (Acts 9:9). Ananias is instructed in a vision to heal Saul, "for he is an instrument whom I have chosen to bring my name before Gentiles and kings and before the people of Israel" (Acts 9:15). He goes to Saul and heals him. "Then he [Saul] got up and was baptized" (Acts 9:18). Later in Acts when Paul narrates for King Agrippa this same experience, he characterizes it as a "heavenly vision" (*optasia*), a word he does not use in the description of his *apocalyps*-revelation in his letters.

All of this is very dramatic and memorable, but incompatible with what we know from Paul. Luke's version of events has dominated the imagination of later Christians, while Paul's remains almost unknown. What we forget is that this dramatic story was in the service of Luke's program of distinguishing between Paul and Luke's fabrication of twelve apostles—and to subordinate Paul to the Twelve. The apostles see the resurrected Christ in the semi-flesh, Paul has a vision.

Peter

Traditionally, Peter (or Cephas) is the foundation of the resurrection. While Cephas is first on Paul's list, that does not imply foundation or priority. Being on the list is what counts, not the order on the list. Paul's being last on the list does not make him inferior to Cephas who is first on the list. Besides, Paul's list is more extensive than we have commonly understood.

In Mark's gospel the young man tells the women to "go and tell his disciples, including 'Rock,' 'He is going ahead of you to Galilee'" (Mark 16:7); but of course they famously tell no one, creating a conundrum for an ending. While in Matthew's gospel Peter gets the keys of the kingdom, he gets not a single mention in the resurrection narrative. Furthermore, the first appearance of Jesus is to the two women.

In the fourth gospel Mary Magdalene informs Peter and the other disciple that "They've taken the Master from the tomb" (John 20:2). The other disciple arrives first, then Peter checks out the tomb and appears confused. The other disciple then likewise checks it out and "He saw all this, and he believed" (John 20:8). Mary Magdalene is the first to recognize Jesus—it happens when he speaks her name, for it is his voice that clues her—and she proclaims to the disciples, "I have seen the Master" (John 20:18). Hearing prompts seeing. In the remaining appearance stories of John 20, Peter is not singled out.

Luke's gospel, as we have seen, puts Peter at the center. The role of the women is minimized, and after the couple from Emmaus return to Jerusalem but before they can report to the Eleven, the Eleven say, "The Master really has been raised, and has been seen for Simon!" (Luke 24:34, SV modified). This quick editing gives the first appearance to Peter, but interestingly there is no narrative to support that appearance. Apparently Luke does not know one, so he repeats the traditional formula, "he has been raised and has been seen for," the language from Paul's list. Luke feels free to construct the elaborate narrative of the couple on the road to Emmaus, but apparently not a story of an appearance to Peter.

For that narrative one has to wait until the early second century in the appendix to the fourth gospel, chapter 21. There a story about a miraculous catch of fish is converted into an appearance story and a restoration of Peter. "Feed my sheep" (John 21:17). Only in the second century does a narrative of an appearance to Peter appear.

My Hypothesis Again

Since the dramatic, big-bang type stories are all later, post 85 CE, I am driven back to my original hypothesis. Rome crucified Jesus, and Jesus' group still continued to experience the empire of God. To explain this, they turned to their tradition—to the stories of their ancestors. "He has been raised up," "he has been seen for," "he has been exalted to the right hand of God." All of these formulaic confessions are ways of saying that Rome's apparent victory was futile and that the empire of God is here.

Actually, even the later dramatic stories make the same point. In the Emmaus story when Jesus performs the ritual of the breaking of the bread, the couple's "eyes were opened and they recognized him" (Luke 24:31). It is not the appearance or the explanation of scripture that convinces, but the breaking of the bread, the common meal shared. At the conclusion of Matthew's gospel the Eleven are commissioned to "go and make disciples of all peoples" (Matt 28:19) and Jesus promises "I'll be with you day in and day out, as you'll see, until the culmination of the age" (28:20). Even in the appendix to John's gospel, "Jesus comes, takes the bread, and gives it to them, and passes the fish around as well" (John 21:13).

These stories all make the same point: Jesus remains present in the community's activity. This is a part of the empire of God. For the earliest group to say that God has raised Jesus from the dead invokes the promise from Daniel. Such a confession is based on the continued presence of the empire of God after Rome's crucifixion of Jesus. Thus we are driven to the empire of God both to understand Jesus and for insight as to what the earliest followers thought happened after he was crucified.

To say the God raised Jesus from the dead, that he is at the right hand of the father, that he has been seen for, are all ways to confess that the empire of God—proclaimed and present in Jesus' healings and exorcisms, parables and aphorisms, the meals shared together—is still effective. It is also a profound political statement against the Roman empire and all imperial authority. It represents a rejection of Rome's claim to represent the divine presence in the figure of Augustus and his successors. To say the resurrection is a profound political statement is putting it mildly.

In this book we have followed a methodology ordered by chronology to discipline our inquiry. We agreed at the beginning to set aside the question "what really happened" and instead to follow the evidence where it led. Following chronological order helps us avoid the historical fallacy of the inevitable, the false notion that things had to happen that way. It blocks reading later evidence into earlier situations. This discipline has led us to see that the early Anointed-believers used four different models to explain their experience and that the stories in which the resurrected Jesus appear all come from after 85 CE.

Only at the end have we asked what happened, and even then we have led with the best historical evidence, the earliest (pre-70 CE) Anointed-believers' interpretation, and what that implied about their experience. Only in that sense have we asked what happened. All that we have access to is their accounts of their experience. These are not eyewitness reports taken down by disinterested observers, but rather their encapsulations of their experience in traditional formulaic language.

How do we get from the historical fact that Jesus was crucified to the earliest Anointed-believers first extant interpretations? When we get there all four models are in play. In my judgment, what best accounts for that transition is the conviction that in Jesus' crucifixion Rome did not defeat God, that the empire of God was still present just as it had been before, that Rome was an empty corpse, and their task was to proclaim that good news. On that conviction, resurrection emerged in early Christianity as the only explanation.

Postscript

Reclaiming Resurrection

How might we make sense of resurrection today? How might we reclaim this ancient belief? Should we even try to reclaim it or should we just let it go as the baggage of a bygone era?

I would argue that rebirth, new life, resurrection is a fundamental theme and need of human life and the effort to reclaim and restore it is worthwhile. On the one hand, the experience that underlies resurrection is always trying to come to language, to find expression in words and story. On the other hand, many of the metaphors in which this experience has been embedded are now dead or dying.

Updating Resurrection

In the post-biblical era efforts were made to update or make sense of the resurrection. Chief among these was the doctrine of the immortality of the soul which in many ways replaced resurrection. In the modern period, Rudolf Bultmann made a major effort to demythologize the New Testament preaching. After examining these two attempts, I will turn to three different ways of envisioning resurrection in our situation.

Immortality of the Soul

Modern-day Christians are often surprised to find out that the immortality of the soul is missing from the New Testament and even more surprised to find out that a beatific life after death

225

is by and large missing from the Hebrew Bible. The Bible never imaginatively draws a picture of life in heaven. Most of that comes from Dante or Bunyan. Neither does the New Testament contain a clear belief in the immortality of the soul. That becomes firmly established only during the Neoplatonic revolution of the third and fourth century. In the fifth century Augustine represents the consensus when he defines "a human being, as seen by a human being, is a rational soul using a mortal and earthly body" (*De moribus ecclesiae catholicae* 1.27.52).

The resurrection of the dead is a distinctly Jewish idea, distasteful to the Greeks. Greek anthropology preferred a notion of the immortality of the soul, a notion rejected by Paul in his debate with his Corinthian converts. Early Christianity remained devoted to bodily resurrection, even to the point of Luke and the fourth gospel imagining it in an increasingly physical manner—although not totally physical, since their image of the resurrected body is capable of performing non-physical activities.

There is a double fault line in the Pauline view.

- The nearness of the end time
- The Greek resistance to body in favor of soul

Both of these fault lines appear in Paul's letters. Paul thought Jesus would soon return, most probably before Paul's own death. This being the case, he could say of those who had died that they were dead in Christ (1 Thess 4:16). The solution is tolerable as long as the Parousia is not delayed too long. But the longer the delay, the greater the tension.

While Greeks resist the raising of the body, even thinking it ridiculous, they have an apparent solution to the problem of the delay of the Parousia—the immortal soul.

Judaism resisted the immortal soul because of the divine characteristics implied by immortality. "By nature immortal" is the definition of a god. It is a divine spark. This offends Jewish notions of monotheism. But this problem is solved by having God create the soul and at death having the soul judged and consigned to heaven or hell. Christianity later added purgatory to solve the problem of those who should not go to heaven but also should not go to hell. This notion of the immortal soul as created by God at birth and judged at death has come to dominate Christianity to such a degree that saving souls is a common description of the Christian vocation.

There are several problems with the adoption of this model.

- Jesus' resurrection is divorced from ours.

Jesus' resurrection becomes the proof of his divinity and our resurrection is pushed off to the general resurrection at the end of time. It becomes an article of the Creed with no real force. We die, our soul is judged, the soul goes to heaven or hell, and only on the last day are we raised up in the general resurrection, when our souls and bodies will be rejoined. In this model resurrection is actually relatively unimportant; the immortal soul is much more so. *The Baltimore Catechism* (1891) is typical in this regard.

> Q. 133. What is man?
> A. Man is a creature composed of body and soul, and made to the image and likeness of God.
> Q. 136. Is this likeness in the body or in the soul?
> A. This likeness is chiefly in the soul.
> Q. 137. How is the soul like to God?
> A. The soul is like to God because it is a spirit that will never die, and has understanding and free will.

The second and third losses are correlated.

- The body becomes evil
- The soul is good

The soul is what is saved. Creation becomes devalued, something to be used up. Salvation is escape from this world to the heavenly abode where the soul naturally dwells. In this context Marx accuses Christianity of being an opium of the people, that the immortal soul teaches people to accept the oppression of this life in favor of the heavenly life to come.

Demythologization

In the depths of World War II, in 1941, the great German New Testament scholar Rudolf Bultmann (1884–1976) published his famous essay "The New Testament and Mythology," which lays out his program of demythologization. Both influential and controversial, Bultmann deserves credit for focusing the problem squarely.

Bultmann begins his essay with this statement:

> The cosmology of the New Testament is essentially mythical in character. The world is viewed as a three-storied structure, with the earth in the centre, heaven above, and the underworld beneath. (p. 1)

He finds this mythical worldview unacceptable and incredible to moderns. He argues that the kerygma (preaching) of the New Testament is contained in a "cosmology of a pre-scientific age" and is not the truth of the kerygma "quite independent of its mythical setting?" (p. 3). Demythologization involves taking both the scientific worldview and history seriously. For Bultmann, the failure to do this has made faith incredible.

Bultmann's program is very radical; he argues that taking science and history seriously is the task facing theology and the churches, a task that for the most part has been avoided since the Enlightenment and Darwin. It means that no preconditions can be set on the part of theology. Bultmann formulates this issue clearly and unambiguously:

> [Our] knowledge and mastery of the world have advanced to such an extent through science and technology that it is no longer possible for anyone seriously to hold the New Testament view of the world—in fact, there is no one who does. What meaning, for instance, can we attach to such phrases in the Creed as "descended into hell" or "ascended into heaven"? We no longer believe in the three-storied universe which the creeds take for granted. The only honest way of reciting the Creed is to strip the mythological framework from the truth they enshrine—that is, assuming that they contain any truth at all, which is the question that theology has to ask. (p. 4)

His program has a two-pronged thrust:

- An historical understanding of the New Testament
- Taking the modern (scientific) worldview seriously

The first part of this program we have pursued in this book. The second pre-occupies us now. Bultmann defined this second prong primarily in terms of science, and that is the primary issue. Labeling the question Religion and Science or the Challenge of Science misses the point Bultmann is trying to make. He wants to demythologize faith in light of science or, as I would put it, to re-think and re-express faith in the light of science.

A common critique of Bultmann is that his understanding of myth was too narrow and does not reflect the positive effect of myth in religious language. The efforts of Paul Ricoeur and others have shown the positive value in myth. What Bultmann is rejecting is myth understood as a literal description of reality. The three-storied universe was taken literally in the pre-scientific period. Today it must be rejected as a literal description.

My basic critique would be that Bultmann's program is essentialist and idealist in nature, perhaps unavoidably so. He seeks a kind of pure essence that is translatable to existential categories. In the process what is at risk of being lost is the narrative and metaphorical possibilities. We will pay attention to this aspect in the following examples.

Coordinates of Resurrection

The analysis undertaken in this book has been an effort to open up space in which to imagine resurrection. What does that space look like? Let me suggest that the contours of that space would have the following coordinates, and that by taking these coordinates seriously we can reclaim the degraded view of resurrection that has dominated Christianity since the Neoplatonic revolution.

Corporate

Current belief in the resurrection tends to view it as personal, as something that happens to "me." This is often seen in the notion of Jesus as my personal savior, an idea the ancient world would have found ludicrous. In ancient Israel the notion of raising up was first connected to the people of Israel, and it always maintains a corporate sense. For Paul, Jesus' resurrection is the first fruits of the corporate resurrection of those who trust in God as he, Jesus, has trusted in God. Even Jesus' resurrection is not personal, but part of ours. The restoration of a corporate sense of resurrection enables us to expand the notion to creation itself, which is ultimately what resurrection is about. Resurrection is the restoration of creation to the state in which God intends it.

Justice

The second coordinate of resurrection concerns justice, because that is what drives the original notion of raising up from the dead. Elements of Judaism accepted the raising up from the dead because the martyrdom of the pious ones violated God's justice, and the only way to restore that justice is by raising those martyrs up. This same model drives the earliest understanding of Jesus' death. Jesus died a martyr, and God has raised him up from the dead. Of course, the coordinates of justice and corporate are interrelated. Justice is not simply for the individual martyr, but for the whole people.

Scenario

The raising up of Jesus implies a story—the death of the martyr, God's vindication of the martyr, the ultimate vindication of God's justice. This was early and easily elaborated into an apocalyptic scenario. Narrativity is an important aspect and not just an accident to be ignored. Narrative helps make sense of existence and is the basis of myth. While agreeing with Bultmann that we must demythologize the myth, I do not want to jettison the scenario, the story. In this sense it is important to see that the story is not literal, but rather presents a promise and a demand. The story imagines the way a world should be, can be.

Not about Jesus but God

The final coordinate indicates that the raising up is ultimately about God. God's justice is at stake, God's creation is at risk, God's action is celebrated.

Resurrection in a New Key

In an effort to flesh out these coordinates of resurrection, to explore their dimensions and interactions, I will explore three examples of resurrection in a new key. Two examples will come from films, while the final one will examine a modern martyr.

Literal Resurrection

I am no fan of Jesus movies. As a group they are a sad collection. Great directors have tried their hand, for example, Martin Scorsese (*The Last Temptation of Christ*) or George Stevens (*The Greatest Story Ever Told*), but they inevitably have not been the best examples of these directors' work. In my judgment the best of these films is *Jesus of Montréal* (1989), written and directed by the French Canadian Denys Arcand. It deals imaginatively with the fundamental problem of a Jesus film—how to make a movie about a perfect person. The director solves this problem by making the film not about Jesus but the character who plays Jesus and in the process becomes Christ-like.

A Catholic pilgrimage church hires a group of five young actors to revitalize an old-fashioned passion play. The film constantly interweaves scenes in their lives that parallel familiar gospel scenes and their efforts to re-create a passion play. For example, Mirelle (Catherine Wilkening), one of the two "Marys" of the troupe, is auditioning for a television advertising job. The casting director, who demeans the auditioning actresses, asks her to take off her sweatshirt and expose her breasts. The scene ends with Daniel (Lothaire Bluteau), who plays Jesus in the passion play, grabbing the cords of the TV camera and "cleansing the temple."

As the film progresses and the passion play emerges, Daniel is transformed more and more into a Christ-like figure by taking on the values of Jesus. The film employs two very traditional models: a passion play and the imitation of Christ. These two traditional models give the film a traditional form, while being theologically radical.

The Fourteenth Station

The passion play follows the fourteen stations of the cross. At the final station, the audience is led down a stairwell to a long tunnel. There sit three of the characters, somber and silent. Then one of the Marys speaks: "He'd been long dead. Five years, perhaps ten. His disciples had scattered, disappointed, bitter, and desperate." This is not the traditional way to inaugurate the resurrection story, but it fits with the story that this film is telling.

One of the male characters recites a portion of Hamlet's famous soliloquy "To be or not to be," beginning with "to die, to sleep / No more." The music rises in a haunting female voice and at the tunnel's end through a bright light comes running the Mary Magdalene figure shouting, "I saw him!" But the Peter character refuses to believe. Peter and the other Mary walk slowly forward and then see a shrouded, ghostlike figure. The scene has strong overtones of the Emmaus story in Luke's gospel. When the figure offers them bread and breaks it, Mary hugs and shouts, "Lord! It's you!"—much as did Mary Magdalene in the fourth gospel.

Then, joined by the other two male disciples, the two Marys conclude:

> Slowly people were convinced. He had changed. No one recognized him at first. But they all came to believe he was there. Except Peter and John, the disciples were new: Paul, the Pharisee, Barnabas, Stephen, and foreigners, and Greeks and Romans. They were ready to die for their convictions. They too were beheaded, crucified, stoned. They were steadfast: Jesus awaited them in his new kingdom. They personify the hope, the most irrational and unyielding of emotions. Mysterious hope that makes life bearable lost in a bewildering universe. You must find your own path to salvation. No one can help you. Look to yourself with humility and courage. Overcome the void between you and others. Love, fear, beg, walk beside them. Life is really very simple. It just seems overwhelming when you think only of yourself. If you forget yourself and asked how to help others, life becomes perfectly simple. Jesus is alive, we have seen him. Love one another. Seek salvation within yourselves. Peace be with you and your spirit.

In this retelling the radical is combined with the traditional. The explanation of the origin of the resurrection is radically reconceived, but its meaning is the imitation of Jesus in a new context as a way of life.

Daniel's Resurrection

The passion play turns out to be a big success, a hit with the media, but unfortunately the leaders of the church find it unacceptable and determine to cancel it and return to the old passion play. The players reject this and put on the play one last time. During the crucifixion scene a security guard enters with the police to shut down the play. The audience becomes aroused and one member of the audience, who looks like a weight lifter, comes to the actors' rescue. In the process the cross on which Daniel/Jesus is hanging is knocked over and Daniel suffers a concussion. This scene is powerfully ironic, since a viewer cheers for the hero coming to the rescue of the abused actors, but the unintended consequences lead to a tragedy. The result is a powerful rejection of violence, even apparently justified violence.

Daniel's concussion becomes life-threatening and he dies in the Jewish Hospital. This offers the film a second opportunity to envision the resurrection. The dead body of Daniel is laid out on an operating table in a crucified form, while the doctors begin removing his organs, packing them in ice and we see them being delivered to other hospitals. As Daniel's body is cremated, a man gets a new heart and a woman sees again.

Jesus of Montreal re-imagines the resurrection of Daniel as an almost literal version of Paul's body of Christ or even the eucharist. Daniel's organs give new sight and a new heart to those who receive the transplants. Thus he lives on in these others.

Denys Arcand's film demonstrates the power of the Jesus story. Like the gospel writers, he casts that story in a new and compelling way. He views the resurrection as corporate: it is about founding a new community with a new way of life. It is literally corporate in the sense that Daniel's body becomes part of the bodies of others. The whole film, which provides a bitingly ironic commentary on society, business, and the church, focuses that commentary on the violation of justice. For example, in the scene in which Daniel objects to Mirelle's taking off her sweatshirt to expose her breasts for the titillation of the director and the clients, he objects not out of prudery, but because it demeans her, it denies who she is. She is, he tells her, better than that. Finally, the transformation of Daniel into the Christ-like figure not only employs the traditional model of the imitation of Christ, an important element in the tradition, but also underlines the idea that what counts is the transformation, not Jesus *per se*.

Metaphorical Resurrection

Stranger than Fiction (2006) brings yet another change on the meaning of resurrection. Directed by Marc Forster and written by Zach Helm, the film contains a highly improbable plot. Harold Crick (Will Farrell), an IRS auditor who leads a very humdrum life governed and determined by numbers, begins to hear a voice narrating a story in which he is the chief character. When he rejects a diagnosis of schizophrenia, the psychiatrist recommends him to Professor Jules Hilbert (Dustin Hoffman) who teaches English literature. Professor Hilbert attempts to determine what kind of story he is in, all the time offering appropriate literary quips and bows to literary method. At one point Harold overhears the narrator/voice refer to his imminent death: "Little did he know that this simple, seemingly innocuous act would result in his imminent death."

Eventually the author is discovered, and she turns out to be a reclusive, neurotic writer named Karen Eiffel. As her name suggests, she lives at the top of a tower like building, her rooms all in white with minimalist decoration. Upon discovering who the author is, Professor Hilbert announces that she always kills the heroes of her stories. She, meanwhile, is quite surprised that Harold is a real person and is hearing her voice narrating the story as she writes it. This leads to a blurring of the line between reality and fiction, something the film has been about since the opening credits.

Not Typed

Three key scenes towards the film's end advance our theme. After learning the identity of the author, Harold, with the help of her assistant Penny (Queen Latifah), persuades her to let him read the manuscript. And since the ending has been handwritten, but not yet typed, Harold is, following the film's logic, not dead—just almost dead.

After asking Professor Hilbert to read the manuscript, Harold is told, "You have to die. . . . It's her masterpiece." In obvious anguish, he responds, "You're asking me to knowingly face my death?" This is the first place in the film that we get a hint of the subtext, the story of Jesus' death, of the hero who willingly faces his own death. Harold is neither Jesus nor a hero. He is an every-man, a rather ordinary, humdrum human being, an IRS tax audi-tor who in the course of the film has transformed his life, a change that is symbolized by a Stratocaster guitar.

In response to Harold's protest against his imminent death, Professor Hilbert tells him:

> [I]n the grand scheme it wouldn't matter. . . . No one wants to die, Harold, but unfortunately we do. . . . Harold, you will die someday, some time. Heart failure at the bank. Choke on a mint. Some long, drawn-out disease you contracted on vacation. You will die. You'll absolutely die. Even if you avoid this death, another will find you. And I guarantee that it won't be nearly as poetic or meaningful as what she's writ-ten. I'm sorry but it's the nature of all tragedies, Harold. The hero dies, but the story lives on forever.

The setup is Harold's question, "You're asking me to know-ingly face my death?" The scene goes on to provide an imagina-tive commentary on Jesus' agony in the garden. Professor Hilbert instructs him in a fate that he wants to avoid at all costs, for he has found new life and wants to keep it. Professor Hilbert insists that Karen Eiffel has created for Harold a poetic and meaningful death, one that by implication gives his life meaning in a way that another death would not. He concludes by noting the power of fiction: that although the hero dies, the story lives on. The poeti-cally meaningful death lives on in the story, giving meaning to life. The blurring of the line between reality and fiction in which this film has engaged helps us to see that "fiction" does not mean "un-true" or "unreal" but describes that which is powerfully imagined and remembered. Fiction is a powerful way of unmasking truth or reality. *Stranger than Fiction* reminds us of the power of the scenario—resurrection is not a moment but a story. Its truth is not in its literalness, but its poetic vision.

Harold now reads the manuscript himself and tells Karen Eiffel, "It's lovely. I like the part about the guitars." Thereupon Karen interjects a stumbling suggestion for a rewriting, perhaps of the ending. . . . But Harold objects.

> No, I read it and I loved it. And there's only one way it can end. I mean, I don't have much background in literary any-

> thing but it seems simple enough. I love your book. And I
> think you should finish it.

Harold has come to terms with his death. He has accepted professor Hilbert's judgment. As someone who has spent his whole life in numbers, in the literal, he finally sees the power of the poetic, of fiction, of metaphor. He is ready to die for it.

Author as God

Karen Eiffel as the author is a somewhat godlike character. She literally creates worlds in the imagination. At one point in the film, after Harold has become real and not simply a character in a novel, she agonizes over her life as an author. She asks her assistant Penny, "How many people do you think I've killed?" She has killed eight people, and, she remarks, they were really nice people. Here again the subtext is the notion that if death is part of God's plan, then is God not a murderer?

In the novel, Harold dies, but in the film he cannot. Hence the paradox of the narrative. Early in the morning on which Harold is to die, Karen Eiffel goes to the office of Professor Hilbert. She gives him the manuscript and says, "I think, perhaps, you may be interested in the new ending." He reads the new ending and says it's okay, clearly implying that it is not the masterpiece of the original. She replies that she is okay with okay and goes on to say, "but if the man does not know he's going to die and dies anyway, dies willingly, knowing he could stop it, then I mean, isn't that the type of man you want to keep alive?" Here Karen Eiffel sums up the justice issue that motivated the turn towards raising the martyrs up from the dead in the Maccabean period. God's justice demands that they be kept alive. This notion is reinforced in the film when Harold, who is in the hospital with multiple injuries from stepping in front of a bus to save a young boy, tells his girlfriend Ana Pascal (Maggie Gyllenhaal), "I didn't have a choice. I had to." Having read the novel with its original ending, Harold stepped in front of the bus to save the young boy knowing he would die anyway. He had to. This defines the necessity of dying for the other: it is not a choice, but a necessary part of the story both for Harold and Jesus and the martyrs. "Had to" provokes the need, the demand for resurrection.

A New Ending

The film ends with the Karen Eiffel narrating the novel's new end.

> Sometimes, when we lose ourselves in fear and despair, in routine and constancy, in hopelessness and tragedy, we can thank God for Bavarian sugar cookies. And fortunately, when there aren't any cookies we can still find reassurance in a familiar hand on our skin or a kind and loving gesture or a subtle encouragement or a loving embrace or an offer of comfort. Not to mention hospital gurneys and nose plugs and uneaten Danish and soft-spoken secrets and Fender Stratocasters and maybe the occasional piece of fiction. And we must remember that all these things, the nuances, the anomalies, the subtleties which we assume only accessorize our days are, in fact, here for a much larger and noble cause: they are here to save our lives. I know the idea seems strange. But I also know that it just so happens to be true.

As the narrator's voice intones the new ending, the camera shows examples of each and every one of these items drawn from the film's various characters. The very first example shows Ana breaking a heart-shaped Bavarian sugar cookie as though it were a communion wafer and serving it to Harold. This new ending argues that resurrection is about everyday life, about making everyday events sources of a new life.

We Shall Overcome

One of the most powerful and inspiring speakers in the history of the United States was Martin Luther King. His "I Have a Dream" speech, at the March on Washington, stands beside Abraham Lincoln's Gettysburg Address and Franklin Roosevelt's December 8, 1941 request to the Congress asking for a declaration of war against Japan.

As a black preacher, his oratory drew upon the Bible and Negro spirituals and recast these traditional texts for a new day and new situation. But he moved that oratory out of the church, onto the streets, and into the conscience of the nation. He forged a new rhetoric that was both religious and political.

I Have a Dream

The March on Washington took place in the sweltering heat of August 8, 1963. In this speech King combines images from the Bible, Negro spirituals, and American history. It rings out as a prophetic call for America to live up to its promises.

The speech begins by recalling the famous words of Abraham Lincoln's Gettysburg address: "Fivescore years ago, a great American, in whose symbolic shadow we stand today, signed the Emancipation Proclamation." This sets the promise. "But one hundred years later, the Negro is still not free" (p. 102. All quotes from King's speeches are from *I Have A Dream*). This defines the current situation. Justice is the promise, but the reality demands a coming judgment, an apocalyptic future.

With the theme of the apocalyptic future strangely muted, the speech oscillates between the promise and the reality as it creates a strong sense of present crisis.

> We have come to this hallowed spot to remind America of the fierce urgency of now. . . . Now is the time to make real the promises of democracy; now is the time to rise from the dark and desolate valley of segregation to the sunlit path of racial justice; now is the time to lift our nation from the quicksands of racial injustice to the solid rock of brotherhood; now is the time to make justice a reality for all God's children. It would be fatal for the nation to overlook the urgency of the moment. (p. 103)

The fivefold repetition of "now" and the phrases "fierce urgency" and "urgency of the moment" not only create a sense that now is the time for the promise, but the urgency of now almost creates the experience of the promise. The resurrection theme lies just below the surface: "lift our nation from the quicksands."

The same theme reappears in King's warning to his people: "But there is something that I must say to my people who stand on the warm threshold which leads into the palace of justice" (p. 103). Again "palace of justice" echoes a biblical image. He concludes his warning recalling the theme of resurrection, "Again and again we must rise to the majestic heights of meeting physical force with soul force."

King notes the suffering of his people:

> Some of you have come from areas where your quest for freedom left you battered by the storms of persecution and staggered by the winds of police brutality. You have been veterans of creative suffering. Continue to work with the faith that unearned suffering is redemptive. (p. 104)

Suffering and storms of persecution link these blacks to the martyrs, so King calls out, "knowing that somehow this situation can, and will be changed. Let us not wallow in the valley of despair." This leads to the titular passage:

> I still have a dream. It is a dream deeply rooted in the American dream that one day this nation will rise up and live out the true meaning of its creed—we hold these truths to be self-evident, that all men are created equal. (p. 104)

He has linked the martyrs' narrative to the nation's narrative and hopes the "nation will rise up," be restored to life, live up to its creed, and like Lincoln turn the Declaration of Independence into a sacred document.

But the dream is not just about the future—"I have a dream today!" King's anticipated future collapses into the present. The speech's great climactic ending continues this theme of collapsing future hope into a realized present: "Let freedom ring" he calls out over and over again until the final call:

> And when we allow freedom to ring, when we let it ring from every village and hamlet, from every state and city, we will be able to speed up that day when all of God's children— black men and white men, Jews and Gentiles, Catholics and Protestants—will be able to join hands and to sing in the words of the old Negro spiritual, "Free at last, free at last, thank God Almighty, we are free at last." (pp. 105–6)

Like the apostle Paul, King imagines that future time as somehow already here in the shout "Free at last." His speech demonstrates that prophecy is not about the far away future but declaiming the here and now, naming it for what it is and should be. His concern is not only for his people, but all the people, all the nation and all the nations. He sees God's justice as denied and he calls for the raising up of a dead nation, a nation unfaithful to its creed. While never mentioning Jesus' resurrection, the theme of new life, of rising up from the dead, runs through the speech like a mighty river giving hope to the future and promise to the present.

The Arc of the Moral Universe

1965 was a difficult year. The Civil Rights Act had passed in 1964, but throughout the South blacks were still not allowed to vote. Demonstrations were organized in Selma, Alabama to dramatize the situation. More than 3,000 demonstrators were arrested in the first week of February. From his cell in Selma's jail, King wrote to the New York Times:

> THIS IS SELMA, ALABAMA. THERE ARE MORE NEGROES IN JAIL
> WITH ME THAN ARE ON THE VOTING ROLLS.

On February 21, Malcolm X was murdered in New York City. A march was planned from Selma to Montgomery, where George Wallace sat as governor. On March 7, as the marchers approached the bridge leading out of Selma, the state troopers attacked with clubs, gas, and horses. Dozens of the injured were taken to the Good Samaritan, a black hospital in Selma. That evening ABC interrupted its TV special with "a report of the assault on Highway 80."

The nation was outraged. On March 15 President Lyndon Baines Johnson addressed a joint session of Congress, pleading for it to pass legislation that would guarantee voting rights. In condemning "the crippling legacy of bigotry and injustice," he declared in the words of the civil rights anthem, "we shall overcome."

King called for another march from Selma to Montgomery, and when it reached there on March 25, he delivered another ringing sermon. At the sermon's conclusion he turned to the haunting question, "How long?"

> I know you are asking today, "How long will it take?" I come
> to say to you this afternoon however difficult the moment,
> however frustrating the hour, it will not be long, because
> truth pressed to earth will rise again. (p. 124)

King returns to the fundamental paradox created by martyrdom. God cannot delay "because truth pressed to earth will rise again." He enunciates the fundamental faith of resurrection. Why go through the agony of suffering for justice? Because truth will rise again.

> How long? Not long, because no lie can live forever.
> How long? Not long, because you still reap what you sow.
> How long? Not long. Because the arm of the moral universe is
>   long but it bends towards justice.
> How long? Not long, 'cause mine eyes have seen the glory of
>   the coming of the Lord. (p. 124)

King was no dewy-eyed Pollyanna. He knew that hard times were ahead, that racism is a real evil capable of exploding in violence at any moment. But like the "I Have a Dream" speech, this sermon draws upon the rich resources of the story of resurrection, of faith in God's vindication to bring the hoped for future justice into the present. In the process he demythologizes the literal language of the tradition and defangs apocalyptic of its violent revenge motif. The way of nonviolence is the way of God.

I've Been to the Mountain Top

On April 2, 1968, the night before he was martyred, King preached a sermon that turned out to be truly prescient. He was a much different person with a much larger vision than when this quest had begun with the Montgomery bus boycott (1955). The now famous words at the conclusion of the sermon compel our attention:

> Well, I don't know what will happen now. We've got some difficult days ahead. But it doesn't matter with me now. I've been to the mountaintop. And I don't mind. Like anybody, I would like to live a long life. Longevity has its place. But I'm not concerned about that now. I want to do God's will. And he's allowed me to go up to the mountain. And I've looked over. And I've seen the promised land. I may not get there with you. But I want you to know tonight, that we, as a people, will get to the promised land. And I am happy, tonight. I'm not worried about anything. I'm not fearing any man. Mine eyes have seen the glory of the coming of the Lord. (p. 203)

Adopting the role of Moses, King abandons his life. This is a clear statement of the martyr's mindset. While resurrection never occurs in the passage and he assumes the role of Moses, the theme of the promised land—that future grasped in the present and somehow lived out of—has overtaken his life. If he loses it, he will gain it.

King and Resurrection

Martin Luther King was a prophet. He was vilified and persecuted; he was a martyr, just as much as any prophet of ancient Israel or martyr of the early church. He deserves his place over the west door of Westminster Cathedral with three other modern martyrs: Mother Elizabeth of Russia, Archbishop Oscar Romero, and Pastor Dietrich Bonhoeffer.

Just as much as Jesus, King was a martyr. But God raised Jesus from the dead and not Martin Luther King. Or is that true?

God did raise Martin Luther King from the dead. King's prophetic words and martyrdom helped raise up a nation to a new standard of God's justice, helped it live up to its creed. The importance of Bultmann's program of demythologization is that it de-literalizes the language of resurrection. Once we see that resurrection is not literal language but a metaphor used to explain the experience of God vindicating the martyr, then we can see that King stands foursquare in the tradition inaugurated in Jesus.

Some will object that King's program was political, that he was not martyred but assassinated. But then, Jesus was assassinated by Rome.

King's program was clearly political, but it was driven by religious convictions, and his speeches were interwoven with images from the Bible and Negro spirituals. I do not intend to challenge the wall between church and state. That wall is there to protect both the freedom of the practice of religion and the freedom of government. The line is a useful and important fiction. Yet it is an illusion we create to protect democracy. God ignores the line. We must observe it.

Martin Luther King's speeches help us to appreciate, even experience again, the power of resurrection, of being raised up from the dead, of being taken up into heaven. To listen to King's "I Have a Dream Speech," to hear that last triumphal shout, "Free at last, free at last, thank God Almighty, we are free at last" is to be drawn into the kingdom of God, to be raised from the dead, if only for the moment. That is the transcendent moment.

Conclusion

Once we open up space by exploring the variety of metaphors for resurrection employed by the early Anointed-believers and see the way others have exploited its language in film and speech, we can re-imagine it in ever-different categories and occasions. The whole ecological crisis we have thrust upon ourselves results in part from a rejection, even a martyrdom of God's creation. But that is yet another topic that opens before us.

The trouble with resurrection is that we have literalized, narrowed, and constricted it, turned it into a credal belief, and in the process forfeited its great claim and hope.

There are fundamental differences between our worldview and that of the ancients. Bultmann stands witness to that difference and the need to take it seriously. One major aspect of that difference is that for them God was all powerful. That is why martyrdom was such a challenge to the very notion of God. How could God let them die? God must act. But we lack this surety. Instead of God acting, we see the number of martyrs continuing to pile up. And still God does not act. Ironically it is in precisely this situation that we need the hope of resurrection. Crucifixion is not the end, Rome did not win, cannot win. "The arm of the moral universe is long but it bends toward justice." God's justice is always coming to life; the kingdom of God is like. . . . In the end we are driven back to faithfulness and a world that should be.

Further Reading

Grossi, Vittorino. "Soul, Human." In *Encyclopedia of the Early Church*, edited by Angelo Di Berardino, 789–90. New York: Oxford University Press, 1192.

Perrin, Norman. *The Promise of Bultmann*. Philadelphia: Fortress, 1969.

Ricoeur, Paul. *The Rule of Metaphor: Multi-Disciplinary Studies of the Creation of Meaning in Language.* Translated by

Kathleen McLaughlin and John Costello. Toronto: University of Toronto Press, 1977.

Staley, Jeffrey L., and Richard Walsh. *Jesus, the Gospels, and Cinematic Imagination*. Louisville: Westminster John Knox, 2007.

Stern, Richard C., Clyton N. Jefford, and Guerric Debona. *Savior on the Silver Screen*. New York: Paulist Press, 1999.

Tatum, W. Barnes. *Jesus at the Movies: A Guide to Its First Hundred Years*. Santa Rosa, CA: Polebridge, 1997.

Works Cited

Bultmann, Rudolf. "New Testament and Mythology." In *Kerygma and Myth, A Theological Debate*, edited by Hans Werner Bartsch, 1–44. New York: Harper Torchbooks, 1961.

King, Martin Luther, Jr. *I Have a Dream, Writings and Speeches That Changed the World*. Edited by James M. Washington. San Francisco: HarperSanFrancisco, 1992.

Index

Hebrew Bible and Septuagint

Old Testament Pseudepigrapha

Early Christian Writings

Gospels

LaVergne, TN USA
01 December 2010
207036LV00002B/1/P